MW00437438

How to Make Money with Commodities

Andrew T. Hecht
with
Mark S. Smith

New York   Chicago   San Francisco   Lisbon   London
Madrid   Mexico City   New Delhi   San Juan
Seoul   Singapore   Sydney   Toronto

In loving memory of Barbara Kallins Werner

The **McGraw·Hill** Companies

Copyright © 2013 by Andrew T. Hecht. All rights reserved. Printed in the United States of America. Except as permitted under the United States Copyright Act of 1976, no part of this publication may be reproduced or distributed in any form or by any means, or stored in a data base or retrieval system, without prior written permission of the publisher.

1 2 3 4 5 6 7 8 9 0   DOC/DOC   1 8 7 6 5 4 3 2

ISBN: 978–0–07–180789–0
MHID: 0–07–180789–6

e-ISBN: 978–0–07–180790–6
e-MHID: 0–07–180790-X

This publication is designed to provide accurate and authoritative information in regard to the subject matter covered. It is sold with the understanding that neither the author nor the publisher is engaged in rendering legal, accounting, or other professional service. If legal advice or other expert assistance is required, the services of a competent professional person should be sought.
    —*From a Declaration of Principles Jointly Adopted by a Committee of the American Bar Association and a Committee of Publishers and Associations*

McGraw-Hill books are available at special quantity discounts to use as premiums and sales promotions, or for use in corporate training programs. To contact a representative, please e-mail us at bulksales@mcgraw-hill.com.

This book is printed on acid-free paper.

Contents

Acknowledgments

In writing a book that encompasses so much of one's knowledge base and career, there are many people to recognize and thank. I apologize to anyone I missed.

I would like to start by thanking my dear friend, Marc Fontaine, who introduced me to the world of trading commodities at the tender age of 16. My thanks go also to Sid Gold and Ralph Mizrahi for taking a chance on such a green young man and giving him the opportunity to learn how to trade commodities and commodity options. I would also like to express my gratitude to Andy Hall for sharing his knowledge and for his faith in me during the years I worked for him at Phibro.

I am indebted to Guy Adami for writing the foreword to this book. And I am also grateful to Lynn Johnston, my literary agent, who took me on as an unpublished author. Your advice, guidance, and suggestions have kept me on the right path. Thanks also to Zach Gajewski for giving me the chance to write this book for McGraw-Hill, and thanks for your help and most of all for calmly listening to me rant and rave during the process. I am also grateful to the writer and journalist, Mark S. Smith, who is my friend and editor. I could not have completed this book without him.

Michael and Laura Pisnoy, Mark and Sharon Dershowitz, Steve and Joanne Schofield, Marc and Halina Fontaine, Mindi Bornstein and Craig Werner. We all are more than friends. We are family. You have helped and emotionally supported me over the years. Finally, thanks to my parents, Joan and Jerry Hecht, and my brother, Eric Hecht, and his wife Sue, all of whom have consistently encouraged me to follow my passion for writing. My biggest thank you goes to my sons, Marc and Jason, who are the light of my life.

Foreword

GUY ADAMI

On October 9, 2009, a headline ran across my computer screen that made me do a double take. It read simply, "Occidental Petroleum Announces Acquisition of Phibro." To most market participants, this was just another headline about another merger-and-acquisition (M&A) deal. For me, it was something much more. You see, when I started my career as a professional trader at Drexel Burnham Lambert in the spring of 1986, Phibro was *the* name in the commodity trading business—it also happened to be where a young commodities trader named Andy Hecht worked in the 1980s and 1990s.

Andy spent much of his career at Phibro, starting as a commodity options trader in the mid–1980s, moving up to managing director in charge of precious metals sales and trading a few years later, and eventually becoming the president of Phibro Energy Metals in the 1990s. As an integral part of the company, Andy made a name for himself there, particularly after a series of highly courageous multi-billion-dollar precious metals trades that proved Phibro was a company to be reckoned with. In 1993, *A Bronx Tale*, starring Robert De Niro and Chazz Palminteri famously asked the question, "Is it better to be feared or respected?" In the case of Phibro there was no question. It was both feared and respected by the entire financial industry. It was the commodity king.

Commodity trading has taken place throughout history. In many ways, it is the essence of supply and demand. Commodity speculators today are often ridiculed and lambasted in the press for driving the prices of goods higher. Of course, they are easy targets. As far as I am aware, no lobby exists that fights on the side of commodity traders. These critics, however, often forget that speculators speculate on prices going higher *and* lower. During the spring and early summer of 2012, for example, there was a 30-percent–plus drop in the price of crude oil. Not surprisingly, there was no public outcry that accompanied such a dramatic move.

I am fond of the expression, "Price is truth," and commodities, whether gold, silver, crude oil, or soybeans, will find their fair market price. Sure, over the course of hours or a couple of days, price disruptions can occur for any number of reasons—geopolitical, weather-related, or short-term supply-chain failures. In the end, however, markets will always self-correct.

Commodities impact all of our daily lives. Consider those of us who use oil to heat our homes or go grocery shopping and buy a gallon of milk or a box of cereal. Though these are seemingly small actions or decisions, they are highly affected by the change in commodity prices. Although prices rise and fall, however, we typically take note only when they rise.

People often ask me, "Why do prices go up faster than they go down?" The short answer is that the size of our planet is the same as it has always been, but our world is growing. Asia's demand for goods has risen almost exponentially over the past few decades. Within the next 15 to 20 years, China will have the largest economy on the planet. China's growth, as well as growth in other developing nations, has put a tremendous strain on commodity markets. In turn, that strain has put an immense pressure on our personal pocketbooks.

Without knowledge and understanding of the commodity market, most people have no recourse but to "grin and bear it." With the release of this book, however, Andy Hecht and Mark S. Smith have provided a well-written, highly educational guide for investors. It's something people can arm themselves with and use to help them prosper in this changing world.

Introduction

If the world was perfect, it wouldn't be.

—YOGI BERRA

I learned the commodities business from the bottom up. My working life began in the late 1970s at Philipp Brothers, a Wall Street commodities trading giant. My training took me from the telex room to the traffic department and then onto the trading floor. Each step taught me something new about the business of trading commodities. In the telex room, I learned about markets from reading the many messages that came into the firm each day. As a traffic clerk, I found out how physical commodities, such as gold, silver, coffee, and crude oil, were transported from production sites to centers of consumption. As a trader, I needed to know why prices of commodities moved and how to make money off these essential goods. I also learned about the global nature of commodity markets. It was not until many years later, however, that I realized how commodity prices affect virtually every business in the world.

I discovered early on that commodity knowledge is not ubiquitous—although it should be. Most people outside the world in which I worked know little about the importance of commodity prices. A giant chasm exists in comprehension and knowledge of how this little-known world affects not only the companies for which we work and invest in, but every company and government around the globe. Many investors know the nominal price of gold and oil, but most don't understand what those prices mean or why they move. When it comes to commodities like corn, soybeans, coffee, aluminum, or live cattle, even the most sophisticated investors are often in the dark. In a perfect world, investors would have complete information at their fingertips, but, of course, this is not a perfect world. However, there is a wealth of knowledge, data, and information out there ripe for the picking. The problem is that most investors don't know how to access it or interpret it.

Every mathematician knows that is impossible to solve an equation without the key variables. The same is true for the world of investing. Commodity prices should be a key variable in the investment calculus of every investor. This is why I decided to write this book, and this is the reason you are reading it—to understand these key components of daily life, from the sugar in your morning coffee and the gasoline in your automobile to the materials that go into making the home you live in, and then how to use this knowledge to enhance your investment portfolio.

With an understanding of commodities and the markets in which they operate, an investor will experience something akin to a light being switched on in a darkened room. You will come to understand the "why" and be able to improve your investment results with the tools this book provides. Knowledge of global commodity markets will furnish you with the ability to invest directly in the commodity markets. It will also help you make better decisions when investing in the equities of companies or other risk assets. Whether you choose to invest and trade commodities directly or use the book as a guide for other investment pursuits, the knowledge gained will be invaluable. Adding commodity knowledge to your investment calculus will give you a huge advantage, and this knowledge will help you make money and increase the returns on all your investments.

Demand for staple goods is growing as the world's population rises in tandem with levels of global wealth, particularly in emerging markets. This demographic trend has driven the prices of many essential products significantly higher. Meanwhile, the value of paper currencies is declining. This environment has led to increases in the production costs of many commodities. Higher production costs and greater demand have also resulted in increased volatility. Consequently, commodity prices move around a lot.

Every citizen of the world is a commodity consumer. So you, the reader, have more intuitive knowledge about the subject and more personal exposure than you probably realize.

WE ARE ALL COMMODITY CONSUMERS

Since the beginning of the millennium, commodities have become a mainstream investment sector, particularly for many professional traders and investors. Rapidly rising global populations have put strains on essential goods, which are commodities. Commodity prices began a long-term uptrend—known to economists and traders as a secular bull market—in the year 2000. Prices for many commodities have doubled, tripled, quadrupled, or more since the start of the new millennium. Commodity markets have always been more volatile than stocks, bonds, or foreign exchange markets. In the 1980s and 1990s, commodities were considered alternative investments. During that period stock and bond markets provided better returns. But if you look back in history, commodities have always attracted key investors. For example, governments have held gold as a reserve asset for millennia. Commodities are basic staples in our daily lives, and the prices we pay for these staples affect each of us directly.

When we fill up the tanks in our cars, trucks, or motorcycles with gasoline, we consume crude oil and oil products. The same is true when we board an aircraft. Lovers of sweets and chocolate desserts are consumers of cocoa beans, wheat, and sugar cane. That cup of morning java we take for its injection of caffeine makes us daily consumers of coffee beans. The tasty slice of bacon we eat with our breakfast is produced from pigs, which trade as a commodity. Our lunchtime sandwich consists of two slices of wheat product. We consume soybeans when we dip our sushi in soy sauce. At a summer barbecue, the corn on the cob and steak we consume are traded commodities. Corn is also filling our gas tanks in the form of ethanol and feeding the cattle raised to produce that juicy steak. On a hot, summer day, we flip on the air conditioner and we flip a switch for light, both of which require electricity, generated by using natural gas, nuclear power, or coal—all commodities. The water in our glasses has already flowed through pipes, which are often made of copper. Many of the clothes we buy are made of cotton. A ring made of precious metals symbolizes marriage. The list of commodities is enormous.

In our personal lives, we spend more money as prices for staple goods rise. We all have exposure to commodity price risk. As investors we are keenly aware of the stock, bond, and even the foreign exchange markets. We watch them closely because we have invested our money into these assets. Often, we have a portfolio with the aim of retiring one day with a sizable nest egg. We call our brokers, check our accounts online, and watch as our portfolios rise and fall. We feel good on days when our assets increase and bad when our portfolios shrink. Most of us, however, do not watch, understand, and analyze commodity prices. To me, this is an odd phenomenon because the influence and impact of commodities is huge. The vast majority of investors is not in the market buying and selling financial assets every day. But every one of them is a daily commodities consumer, and the prices of those commodities impact directly the performance of their investment portfolios.

COMMODITY PRICES IMPACT ALL INVESTMENTS PORTFOLIOS

While inflation eats away at our money and investments, it also causes commodity prices to rise. Just as history tends to repeat itself, markets tend to trade in cycles. Jim Rogers, the famous investor, said on his website, JimRogers.com ("Breakfast of Champions?"), "Historically, there has been a bull market in commodities every 20 or 30 years." Market cycles, as Rogers described them, represent the replication of history. In history, as in everyday life, commodities have always played a central role. The last commodity bull market ended in 1980. The next two decades saw stock and bond markets provide investors with their most obvious and pressing opportunities. However, the start of the new millennium hailed a new and exciting bull market in commodity prices, and this affected every asset in your investment portfolio. There is not a manufacturer on the planet that does not use basic commodities to produce its wares. And at the end of the manufacturing process, finished goods are shipped from factories to stores or directly to consumers, thanks to another commodity—fuel. The value of every stock in your portfolio is affected by commodity prices, because the cost of goods sold is linked directly to a company's earnings, which raise or lower its share price.

Commodities also impact bond values, because bonds are interest-rate instruments. Often referred to as fixed-income investments, bonds pay a rate of return, but they move up and down in value. When commodity prices rise, inflationary pressures tend to rise. The consumer price index (CPI) and the producer price index (PPI) often directly affect the price of bonds, because, at base, these indexes merely measure the effect of commodity prices on finished goods.

Foreign exchange rates, which are the value of currencies of various nations around the world, are also sensitive to commodity prices. The Norwegian krone, for example, often moves higher as oil prices rally because Norway is an influential exporter of crude oil. The Australian and Canadian dollars both tend to rise and fall with commodity prices because these nations are big commodity producers. Indeed, the vast reserves of farmland, energy, metals, and ores within Canadian and Australian borders make their currencies commodity proxies. Whether your portfolio is focused on specific stocks, bonds, mutual funds, or foreign exchange instruments, your investments will rise and fall based on movements in the commodity markets.

WHY DO COMMODITY PRICES MOVE?

Commodity markets are global. Designated exchanges in the United States, Europe, or Asia centralize trade in these essential goods, but they remain world markets. At the same time, commodities tend to have localized production. Chile, for example, produces the most copper in the world, while natural gas production is concentrated in the United States and Russia. Meanwhile, the vast majority of cocoa beans comes from the Ivory Coast, Ghana, and Brazil. The bulk of the world's coffee is grown in Colombia, Vietnam, and Brazil. The United States, China, and Brazil are the world's largest corn producers. South Africa and Russia produce almost 90 percent of the global annual supply of platinum. The list is as long as it is varied. And the consumption of commodities is ubiquitous. Producing countries export surplus commodities around the globe.

Commodity prices move for a variety of reasons. There are macroeconomic factors, such as supply-and-demand imbalances that drive the prices up or down. Geopolitical events, such as wars, weather, climate change, natural disasters, and even trade policies between nations, also can cause the price of a commodity to move.

Demographics are another big factor when considering long-term trends. Commodities are finite resources, but population growth expands the market for these goods and thus increases global demand. Two hundred million human beings inhabited the earth in the year 1 AD. By the year 1500, the population had more than doubled to 450 million. It took an additional 304 years for the world's population to reach 1 billion inhabitants. On October 31, 2011, there were 7 billion human beings in the world. The year 2525 will see the population hit 8 billion. The rate of growth of humans on planet Earth has been nothing short of astonishing, and every birth adds potential new demand to the global commodity story.

Meanwhile, as the population has increased, so has technology and mining. Farming, commodity-sourcing technology, and ingenuity have kept up with the needs of the human race on planet Earth. However, just as commodities are finite resources, arable land and water are also finite. In spite of all the ingenuity and improvements in commodity-sourcing technology, demand will increasingly outstrip supply. Population growth rates will put a strain on the supplies of commodities, and competition for these finite resources is sure to increase in the years ahead.

In addition to population growth, there is another dynamic that has emerged over the past couple of decades that will increase the strain on commodity staples. Emerging markets have been booming since the late 1970s and early 1980s, China in particular. Over that period, the Chinese economy grew at an average annual rate of almost 10 percent, or triple the global average. China's gross domestic product (GDP) grew from $147.3 billion in 1978 to $4.9 trillion in 2009. Economists estimate that China will overtake the United States to become the largest economy in the world by 2019. In terms of population, there were more than 1.3 billion people in China in 2010, more than four times the number of inhabitants in the United States. As the Chinese population and GDP grew, a rising middle class has emerged. This middle class has money to spend as its members endeavor to raise the standard of their lifestyles—both for themselves and their families. Better living means a more sophisticated and better-quality diet. It also means more possessions, such as televisions, laptops, smartphones, and cars. This equates to a greater consumption of commodity staples.

A larger addressable market, which largely comprises rising population and wealth in formerly poor nations, is now chasing a finite supply of commodities. As a result, commodity prices since around the year 2000 or so have become increasingly volatile. Commodity prices react, sometimes violently, each time GDP numbers are reported from leading countries around the world. As global GDP expands, commodity prices move higher. This is hard evidence of the strain on the fundamental supply-and-demand equation for commodities, given the finite characteristic of supply. Competition for commodities has never been fiercer.

Market psychology also plays an important role in determining prices for each commodity sector and each individual commodity product. Rumors of shortages and surpluses can move commodity market prices in the short term. The same is true for the price of stocks and bonds. Traded assets are all susceptible to short-term market repricing based on the perception of market participants.

Microeconomics has an important role in commodity prices movement as well. The price of a commodity sometimes becomes so high that consumers substitute a cheaper commodity for a more expensive one. This occurred in 2011 as cotton prices hit historically high levels. The price of cotton climbed to dizzying heights because corn prices in 2008 exploded higher and farmers decided to plant corn instead of cotton. But the lack of a sufficient cotton crop led to a deficit and a consequent price surge.

However, rather than pay extra high prices for cotton, Chinese garment manufacturers decided they would instead use less expensive synthetic fibers to produce garments. Chinese manufacturers knew that their customers would not pay five times the regular asking price for a cotton sweater or blouse. This is a perfect example of how individual behavior will affect the price of a commodity. Another example is when the price of corn shoots up, a farmer may decide to plant more corn than other agricultural products. The rationale is simple. The farmer will make more money planting a crop that is expensive rather than planting one that is cheap.

Sometimes an event triggers a change in consumer behavior. This was the case during the bovine spongiform encephalopathy (BSE) hysteria in recent decades. BSE, also known as mad cow disease, was first reported in the United Kingdom in 1986 and emanated from cheap feed made with animal parts. Once the media got hold of the story, cattle prices plunged—not only in the United Kingdom, but around the globe, as governments feared importing tainted meat and meat products. Indeed, the scare over mad cow disease directly impacted cattle prices for 20 years. However, in 2006, Hematech, a biotechnology company based in Sioux Falls, South Dakota, used genetic engineering and cloning technology to produce cattle that are immune to mad cow disease. Since Hematech's discovery, cattle prices have traded higher.

Many variables go into the ultimate selling price of an individual commodity. There are macroeconomic reasons, such as demographics, geopolitical dynamics, GDP, world events, and weather, to name but a few, as well as microeconomic reasons, such as the individual behavior of consumers and producers. Any variation in these factors will move commodity prices.

WHY SHOULD YOU CARE?

You should care about price movement not only because the price movements of individual commodity markets impact your pocketbook as you shop for the necessities of life, but they also affect your investment portfolio. When higher cotton prices in 2011 affected Chinese manufacturers, Chinese economic reports, such as CPI and GDP, were also affected. This, in turn, affected your portfolio, because all markets today are hypersensitive to Chinese growth statistics.

Meanwhile, mad cow disease had a direct impact on the share prices of companies that sold beef products, such as McDonald's, Tyson Foods, and other similar firms you may hold in your investment portfolio. When farmers decide to plant more corn, it may create soybean shortages, which will affect the price of many manufactured food products as well as the share prices of companies, such as General Mills and Kraft. So the ups and downs of commodity markets are key factors in determining both your monthly expenditure and your retirement assets.

One of the most interesting things I've learned about commodities markets during my career is just how much governments care about production, consumption, and strategic stockpiles of these essential goods. They also care about prices and availability. Gold, for example, is held as a reserve asset by governments. Another example is the Organization of the Petroleum Exporting Countries (OPEC), the cartel formed by several of the largest oil-producing governments, which serves to control oil flows and the price of crude oil around the world.

Governments have always been concerned about their ability to feed their people. For example, bread prices have been the source of many uprisings throughout history. On September 4, 1793, the French revolution started with a demonstration for more wages and bread. New York City experienced the bread riot of 1873. On February 10 of that year the following notice appeared, "BREAD, MEAT, RENT, FUEL. Their prices must come down! The voice of the People will be heard, and must prevail. . . ." The Arab Spring of 2011 began as a demonstration against rising food and bread prices in Tunisia.

When I first visited Russia as a commodities trader during the mid–1980s, I learned firsthand that governments care deeply about the prices of commodities. Just as governments watch each other, they also watch commodity flows. By extension, this means that they watch people like me.

After checking in at Mezhdunarodnaya Hotel in Moscow, the unsmiling woman at the desk handed me a room key and four squares of toilet paper. This was no ordinary toilet paper; it could also have doubled as fine sandpaper. When I got to my room and saw no roll in the bathroom, I understood that there must have been a paper shortage in Russia. But it wasn't just paper. There were shortages of everything. This was a four-star hotel, but the shower did not work, and there was no bathtub plug.

Later that evening, I had dinner with people from the Bank for Foreign Trade, the government arm that controlled gold and silver sales for the USSR. At the time, the Soviet government set up specific agencies to trade with foreign business entities, like the one I represented.

I met the traders from the Bank for Foreign Trade at a Moscow restaurant, and we proceeded to talk business, laugh, eat, and drink for hours. Eight people attended this dinner, including a colleague from London. We consumed a tremendous amount of Russian vodka which is made from potatoes. (Other intoxicating libations are made from grains—which are traded commodities!) My hosts arranged for a car to take us back to the hotel around 1 a.m., and my colleague and I wandered through the lobby to the hotel bar. We decided that we desperately needed a walk to breathe in some of that brisk Moscow air and clear our heads. It was mid-February and the temperature was around 15 degrees below zero. The air felt good as we made our way down the cold and empty streets around the hotel.

A long black car pulled up and stopped beside us. A well-dressed man jumped out showed us his KGB identification, and in perfect English addressed us both by name.

"Mr. Hecht," the KGB officer said, "it is not safe for you to walk on the streets of Moscow at this hour. Please get in the car." We got in the car. Our protector told us, "Please stay in your comfortable hotel at night. We have been assigned to ensure your safety in Moscow."

When it comes to commodity production, Russia has it all. Russia is one of the biggest producers and exporters of raw materials and energy in the world. It is a significant producer of precious metals, including gold, silver, and most notably platinum group metals (PGMs). Russia is the world's top producer of nickel and the world's third largest producer and exporter of steel and aluminum. The country also produces copper, and it also possesses enormous natural gas reserves. At the same time, it has the world's third largest coal reserves and the eighth largest reserves of crude oil.

Today, Russia comprises more than three-quarters of the territory of the old USSR and remains a huge producer of livestock and grains. It exports its commodities all over the world, and its main trading partners are Western Europe and China. Western Europe imports Russian natural gas via pipelines. Indeed, as this book is being written, the Russians are in the final stages of opening the Altai natural gas pipeline from western Siberia to northwestern China. Russia has always been a rich country when it comes to natural resources. Only its own history has held mother Russia back from reaching its full potential.

Russia is much different today from the way it was in the mid–1980s, but it is still a commodity-producing powerhouse. Keep an eye on all commodity-producing powerhouses. Governments around the world are well aware of Russia's potential. The Russian commodity business is on their radar; it should also be on yours. This knowledge will keep you steps ahead of other investors and will yield fruitful investment opportunities in the years to come.

Remember, commodity markets are global markets. Consumption is ubiquitous, but production is usually highly localized. Governments attempt to keep a tight leash on commodity prices and flows and must make sure that staples reach their citizens.

This book will help guide you through the various commodity markets, as well as inform you of how and why these markets operate and why prices move. A basic education in the science of commodity trading will enhance and complement your investment activities. You will find that this important variable in the calculus of investing will help you make better and more informed decisions.

CHAPTER 1

A "Technomental" Approach

FUNDAMENTAL AND
TECHNICAL ANALYSIS IN THE
COMMODITIES MARKETS

Human sacrifice, technicians and fundamentalists living
together ... mass hysteria!
—GHOSTBUSTERS (MOVIE, 1984)

borrowed the above opening quote from an article in *Futures* maga-
zine, published on July 15, 2008. The author, James T. Holter, wrote:

> All right, so maybe Dr. Peter Venkman (a.k.a. Bill Murray)
> didn't foretell exactly that in the 1984 movie *Ghostbusters*, but
> such a proclamation would have been just as ominous. ... Over
> the years, the relationship between technicians and fundamen-
> talists, who examine supply and demand data to forecast future
> prices, has been just as strained as that of felines and canines,
> with both often derisively attacking the others' approach.
> Technicians call fundamentals "funny" mentals. Fundamen-
> talists refer to technical analysis as "voodoo science."

Holter hit the nail on the head. He goes on to describe that with respect to both forms of market analysis, the sum is much greater than the two parts individually. Fundamental and technical analysis in concert create a more vivid picture of the price structure of a market and are a far more effective investment and trading tool.

In this chapter we review how these two forms of analysis used together will enhance your understanding of commodity prices. We also demonstrate how, used independently, both forms of analysis are flawed.

FUNDAMENTAL ANALYSIS

Commodity fundamentals are defined as an equation involving supply and demand. The equilibrium price of a commodity is the price that occurs when sellers and buyers meet in a free marketplace. The goal of fundamental analysis is the estimation of total production compared to total consumption of a commodity over various time periods.

When the supply of a commodity is greater than the demand, a surplus is created and, according to fundamental analysis, prices will fall. Fundamentalists regard surplus conditions as bearish for prices. By the same token, a deficit is bullish, and prices will rise. A deficit in wheat, for example, may be the result of poor or damaged crops in major growing nations such as China, India, Russia, or the United States.

Deficits can create dangerous social situations for individuals and governments alike. Imagine making a trip to the grocery store and finding no bread for sale because of a sudden deficit in the global wheat market. Picture no gas at the pump because of a sudden deficit in crude oil. Such situations have the makings of social unrest; therefore, governments often hold stockpiles of commodities as safeguards.

While stockpile levels are easily obtainable from some countries, such as the United States, or the nations that comprise the European Union where there is a higher degree of transparency, other countries, such as China and Russia, regard the data on their commodity stockpiles as strategic state secrets. In the United States, the Department of Energy periodically releases data on supplies of crude oil and natural gas in storage, and the U.S. Department of Agriculture releases crop reports and data on stockpiles of various grains and other agricultural commodities. For example, the United States currently holds more than 700 million barrels of oil as its strategic petroleum reserve (SPR). At the same time, the International Monetary Fund releases data on reserve assets, such as gold and silver, held by nations around the world. It is nearly impossible to calculate accurately the global stockpile of any one commodity at a particular time. Analysts make estimates in each market, but these are, at best, educated guesses. Fundamental analysis becomes more of an art than a science when it involves a commodity-producing country that holds its cards close to its vest.

The job of a fundamental commodity analyst is to "guesstimate" a commodity's total annual supply, annual demand, and the level of stockpiles. These are the calculations that reveal whether a commodity is in surplus, deficit, or equilibrium. Many companies rely on this analysis to make key business decisions and projections involving the availability of commodities for their manufacturing processes, future costs, and pricing calculations for consumers. A producer sensing a market deficit in a particular commodity may postpone sales in anticipation of higher prices. At the same time, a consumer expecting a deficit may stockpile at present prices for fear of future price hikes and availability problems. The consumer, for example, might be a manufacturer that needs to source aluminum to make cars. A deficit in aluminum could have serious consequences on the business because if the company is unable to purchase the aluminum below a certain price, the cost of finishing the car could end up higher than it can be sold for. Analysts go to great lengths to understand fundamentals, and industries around the world depend on the accuracy of their data and forecasts.

Commodity Production

Fundamental analysis usually begins with the calculation of the annual production of a commodity. This tends to be concentrated in a few areas of the world. For example, just as there are a limited number of countries with arable land suitable for growing certain crops, there are a limited number of countries with mineral deposits for certain metals. Many of these countries, such as Chile for copper, Ukraine for wheat, the Ivory Coast for cocoa, and Nigeria for oil, are not on the radar of many investors. However, there are times when it is highly profitable to keep tabs on these countries. When attempting to understand commodity risk that will affect a specific investment, it is important to pay attention to events in countries that are significant producers of that commodity.

A fundamental analyst can sometimes be the most powerful force in a market. The Ivory Coast and Ghana, two small African nations, routinely produce more than 50 percent of the world's cocoa beans. The control of a market that produces one of the world's most beloved products, chocolate, puts those two countries in an enviable position. One would think they would be the most powerful forces in the global cocoa market, but this is not the case.

The most powerful force in the cocoa market over the past 50 years has been Johannes "Hans" Kilian, a German cocoa-pod counter, who turned 75 in 2012. Kilian, a fundamental supply-side analyst, started his career in the 1960s at a German cocoa trading company, and over the course of his career has worked for numerous cocoa trading firms, hedge funds, and chocolate manufacturers, including Swiss giant Nestlé. Each season, Kilian visits the cocoa-producing fields of West Africa, Indonesia, Brazil, and other countries, counting cocoapods as he goes, one by one. Since 1991, his company J. G. Kilian and Co. has forecast the annual global cocoa supply in reports that move the price of the commodity. In an article by Emiko Terazono from April 3, 2012, the *Financial Times* described Kilian as, "The man who could single-handedly move cocoa prices 10 percent higher or lower in the space of a few seconds." Kilian has developed a granular method of information analysis for which hedge funds, huge food companies, and cocoa producers pay handsomely. However, Kilian is only one example of the many fundamental analysts who toil to produce reliable production statistics on global commodities.

The supply side is often impacted by exogenous issues, such as weather, politics, and civil unrest. A producing country engaged in civil war, for example, might have a bumper crop—an unusually bountiful harvest of a particular crop—but getting it to market might be impossible and, in spite of its abundance, the crop might rot. Corruption in certain locations also plays a role in crop size and the flow of currency to pay for it.

To complicate matters further, the potential for commodity production is also an issue for the fundamental analyst. How much oil is in the crust of the earth at certain locations around the world? How much natural gas exists between rock formations? What is the best way to quantify the level of reserves of copper, gold, bauxite, silver, nickel, lead, and other metals and ores? How much arable land is available on the planet for corn, wheat, soybeans, rice, sorghum, sugar, cocoa, coffee, and other food staples, and how much will this land yield under perfect and not-so-perfect growing conditions? Together, the compilation of annual supply, worldwide stockpiles, and proven, probable, and potential reserves will yield a snapshot of a commodity's global supply.

Commodity Demand

Fundamental analysts investigate the demand side of the equation to estimate the annual usage of individual commodities. Just as almost every country across the globe consumes chocolate, the same holds true for energy sources, such as oil, natural gas, and coal. And just as building infrastructure requires metals, agricultural commodities like grains help sustain life across the entire face of the earth. While global economic, demographic, and political conditions influence the demand side of the equation in fundamental commodity analysis, these components are virtually useless as a sole tool for forecasting the price of any commodity. Mining, agricultural, and energy technologies all sit on the supply side of the equation, and each of them is a form of objective science. Conversely, economics, demographics, and politics on the demand side are all social sciences, and these are subjective and unquantifiable by nature. When you balance physical science on one side against social science on the other, the result will be less than accurate.

Nonetheless, in spite of its imprecise nature, demand is just as important as supply when it comes to understanding commodity markets and prices. As countries build infrastructure, such as new roads and buildings, companies expand and individuals buy more consumer goods. Economic growth increases demand for staples on a global basis. At the same time, the opposite is true during times of economic contraction. As national investment in infrastructure decreases, companies slim down and individuals are more careful about the amount of goods they purchase.

Every microeconomist will tell you that demand for a commodity, or any goods for that matter, decreases as prices rise. Economists call this price elasticity, and it is part of the basic laws of supply and demand. Even if the commodity is a staple, human beings will adapt and find cheaper alternatives if prices become too high. For example, if bread prices were to go through the roof, as they have in many parts of the world throughout history, demand for rice increases; rice is a less expensive starch. By the same token, when the price of a commodity rises, producers increase production as long as production costs do not rise so high that they negate profit margins. Meanwhile, if the price of a commodity falls, demand tends to increase. Imagine, for example, the increased mileage U.S. motorists would put on their automobiles each year if gasoline prices suddenly dropped to $1 a gallon.

Finally, when commodity producers have the opportunity to choose between different commodities to produce, they will generally opt for the one that yields the most profit. This is usually the thought process behind the choices farmers make when deciding which crops to plant. As you can see, the microeconomic behavior of both producers and consumers will affect the ultimate price that a commodity will fetch.

Demographics pack a big punch on the demand side of the fundamental commodity equation. The rate of population growth on planet earth is staggering. More people means more mouths to feed, more housing, and more consumers to whom products can be sold. Greater wealth and higher standards of living across the planet have also increased the demand for commodity staples. However, commodities are finite, and an expanding and wealthier populous will continue to vie for these precious products.

Politics are perhaps the trickiest part of the demand-side equation. For example, crude oil prices would probably fall precipitously if Saudi Arabia decided to flood the world market with oil and double its daily production. If Iran cut off oil supplies by blockading the Persian Gulf, as it has often threatened, oil prices would skyrocket.

Export and import tariffs also affect commodity prices, as do subsidies. A U.S. tariff on steel exports from the United States into China would dampen the demand for steel and might even start a trade war with deeper consequences. Tariffs are politically motivated policies aimed usually at one country and are often designed to level the playing field of trade. For example, politically motivated legislation in the European Union (EU) showers billions of euros in annual subsidies on beet sugar producers. This has served to keep the price of sugar unnaturally high and has resulted in food processors paying more than world market prices for the commodity. In the United States, farm subsidies have supported crop production and have kept the prices of produce at artificial highs for decades—all at a cost to the consumer.

Fundamental analysis often uses sophisticated econometric models to forecast the usage of a commodity by factoring in current and past data to predict future economic conditions. These models use indicators like the consumer price index (CPI), the producer price index (PPI), global currency and interest rates, and gross domestic product (GDP) to forecast demand. The Department of Energy, Department of Agriculture, and other government agencies in the United States and the EU provide demand-side analysis. At the same time, the world's top consumer, China, also releases reports on its economy. There are much data to keep track of when it comes to the demand for individual commodities, and it is often difficult to ascertain whether increased demand for certain commodities is simply the result of increased stockpiling.

Production-Consumption Dilemma

The chief problem with fundamental analysis in the commodities markets is the nature of the markets themselves. Because production is concentrated and consumption is widespread, producers tend to sell regularly and in large quantities. As such, producers depend on the cash flow from production to fund future production. Consumers, on the other hand, tend to buy hand to mouth. They buy commodities as they need them—whether it's mom on a grocery-shopping trip or a manufacturer buying for the manufacture of all types of finished goods.

Indeed, a producer's entire business often relies on the use of a single commodity. A business consumer, on the other hand, may use many different commodities to manufacture its product. This dynamic is also part of the calculus that causes volatility in commodity prices. In a perfect world, consumers would buy directly from producers at fixed prices that would allow a profit margin for the producer and a profit margin for the manufacturer. There would be total and complete transparency, no government intervention or influence, and centralized data on production and consumption. But the world is not perfect, and producers often want to sell at times when consumers do not want to buy; and sometimes consumers want to buy when producers do not want to sell. Hence, we have traders and speculators in the market who often serve to smooth price volatility and provide a constant market for producers and consumers.

As volatile assets, commodity prices tend to trade in a wide range, and predicting short-term movements is no easy feat. While fundamental analysis can provide important clues to long-term price trends, it can often be a blunt and imprecise tool for short-term analysis. The supply-and-demand flows of specific commodities will provide any investor with important clues to the risks and profit potential inherent in most portfolio holdings. It's all about improving an investor's knowledge base. The risk of higher or lower commodity prices can make or break a company, and many investors do not monitor these risks until it is too late. Understanding long-term fundamental commodity risks will not only provide clues to the future earnings of a company, but it can also reveal how its management handles such risk and uncover the expertise or shortcomings that will determine success or failure.

TECHNICAL ANALYSIS

In commodities markets, as in other markets, there are cycles. Understanding the history of cyclical behavior and past price movements can help predict the future. Fortunately, you will not have to pore over thousands of pages of prices and data. All the data required for technical analysis are contained in one picture—one simple price chart. Fundamental analysis examines numerous aspects of an individual commodity market, while technical analysis studies past and current price action in futures contracts.

One of my first bosses in the commodities business was a strict fundamentalist. He considered charts and technical analysis to be something akin to voodoo. That was back in the mid–1980s, and I wanted to buy gold. As proof of my analysis, I provided my boss with a chart. He turned the chart upside down and poured his cup of coffee on it. Then he laughed and demanded that in the future I bring him only fundamental data. He also told me that fundamentals revealed to him that my analysis was wrong. I was young and listened to my boss. I didn't buy any gold. A few days later, when the gold price rallied, my boss didn't say a word. I knew then there was a time and place for technical analysis.

The reason technical analysis works has little to do with commodities themselves, but because every technical analyst in the world is looking at the same price charts, and many of those analysts act on what they see. The more glaring the pattern, the more technically biased traders will act. At heart, this is an issue of mass market psychology.

Even if fundamentals had not supported that rise in the price of gold my boss refuted, the chart pattern had created a self-fulfilling prophecy. One certainty in the volatile world of financial markets is this: they go up when there are more buyers than sellers, and they go down when there are more sellers than buyers. So the advice here is simple: ignore charts and technical analysis at your own peril.

A technician does not follow supply-and-demand fundamentals; a technician follows price patterns, price history, and market trading data to make trading decisions.

Three Types of Charts

Charts provide concise pictures of market activities over various time periods. Technical analysts use a number of different types of charts to analyze price movment.

Line Charts. These represent only closing prices over a period of time. Take a look at the line chart in Figure 1.1, which plots quarterly prices for Intercontinental Exchange, Inc. (ICE) sugar futures. On a daily line chart, only the daily closing prices are used.

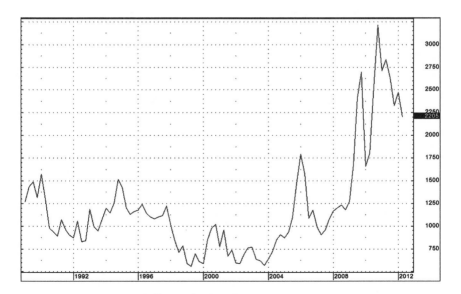

Figure 1.1 **Quarterly ICE sugar line chart**
Source: CQG, Inc. © 2012. All rights reserved worldwide.

This kind of chart provides an excellent picture of long-term trends. However, the range of trading during a period is often important information for a technical analyst, and this is why line charts are rarely used for in-depth technical analysis.

Bar Charts. These expand on the line chart by adding other pieces of key information, including the high and low prices traded. Bar charts represent the total trading activity within a certain time period.

In Figure 1.2, a horizontal dash on the vertical line represents the opening price (on the left side) and closing price (on the right) of the period. On most bar charts, if the left dash is lower than the right dash, the bar will be shaded black, representing an up period. Conversely, if the left dash is higher than the right dash, the bar will be shaded red representing a down period.

Candlestick Charts. These provide an easy view of a period's trading range and contain information similar to that in the bar chart. The wide, vertical lines, or candles, illustrate the difference between the opening price and the closing price.

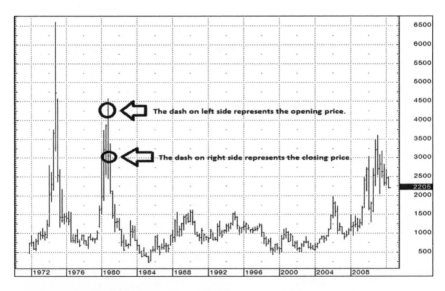

Figure 1.2 **Quarterly ICE sugar bar chart**

Source: CQG, Inc. © 2012. All rights reserved worldwide.

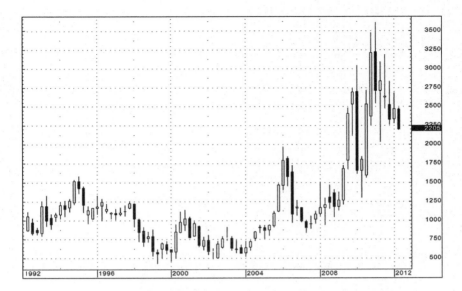

Figure 1.3 **Quarterly ICE sugar candlestick chart**
Source: CQG, Inc. © 2012. All rights reserved worldwide.

In Figure 1.3, the black candles indicate periods in which the sugar price went down, and white candles indicate periods in which the price climbed.

Identifying Support and Resistance Levels

In technical analysis, two concepts can be applied to the three charts—support and resistance levels. A *support level* is below the current price, and it is the price at which technical analysts believe that buyers will outnumber sellers. The *resistance level* is above the current price, and technical analysts believe that it is the price at which sellers will outnumber buyers. The monthly New York Stock Exchange (NYSE) crude oil chart shown in Figure 1.4 provides an example of support and resistance.

A technical analyst will watch these levels of support and resistance carefully because prices tend to correct themselves once a market approaches either of them. If the price approaches the support level, the market will increase. If it approaches the resistance level, the market will decrease. The theory here is that as a market price declines and approaches a support level, there will be more buyers than sellers

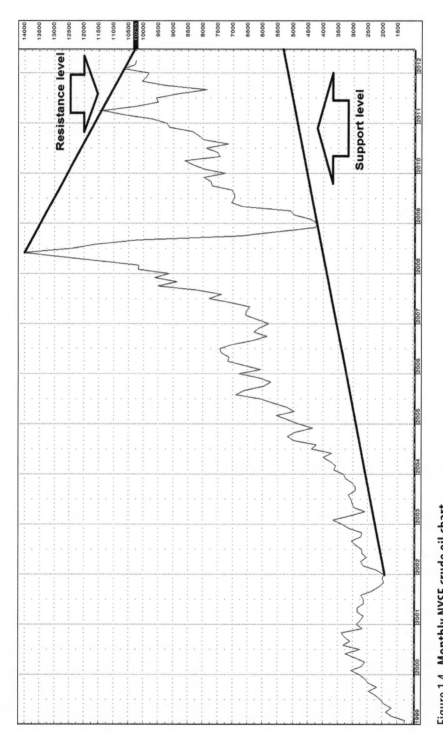

Figure 1.4 Monthly NYSE crude oil chart

causing the market price to move higher or bounce off support. Bounce-off support occurs when a price approaches a support level, does not violate that support, and turns around and moves higher. Conversely, as a market price increases and approaches a resistance level, there will be more sellers than buyers, thus causing the market price to move lower if it does not violate the resistance level. However, if support or resistance is broken, a breakout occurs as a market moves outside the trading range, below support or above resistance. A breakout is a continuation of a price move down below support or up above resistance. The ability to know in advance when a commodity price is ready to move up or down is obviously an enormous benefit to an investor.

Trend Charts

As in other markets, technicians look for the development of price patterns over time. A trend develops when a market moves and continues to move in a particular direction. Figure 1.5, which measures price history on a long-term quarterly basis, illustrates the uptrend in the Commodity Exchange (COMEX) gold price.

The New York Mercantile Exchange (NYMEX) natural gas chart shown in Figure 1.6 illustrates a long-term downtrend in prices for the commodity.

If we combine what we know so far about trends and levels of support and resistance, we can form a pretty good idea of how commodity markets tend to move over long and short time periods. The quarterly Chicago Board of Trade (CBOT) corn chart shown in Figure 1.7 illustrates how, at times, trends can be broken and market prices follow through.

This chart shows how in 1995, a long-term trend line was broken (#1), as corn prices broke a resistance line and then jumped by more than 45 percent in a very short period of time. When the resistance was broken, the previous resistance level became a support level. The following year, corn prices broke the support level (#2), and fell by 37 percent. The chart also reveals that after an initial false breakout in 2007, corn prices broke back above resistance (#3) and soon jumped by more than 90 percent. Investors can expect that, when resistance is broken on the upside, the resistance level will become the market's support level, and when support is broken on the downside, that support level becomes the market resistance.

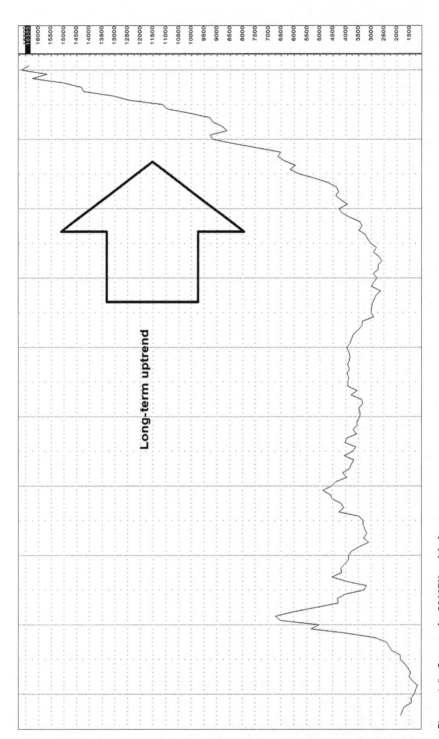

Figure 1.5 Quarterly COMEX gold chart

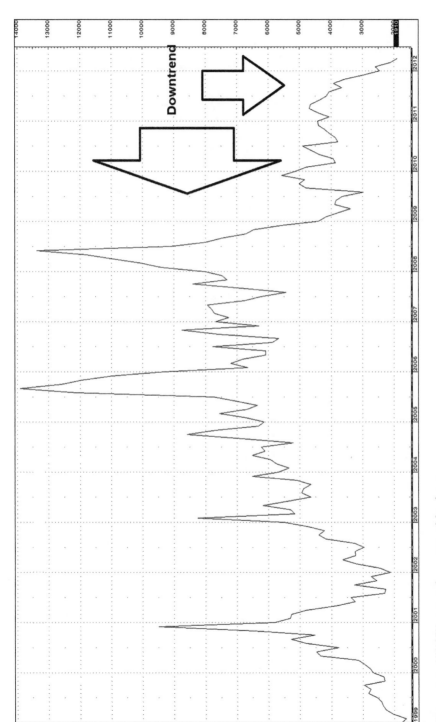

Figure 1.6 NYMEX natural gas monthly chart

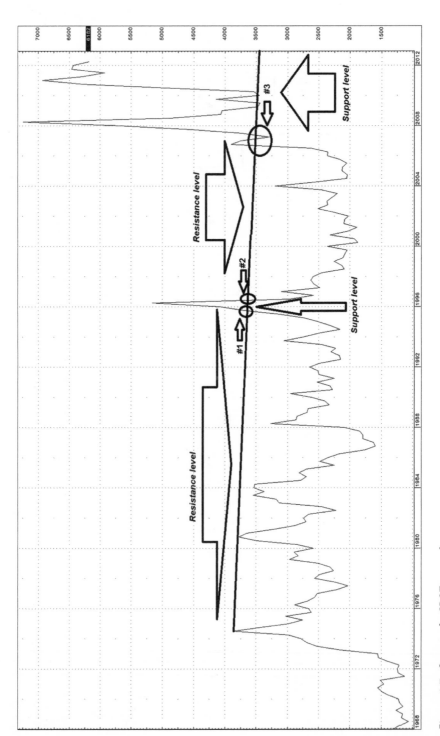

Figure 1.7 **Quarterly CBOT corn chart**

Continuation and Reversal Patterns

Technicians always look for patterns that have caused price movement in the past. However, other patterns also cause technicians to act. Continuation and reversal patterns aim to forecast whether a market will continue within the current trend, or whether it will reverse. The charts below are just the tip of the iceberg in the world of technical analysis, but they are among the most common:

- **Cup and handle.** This bullish pattern (Figure 1.8) illustrates consolidation before a breakout. It gets its name from the way it looks. The length of the breakout usually corresponds to the height of the cup.

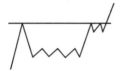

Figure 1.8 **Cup and handle**

- **Flag.** This chart pattern (Figure 1.9) is shaped like a rectangle, or a flag, and is usually found in the middle of a significant advance or decline trend. The flagpole is the distance from the first resistance or support break.

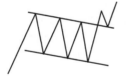

Figure 1.9 **Flag**

- **Pennant.** This particular pattern, the pennant (Figure 1.10), is similar to the flag, but the consolidation narrows into a symmetrical triangle shape before breaking out.

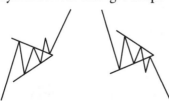

Figure 1.10 **Pennant**

- **Rectangle.** This pattern (Figure 1.11) is one of the easiest to recognize because of its well-defined support and resistance levels. The breakout here often continues in the direction of the original trend.

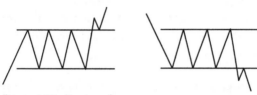

Figure 1.11 **Rectangle**

- **Ascending and descending triangle:** This pattern comes in the shape of a triangle (Figure 1.12). As support and resistance lines converge, the breakout up or down will run as long as the widest part of the triangle.

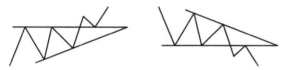

Figure 1.12 **Ascending and descending triangle**

- **Triangle symmetrical.** This one (Figure 1.13) is similar to the pennant but without the flag pole, and it usually represents a period of consolidation. The breakout usually continues in the direction of the original trend. Like ascending and descending triangles, the breakout up or down will run as long as the widest part of the triangle.

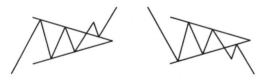

Figure 1.13 **Triangle symmetrical**

- **Wedge falling/rising.** This is a bullish pattern (Figure 1.14) that begins wide at the top or bottom and contracts as prices move up or down. This is a reversal pattern and is bullish when the wedge is pointing down and bearish when pointing up. The breakout up or down will run as long as the widest part of the triangle.

Figure 1.14 **Wedge falling/rising**

- **Double bottom/top.** This is a reversal bullish/bearish pattern (Figure 1.15), depending on direction, and usually occurs after an extended trend. The breakout often extends by the difference from the resistance/support breakout to lows or highs.

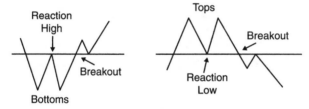

Figure 1.15 **Double bottom/top**

- **Head and shoulders bottom/top.** This reversal pattern (Figure 1.16) is made up of a left shoulder, a head, and a right shoulder. The breakout usually runs as long as the distance between the head and the neckline.

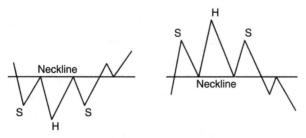

Figure 1.16 **Head and shoulders bottom/top**

- **Rounded bottom/top.** This one (Figure 1.17) is usually a bullish or bearish signal, depending on its direction and indicating a possible reversal of the current trend.

Figure 1.17 **Rounded bottom/top**

- **Triple bottom/top.** All three lows (or highs) should be reasonably equal, well-spaced, and mark significant turning points (Figure 1.18). The breakout expectation is the same as the double top/bottom.

Figure 1.18 **Triple bottom/top**

Three Key Measures

When looking at a technical position in a commodity market, it is helpful to examine three particular statistical measures of futures contracts: volume, open interest, and historical volatility.

Volume. This is the total number of futures contracts traded in a specific market. The higher the volume, the more actively traded or liquid the futures contract or commodity is. Volume is an important tool for technical analysts because it can confirm a price trend. If a market moves higher or lower, a technician will immediately investigate the trading volume during the move. Rising prices along with rising volume generally confirm strong bull market action. Falling prices and rising volume generally confirm strong bear market action. Technicians also monitor volume for trend reversals. If rising or falling prices are combined with decreasing volume, technical analysts will likely conclude that the market is running out of steam in one particular direction. A technician will then search for a correction point where the market will reverse from the current trend.

Open Interest. This is the total number of long and short positions in futures contracts for a particular commodity that have yet to be closed. This is a key tool for understanding what market participants are thinking and doing. Open interest is often used as an indicator of strength in a market and represents only active positions in a market at a particular time. Higher open interest indicates strength behind price movement. Decreasing open interest suggests that a market may be entering a period of less active trading because market participants are not taking new positions.

A technician will regard an increase in open interest coupled with an increase in price as confirmation that the upward price movement may continue. A fall in open interest along with an increase in price indicates that upward price movement may be about to reverse. Commodity exchanges publish volume and open interest data daily and in some cases in real time. The Commodity Futures Trading Commission (CFTC) publishes weekly data called the Commitment of Traders report, which indicates which types of market participants are holding long or short positions.

Historical Volatility. This is a statistical measure of historical price fluctuation for particular commodity futures contracts. Historical volatility, which is expressed as a percentage, is simply the standard deviation of price differences over time. A technician can select any time period for measuring volatility by comparing the width of a commodity's price range over different periods of time.

Predicting Future Prices

The past is always useful when you're attempting to predict the future. What follows is a brief look at some of the analysts' most popular charting tools.

Moving Averages. This is used as an indicator for the direction of a trend and, as the name suggests, it is calculated using a number of closing-price averages over a certain time period. A moving average

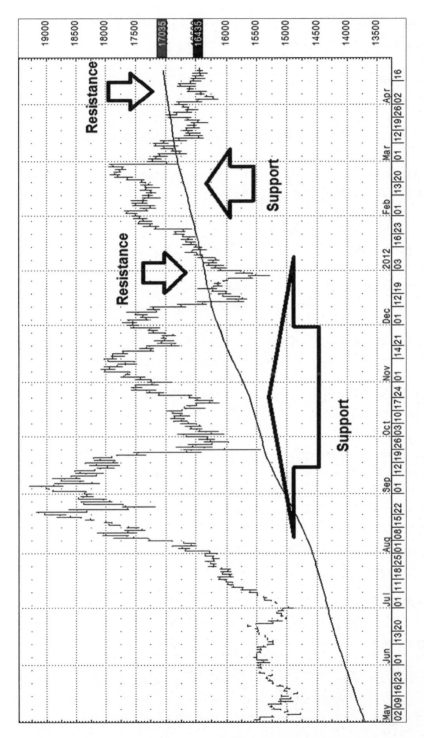

Figure 1.19 Daily gold chart with 200-day simple moving average

Source: CQG, Inc. © 2012. All rights reserved worldwide.

will show support levels in a rising market and resistance levels in a falling market. A simple moving average is equally weighted, meaning that each data point has the same importance. These tend to lag market moves, particularly in volatile markets. To eliminate the lag, many technical analysts use an exponential moving average, which gives more weight to recent prices.

Figure 1.19 illustrates a 200-day simple moving average. When prices are above the moving average, the moving average suggests support; when prices are below, the moving average suggests resistance.

Relative Strength Index. This compares recent gains and losses in a market and indicates whether a commodity is overbought or oversold. Known as the RSI, this index ranges from 0–100. An RSI of lower than 30 indicates an oversold condition, and one greater than 70 indicates an overbought condition.

Figure 1.20 illustrates the RSI for a weekly copper chart. As you can see, an overbought condition led to a fall in prices and an oversold condition led to a rise in prices. But investors should also beware, because as every technical analyst knows, markets can remain overbought or oversold for long periods of time.

Stochastic Oscillators. These aim to quantify the momentum of a price rise or decline. They work by comparing closing prices with price ranges over a time period. The theory behind this technical tool is that prices tend to close near the highs in rising markets and near the lows in falling markets. A reading of below 20 indicates an oversold condition, while a reading of above 80 indicates an overbought condition.

Figure 1.21 shows slow stochastic readings on a daily corn chart. The overbought condition may result in a correction lower (ovals). An oversold condition may result in a correction higher (boxes).

Channels and Bollinger Bands. Bollinger Bands measure the height and depth of a market relative to previous trades, and the channels that are created by these bands measure a market's trading range of prices. As in Figure 1.22, the upper band of a channel represents resistance, while the lower band represents support. Bollinger Bands use a moving average in the middle of a support and a resistance channel to help technicians identify whether a market is trading at the upper or lower end of a range.

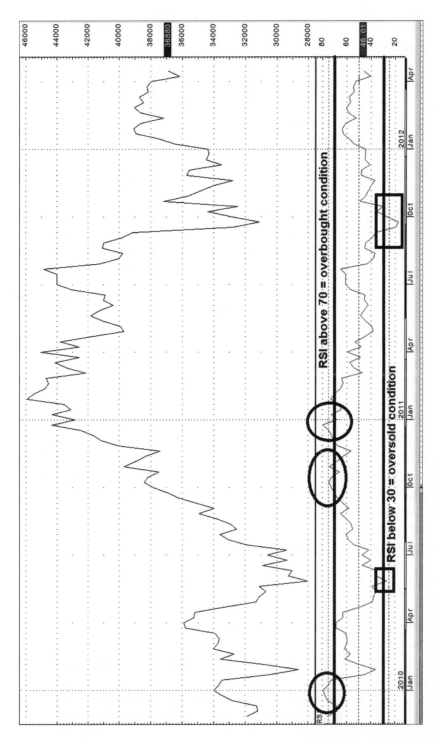

Figure 1.20 Weekly copper line chart with RSI

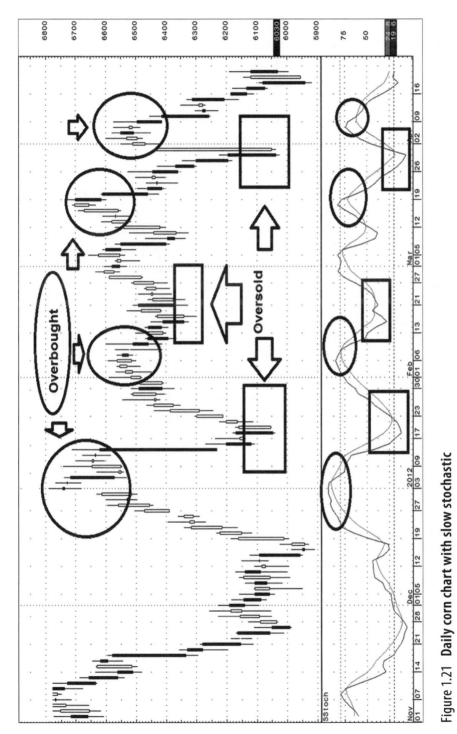

Figure 1.21 **Daily corn chart with slow stochastic**

Figure 1.22 shows a weekly crude oil chart with an upper Bollinger Band, which denotes resistance, and a lower Bollinger Band, which denotes support. There is also a middle moving average value. Wider Bollinger Bands signify a more volatile market.

MACD. The moving average convergence/divergence method uses moving averages to spot changes in market strength, direction, momentum, and duration of price movement.

A crossover occurs when the MACD falls above or below the signal line. A crossover below the line is a bearish signal, and a crossover above the line is bullish. A divergence occurs when a price diverges from the MACD; this generally signals the end of a trend. Finally, a dramatic rise or fall in the MACD signals that a price is overbought or oversold and will soon return to more normal levels or that the market will correct in the opposite direction. (See Figure 1.23.)

Parabolic Indicator. Technicians use parabolic indicators to signal the prices at which to buy and sell. Technical traders will often use this indicator to stop and reverse their market position.

The London Metal Exchange (LME) nickel chart (Figure 1.24) illustrates why a technician might use a parabolic indicator. A parabola above the price is a signal to sell, and a parabola below the price is a signal to buy.

Elliott Wave Theory. This is a technical tool based on the idea that history repeats itself. It uses price history along with a mathematical sequence called the Fibonacci pattern, in which the sum of the previous two numbers equals the third number (i.e., 0, 1, 1, 2, 3, 5, 8, 13, 21, 34, 55, 89, 144, etc.). The Elliott wave theory looks at market cycles and defines them as occurring in a series of price movements or waves.

There are two types of waves—impulse waves and corrective waves. Five subwaves comprise an impulse wave (1–5), and three subwaves comprise a corrective wave (a–b–c).

Elliott wave theory teaches that the waves can be larger or smaller but that the pattern is always similar. Elliott wave technicians scour charts looking for waves within waves to identify the exact point of the market cycle. Once this point is established, they believe that the next move up or down can be predicted.

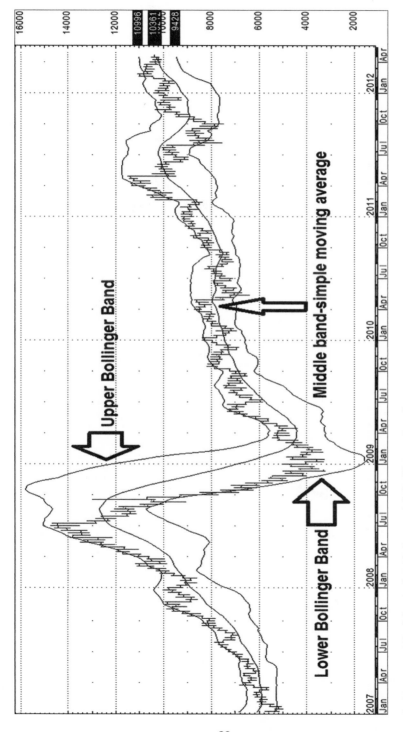

Figure 1.22 **Weekly crude oil chart with Bollinger Bands**

39

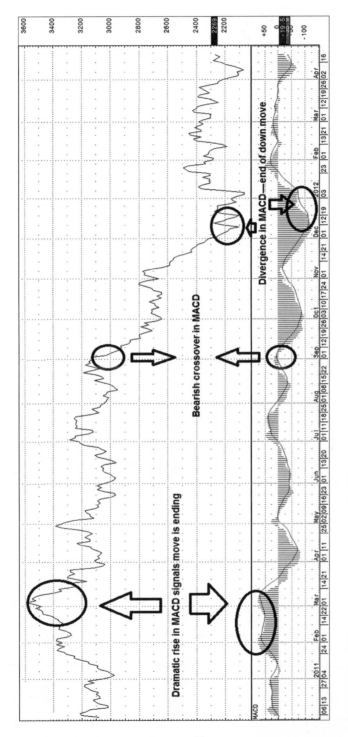

Figure 1.23 Daily cocoa line chart with MACD

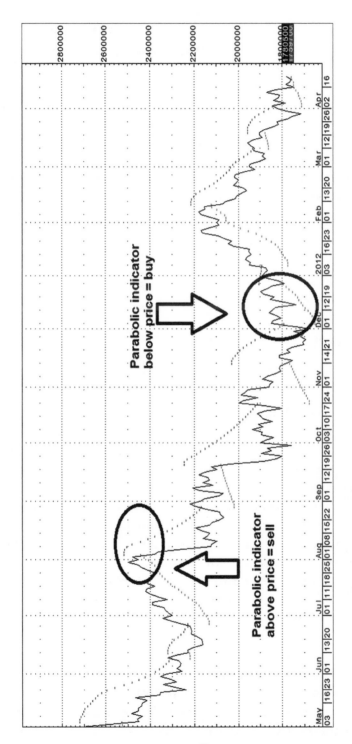

Figure 1.24 LME nickel prices with parabolic indicator

41

The patterns described above (and the Elliott wave pattern shown in Figure 1.25) are road maps for investors. Chart patterns often predict future prices and price trends, especially on a short-term basis. Many market participants use these charts to help them decide whether to buy or sell, and they often become self-fulfilling prophecies. When a bullish pattern appears, a herd of traders will buy and cause prices to rise. When a bearish chart appears, the herd will sell and cause prices to fall. An investor who understands and watches these short-term market movements will be able to predict short-term moves in commodity-related equities themselves. History tends to repeat itself.

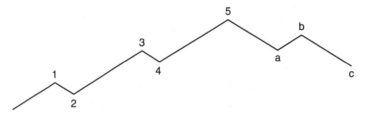

Figure 1.25 **Elliott wave**

Technical Models

Models based on technical analysis operate in all markets at all times. Quantitative expertise is a skill sought by banks, Wall Street firms, and hedge funds. Understanding complex mathematics-based algorithms is important for short-term day traders, whose job is to pick up small profits during each daily market session. At the same time, the development of new technical models and the tweaking of old models that use technical analysis is a constant practice among professional traders.

As technology advances, so does the ability of technical analysts to turbocharge short-term trading results. High-frequency traders often use advanced computer models and a variety of technical analytical tools, such as many of those explained in the preceding pages. In the great trading houses of Wall Street, London, and across Europe and Asia, the models used are often proprietary and contain their own "special sauce," which is generally a variety of tools that are customized and used in a coordinated fashion.

Technical traders often use trial and error to see what works in various markets. When these technicians develop a model that works, they may become extremely active, and they often trade large volumes for small gains, which can be a very profitable venture. However, typical investors do not have to worry about these quantitative geniuses, who use advanced mathematics to trade, although they should be aware of their presence in the markets. The more that market participants use technical tools, the more influence those tools have.

The problem with technical analysis in the world of commodities is that it works well in environments in which volume is significant and consistent. However, commodity markets are often volatile, and prices can move sharply on low volume, which can produce false technical signals. It can often be costly to act on these signals when the unexpected occurs. Trading or investing using only technical signals is as dangerous as relying only on market fundamentals.

And so we come to the optimal method of analyzing commodity markets.

TECHNOMENTAL ANALYSIS

Technomentals are exactly what the word suggests—a combination of technical and fundamental analysis that utilizes the best of both methods. It is important to understand market fundamentals and to access supply and demand equations when trading commodities, and there are massive amounts of data at your fingertips through the Internet to do so. Supply-and-demand data are always the best guide to understanding longer-term trends in commodity markets. Investors must ask, however, how to identify the best time to act. When should you buy that oil refining stock? Higher grain prices may have caused a stock in your portfolio to soar, but when should you take profits? Technical signals are effective tools for entry into and exit from the market.

Technical and fundamental signals often conflict with each other. There are times when the charts signal one direction and fundamentals scream another. An investor with knowledge of both can effectively enhance a portfolio by understanding commodity fundamentals and by using technical signals to get into or out of investment positions.

THE KEYS TO SUCCESSFUL INVESTING

There are two keys to successful trading that I always throw into the mix when I analyze a market and decide to take action and invest. The first is discipline. When I enter a position, I always quantify my risk.

If I buy a stock, I determine how much money I want to risk and what type of reward I am looking for. I never risk more than one dollar to make another dollar. The greater my risk-reward ratio, the greater my chance of success.

Even the world's greatest traders are not right 100 percent of the time. If you risk one dollar to make two dollars, you have to be right only 50 percent of the time to make money. If you are right 60 percent of the time, you will be a successful investor. Identifying your risk-reward position is one of the most crucial aspects of investing. Discipline is most important when a market arrives at your profit target or predetermined loss level. To make money over time, an investor must develop the fortitude to execute at those levels. Most investors let profits turn into losses and losses turn into bigger losses.

The second key is contrarianism. When the fundamentals are screaming buy and the technical traders are selling, it is often the perfect opportunity to enter into an investment position. Additionally, always question the fundamental data you receive with your own intuitive consumer knowledge. Investors have a rich mine of data in their heads. You know what you paid for a gallon of gas, a loaf of bread, a chocolate bar, and a pair of jeans, relative to the amount you paid previously. Sensitize yourself to the prices of goods on a daily basis. For example, is your morning cup of coffee more expensive this month than it was last month? That fundamental microdatum can confirm or refute other data you may come across.

Always trust your own intuition. The funny thing about markets is that they often do stupid things for stupid reasons. Ignore the noise and go with your gut when it comes to investing. Contrarian investing has yielded my best profits over the course of my career.

A technomental approach to investing incorporates the best of both worlds into your portfolio. When it comes to furthering your commodity education and your ability to profit, a combination of fundamental and technical analysis will open up a world of opportunity that many never realized existed.

CHAPTER 2

Commodity Markets

PHYSICAL COMMODITIES, FORWARD/SWAPS, FUTURES, OPTIONS, AND EXCHANGE- TRADED FUND MARKETS

The future ain't what it used to be.

—YOGI BERRA

Commodities flow from producer to consumer, and they pass through many hands before they arrive at their final destination. Often, however, producers want to sell when consumers do not need to buy, and sometimes, conversely, consumers need to buy when producers have nothing to sell. But human beings are adaptable and innovative creatures, and so they have devised a system to deal with this natural phenomenon. This price-risk transfer system, otherwise known as a market or an exchange, ensures that commodities producers always have a consumer to whom they can sell their commodities and that consumers always have a producer from whom they can buy. Transferring price risk ensures the flow of commodities from producer to consumer at variable prices via a series of steps, including ownership at times by different intermediaries, such as governments, financiers, manufacturers, traders, market makers, speculators, and investors.

Understanding how individual commodity prices directly influence the price of all investments in your portfolio requires an education in the underlying commodity markets themselves. This chapter outlines how the various commodity markets work.

THE PHYSICAL SPOT MARKET

The physical spot market operates under a simple principle. The buyer pays the seller in cash for the immediate delivery of a physical commodity. Title passes from seller to buyer upon payment. Dry bulk commodities, such as grains, coal, iron, sugar, or steel, are transported in large amounts. Many dry bulk commodities travel by ocean vessel, train, or truck. Armored cars and airplanes carry precious metals. Other commodities, such as natural gas, crude oil, and oil products also travel by ocean tanker and sometimes pipelines. Electricity is carried from point to point via transmission lines. Nonetheless, in each case, a physical spot transaction occurs when the seller transfers title to the buyer in exchange for cash.

When a commodity transaction is agreed upon, the buyer is often required to open a letter of credit drawn from a mutually agreed upon financial institution. This letter is a document that guarantees payment on delivery. As evidence of goods having been received by a consignor, or a goods shipper, a *bill of lading* is signed by the transporter. Entries of goods shipped in vessels' log books date back to ancient times, but a bill of lading was first used by a shipper in the Italian city of Florence in 1526 to track a consignment. Today, almost 500 years later, when a bill of lading is presented, physical commodity transactions are regarded as settled and title can pass from seller to buyer.

While the final price of the commodity is the most important issue negotiated in physical transactions, there are others as well. Sellers and buyers must agree on terms of the deal, which often include the conditions and date on which title passes. For example, does it pass when the commodity is loaded upon the carrier or when it arrives at the buyer's destination? Who pays for the shipping and insurance? What happens if the transport arrives late or early? It is also possible that the quality of the commodity delivered is not up to the standards agreed upon. What happens then? What if a shipment arrives damaged or if a perishable commodity rots or is contaminated?

Physical-commodity transactions are often plagued by unforeseen circumstances. As an investor, it is always best to be prepared for the unexpected. For example, pirates lurk today in shipping lanes off the coast of Africa. A physical commodity transaction may look sound at first glance, but it is loaded with potential disaster for both buyer and seller. As a commodity trader, I have firsthand experience of physical transactions that went horribly wrong.

The Fiasco of the Giant Sugar Cube

I recall one deal back in the mid–1980s when the price of sugar was particularly low. At one point, the commodity traded below 2.5 cents per pound. In fact, sugar was so cheap that transportation of the commodity made up a huge part of the costs of any physical deal.

Sugar is a dry bulky commodity, and it is carried around the world by ocean-going vessels. Because of the low value of sugar, the ships that transport this sweet commodity are often old and sometimes not in the best state of repair. Raw sugar is loaded onto and off a ship with a device that resembles a vacuum cleaner. Meanwhile, sugar terminals are often located at the ports of major sugar-exporting and sugar-importing countries.

This particular sugar fiasco began when raw sugar was loaded onto a ship at the port of Santos, Brazil. Everything appeared to go well with the loading, and the ship set sail for a destination in Eastern Europe. It arrived at its destination on time, but as it was about to be unloaded, an unpleasant surprise awaited the handlers. At some point during the journey, moisture had leaked into the cargo—so much moisture that the shipment had turned rock solid. The cargo had become one giant sugar cube trapped in the hull of a ship, and it was impossible to use the vacuum cleanerlike equipment.

A serious problem now arose with the terms of the original deal, which had been negotiated by a sugar trader. The trader, who was a friend of mine, bought the Brazilian sugar and paid for it once it was loaded onto the vessel. He then sold the sugar to his Eastern European customer under terms that the buyer would pay once the sugar was unloaded at port. The trader also paid the freight, insurance, unloading, and all costs of transport and built a healthy profit margin into the deal. But that margin depended on everything going smoothly during transport. It turned out that while the margin was healthy, it was not healthy enough.

The trader had to deliver the cargo to his buyer, but he now could not get the sugar off the boat. The trader faced two risks. First, he ran the risk of not delivering the cargo he had promised, and no delivery meant no payment. He would have lost all the money he had already paid to the seller, as well as the cost of transportation. The trader also faced a risk to the owner of the ship, who was charging for each day that the sugar remained onboard his vessel.

Quick thinking provided the trader with an answer that at least reduced his risk. He hired a team of laborers to break up the giant sugar cube with jackhammers. The laborers then had to remove thousands of smaller cubes by hand. The cargo was eventually unloaded and delivered to the buyer, who then demanded a discount because the sugar was not in the form contracted for. While insurance paid for part of the fiasco, the trader's profit margin was not enough to cover the losses, which amounted to several million dollars. The giant sugar cube cost my friend a boatload. Even though he had done everything right, Murphy's law had come into play, and everything went wrong.

The lesson of the giant sugar cube is that the physical commodity markets can often provide important clues to the future price of portfolio holdings. Consider whether it is easy or difficult to transport crude oil through a seaway. When physical commodities flow freely, risk is diminished, and prices can fall. Conversely, when physical flows are impeded, commodity prices can rise. When a crop is damaged, a supply shortage can cause prices to rally. An oil spill in the Gulf of Mexico can affect public policy and restrict drilling and thus result in less production. Physical commodity flows directly affect the business of companies that depend on those commodities and will thus affect the earnings and share prices of those companies.

Storing Physical Commodities

Physical commodities often need to be stored. Postproduction and preconsumption storage arrangements are an important consideration in the physical commodity world. Some commodities wind up in government strategic stockpiles. Companies, investors, or even individuals can hold private commodity stockpiles. When commodities are not in transport, they need to be stored somewhere safe.

For example, governments and individuals hold gold and precious metals. Safes, vaults, and secured warehouses, like Fort Knox, hold gold and silver bullion. Tankers and sometimes even caves can serve as storage places for strategic reserves of crude oil and oil products. Strategic petroleum reserves of the United States are stored in artificial caverns in salt domes beneath the earth near the Gulf of Mexico. Meanwhile, pipelines and storage tanks can hold stocks of natural gas; grains and other agricultural commodities are stored in silos, grain elevators, and terminals. Warehouses store base metals, such as copper, aluminum, and others, while scrap metal, iron, and steel are often stored in fenced-in lots. Storage and insurance can be expensive for the owner of a stockpile. Storage can also prove problematic for agricultural commodities that are perishable and subject to rot. However, commodities such as electricity cannot be stored. Electricity runs along transmission lines, and if not used, is lost.

Trading a physical commodity is often a minefield of potential dangers. Sellers can deliver inferior quality, and buyers can demand a renegotiation of prices if a market moves. At the same time, commodities can perish during transport, and some are subject to mold and fungus. Commodities can also be stolen. Ships can sink. A frozen port can delay shipments of key goods, such as nickel, causing the price of the commodity to spike. Meanwhile, a hurricane can take out a natural gas pipeline or an oil refinery near the Gulf of Mexico, causing the prices of these commodities to rise. Such mishaps are unlikely to impact your investment portfolio in the long run, but they certainly affect prices in the short term. Knowledge of these events and the correct interpretation of the results can save you money, but it can sometimes also make you a lot of money.

THE FORWARD AND SWAP MARKETS

A forward contract is an over-the-counter financial transaction for the future delivery of a commodity. The buyer receives guaranteed access to the commodity at an agreed-upon price, and the seller receives the agreed-upon price as well as a sales outlet from the buyer. These forward contracts also generally call for payment of the commodity upon delivery on the agreed date. Therefore, a forward is an effective hedging tool for both producers and consumers of commodities. However, they can also be fraught with pitfalls.

A pre-export finance transaction is not like a straightforward transaction. It calls for total or partial payment up front, usually upon the signing of a contract. Pre-export transactions are not standardized. They are principal-to-principal contracts, which means that the buyer and seller have agreed upon terms. In this type of deal, the buyer takes a number of risks with respect to the seller. First, the buyer is paying up front for the promise of future delivery. Therefore, the buyer is taking the risk for the entire amount of the deal that is prepaid. Second, pre-export finance transactions generally contain an agreed-upon fixed price. So if the market price drops, it means that the buyer has purchased the commodity at a higher price than it is worth at delivery time. Third, if the seller cannot deliver because of a poor harvest, for example, or a flood in a mine, or a dry oil well, the buyer is at risk of losing the entire investment. Finally, if the price for a commodity promised in a pre-export finance deal rises, the seller could demand a price renegotiation, thus forcing the buyer to pay more than was originally agreed to.

Pre-export finance deals are usually restricted to producers who require cash to manufacture a commodity. For example, if the seller has copper in the ground but does not have the finances to mine the ore, a pre-export contract will enable the producer to cover the costs of production and guarantee a buyer. However, sometimes pre-export finance deals can turn sour and put a company out of business. This was the scenario in which former Wall Street stalwart Philipp Brothers, my former employer, found itself in the early 1980s.

Philipp Brothers and Cocoa—the Last Straw

Philipp Brothers was a physical commodity trading house that in 1980 paid its top executives the highest salaries and bonuses in the United States. In 1981, this wildly successful company bought Salomon Brothers, the private investment bank. I worked for several divisions of the company between 1976 and 1996. When Philipp Brothers purchased Salomon Brothers, the commodities bull market of the late 1970s was winding down. However, Philipp Brothers was flush with cash, and the acquisition of Salomon was probably its best trade ever. The problem was that after the purchase, Salomon made all the money. Philipp Brothers began a steady decline that led to its demise in 1991, and Salomon was ultimately acquired by CitiBank. However, Philipp Brothers' demise came, at least in part, because of a pre-export finance deal gone wrong.

In 1990, Philipp Brothers' management decided to secure a long-term supply of cocoa beans. The Ivory Coast, the world's largest cocoa bean producer, had been a customer of the firm for many years. A hastily prepared pre-export finance agreement gave the cash-starved West African nation a few hundred million dollars up front for the promise of future cocoa harvests at a fixed price. The cocoa market rallied shortly after, and on paper the deal looked great. Philipp Brothers would receive cheap cocoa and sell it at higher market prices to consumers, who wanted the beans to make chocolate.

As the first cocoa beans arrived at the port on the Ivory Coast, however, the West African nation accused Philipp Brothers of manipulating cocoa prices higher. The Ivorians wanted to renegotiate the price for their beans; they wanted more money. But Philipp Brothers had a signed and sealed deal and had paid up front for the beans. And so the company refused to renegotiate. In response, the Ivorians then turned around and sold their cocoa harvest to a French commodity firm. The cost to Philipp Brothers was more than $300 million. It was the trade that helped bury the once giant commodity firm.

Banks, commodity traders, and companies that source commodities all over the world do these kinds of deals often. However, the Philipp Brothers cocoa bean story exemplifies the kind of risks they take. Producers of high-value commodities, such as precious metals and oil, often seek pre-export finance deals. Many of these deals are valued in the billions.

Investors should be on the lookout for signals that these deals may be going sour. Problems on the pre-export finance front can cause problems for companies and for entire market sectors in the equity markets. Your portfolio is certainly at risk.

The Swap Agreement

In 1981, IBM and the World Bank entered into the first-ever public swap agreement. It was the birth of a market that would soon attract huge volume from numerous participants.

A swap is the exchange of a fixed price for a floating price. Swap transactions are popular in fixed income, foreign exchange, and credit markets. In commodities, swaps are similar to forward transactions. These swaps are conducted under strict terms and conditions drawn up by the International Swap Dealers Association (ISDA). The vast majority of commodity swaps occurs in the oil market. Physical delivery does not take place in swaps. They are financially settled instruments, and cash changes hands over the period of the swap.

Financial institutions are particularly active in offering swaps or hedging transactions with their industrial customers. For example, if a consumer of wheat wishes to lock in prices over the next two years, it might enter into a commodity swap by buying a fixed price for wheat and giving the seller of the swap a floating price for wheat. If wheat prices go higher than the fixed price, the consumer will receive payments from the seller of the swap. On the other hand, if wheat prices go lower than the fixed price, the consumer has to make payments against the swap to the seller. Conversely, oil producers can enter into a swap to fix the price they get for oil over the next 10 years. If oil prices go higher than the fixed price, the producer will make payments, but if oil prices go lower than the fixed price, the producer will receive payments. Swaps have been the fastest-growing over-the-counter instruments of the last three decades. According to the Bank for International Settlements, the size of the international swap market had grown to more than $700 trillion by the end of 2011. Swaps are meant to augment, not replace, the physical business. They are strictly financial hedges.

Forwards and swaps are extremely common in commodities markets. Often, one side of these two-party transactions has a consumer or a producer hedging price risk. However, because of volatility, size, and interest in the numerous commodity markets, yet another hedging vehicle is necessary for the transfer of price risk—the futures markets.

FUTURES MARKETS

Futures markets are the most effective tool for the transfer of price risk from one party to another. Futures contracts are simple agreements between buyers and sellers in a common marketplace— a futures exchange. Many of the most actively traded commodities on the planet trade on futures exchanges. And unlike most other markets, futures contracts are uniform and standardized. Understanding risk transfers means gleaning important money-making information that comes from watching whether there are more buyers or sellers in the futures markets. Are prices going up, or are they going down? Are they going up because there is a supply shortage? Are they going down because of a commodity's oversupply? When you understand why the price of raw materials moves, you will understand the risks or opportunities that higher or lower prices present for specific companies.

The world's first futures exchange was the Dojima Rice Exchange, which began operating in Japan in the 1730s. Back then, Samurai warriors were paid in rice. But bad rice harvests were extremely common in those days, causing huge volatility in the price of the staple. The Dojima futures exchange allowed for the exchange of rice for currency in a stable environment. However, the advent of futures contracts at that time actually caused greater volatility. The Samurai panicked over the exchange rate, as speculators and brokers kept vast stores of rice in warehouses, which ensured low prices. Meanwhile, starvation was widespread, and a series of riots erupted as some speculators attempted to corner the market and control prices. The Shogunate then set a price floor and forced merchants to sell above a set minimum. About 130 years later, in 1864, the Chicago Board of Trade (CBOT) introduced futures contracts on grains.

Futures contracts have been successful tools for hedgers, traders, speculators, and investors ever since those days. A futures contract has the following characteristics:

- One stated physical asset or commodity (such as gold, crude oil, soybeans, or even interest rates)
- The type of settlement—physical or cash

- A fixed amount of the asset per contract (i.e., 1,000 barrels of crude oil, 100 ounces of gold, or 112,000 pounds of sugar)
- The currency in which the futures contract is quoted
- The grade or quality of the commodity or asset that is deliverable under the contract
- The delivery month and subsequent delivery months
- The last day for trading
- The minimum price fluctuation per contract, known as *tick value*

Today there are two ways that futures contracts trade on an exchange. In an open outcry environment, floor traders represent their clients' interests and buy and sell futures for them. This "open outcry trading" takes place in the pit, an area designated by the futures exchange for the trading of a specific futures contract. The second method of trading today is via an electronic platform, which matches buyers with sellers through computer-based trading.

Futures markets depend on the confidence of buyers and sellers in each meeting their mutual obligations. A clearinghouse guarantees that both parties perform on the contracts, and it requires market participants to post "margin," a good-faith deposit. It is the clearinghouse that takes the risk of the buyer's purchases and the risk of the seller's sales. The clearinghouse becomes the contract party to an open trade on a futures exchange.

There are two types of margins—*original margin* sometimes referred to as *initial margin*, is the amount required to cover a new position or the amount of cash or securities that at a minimum must be kept in an account against open market positions. Meanwhile, *variation margin* or *maintenance margin* is the minimum amount of cash or negotiable securities that must be held based on the current price of a futures position. If the amount of margin drops below the variation or maintenance margin requirements, the customer is required to immediately put up more money. In theory, this system ensures there will be enough resources available for buyers and sellers to meet their obligations.

The futures exchange itself is responsible for setting margin requirements. In the case of higher market volatility, exchanges will often raise margin requirements. It is also the job of the futures exchange to make sure that buyers and sellers of futures contracts meet their financial obligations to each other. Margin is a good-faith deposit made by market participants who trade and hold positions in the futures markets. Investors who watch the futures market to understand price risk in their underlying investments can often see a move coming when margins change. Exchanges adjust margin requirements based on the volatility of the commodity prices in question. If a commodity becomes volatile, exchanges tend to increase margin because the commodity is more risky. Risky markets often attract speculators. However, when an exchange raises margins, it becomes more expensive for a speculator to participate. Thus, raising margins can sometimes cause a market to reverse, as it can lower participation.

Changes in margin levels are great tools for gauging speculative interest and even the future direction of a commodity market that may have important ramifications on some of the investments that you hold. When the exchange and clearinghouse determine that a market has become more volatile (the price range widens), they will raise margins in order to protect buyers and sellers from potential default.

In April 2011, the COMEX/NYMEX exchanges, which are responsible for the silver futures contract, decided to raise margins because of increased volatility in the price of silver. At that time there were many market participants holding long futures positions in silver. The higher margin requirements made it more expensive to hold those long positions. Higher margin levels cause the liquidation of positions, and the price of silver dropped by almost 35 percent in one month. Investors holding silver in their portfolio with knowledge of the increase in margin requirements would have seen the price correction coming from a mile away.

It is extremely attractive to many market players to be able to control a large portion of a commodity for the price of a margin, which is essentially a small amount of capital. By using this leverage afforded by futures markets, participants can make huge profits or losses for small down payments.

Many futures contracts can be traded with particular commodities. Each contract represents a different time period or "contract month" for delivery and this provides hedgers with the ability to lock in prices for different months or time periods. Most trading activity tends to take place with nearby futures contracts, the so-called active month, when delivery is closest to the date the deal was struck. Some commodity futures are long-dated. Crude oil futures can trade as far ahead as 10 years. Other futures contracts can relate to time periods as "nearby" as only a few months in the future. The futures exchange sets the duration of contracts for all commodities and assets. The durations offered depend on the liquidity of or interest in each particular market.

The largest futures exchange in the world is the Chicago Mercantile Exchange (CME), which has snapped up a number of successful commodity exchanges in recent years, such as the New York Mercantile Exchange (NYMEX), the Chicago Board of Trade (CBOT), and the Commodity Exchange (COMEX) as well as several others. The CME trades energy, metals, agricultural products, currencies, interest-rate derivatives, financial indexes, and other commodities. An Internet-based marketplace, the Intercontinental Exchange (ICE), trades futures on energy and soft commodities. The U.K.-based London Metals Exchange (LME) trades nonferrous metals, sometimes known as base metals, as well as steel and minor metals. The Tokyo Commodity Exchange (TOCOM) trades metals and other commodities. Commodity exchanges also operate in Australia, Brazil, China, Canada, and a number of other countries.

Futures exchanges offer different market participants the abilities to trade futures contracts on commodities on a level playing field. Unlike their earlier eighteenth-century Japanese ancestor, today's futures exchanges operate in a transparent environment where prices to buy and sell are open to the public. The exchanges also provide a plethora of valuable data on volume, open interest, and price history. Volume is the total amount of futures contracts traded while open interest is the total number of long and short positions not yet closed out. Futures exchanges have opened the world of commodity trading to anyone who wishes to participate. They bring together producers and consumers of commodities, as well as speculators, investors, financiers, banks, hedge funds, and market makers, who provide a two-way price to other market participants. The *bid* is the price at which the market maker is prepared to buy, and the *offer* is the price at which the market maker is prepared to sell.

If a market becomes more volatile, the market maker will widen the bid-offer spread on which they are prepared to transact.

Conversely, if a market becomes less volatile, the bid-offer spread narrows.

As the settlement/delivery date approaches, the price of the commodity increasingly reflects the actual physical market price. This is called *convergence*, and it ensures that speculative interest cannot unduly influence prices and create false markets.

A speculator who is long or has bought futures contracts that will expire soon must be willing to take delivery of the underlying commodity or must liquidate the position in the delivery month. A speculator who is short or has sold futures contracts that will expire soon must be willing to make delivery or liquidate the position in the delivery month. The delivery mechanism protects hedgers from speculators and financial traders, who position themselves for profit without a physical underlying interest in the commodity. The delivery mechanism guarantees that prices will reflect the real underlying price of a commodity at the end of the contract period and that these contracts represent an actual commodities market, not just a paper market for gambling purposes.

Meanwhile, as the delivery period approaches, open interest in a futures contract month tends to shrink dramatically. Usually, open interest is transferred, or rolled, to another contract farther in the future. Indeed, the vast number of participants in futures markets never make or take delivery of the physical commodity. Even producers and consumers rarely use the futures delivery mechanism to buy or sell their physical commodities. However, when this does occur, buyers will receive a paper receipt, which entitles them to pick up the commodity at an approved exchange warehouse, terminal, or distribution point.

There are a number of reasons delivery occurs so rarely, including the fact that futures positions are often hedges against physical deals. Producers and consumers take the risk of the price differential between the physical and futures markets, known as the *basis*. And by the same token, speculators and investors rarely make or take delivery, but instead have only a financial interest in the price of the commodity.

The Commodity Futures Trading Commission (CFTC) is the body assigned to regulate the operation of futures exchanges in the United States. In London, the Financial Services Authority (FSA) regulates all U.K.-based exchanges and markets. The Commodity Exchange Law of 1950 guides regulation of the TOCOM in Japan.

Many different points of view have been expressed as to the role of speculators and investors in futures markets. Some argue that these market participants distort the supply-and-demand equation for commodity prices; others say they provide important liquidity and depth in markets. It is the role of the exchange and the regulators to ensure that markets operate efficiently and fairly. Later in this book, we look at how regulation has changed over the years and the direction that it will likely take in the future. I also examine the arguments surrounding the role of speculators in greater detail.

Nonetheless, successful futures exchanges have given rise to another derivative market product that has become increasingly popular over the past three decades. The introduction of options on futures contracts has given market participants yet another tool for managing risk.

THE OPTIONS MARKETS

The first reported use of options occurred back in the sixth century BC, when the ancient Greek philosopher Thales, in the Ionian city of Miletus, bought the rights to an olive harvest. According to the story, which was related by Aristotle, Thales made himself a handsome profit by betting that the following year's olive crop would be abundant. By the year 1636, options were widely used in Amsterdam during the period of the tulip mania, the first recorded financial bubble. During the first half of the following century, options were traded widely in London. However, because of their association with excessive speculation, the 1733 Barnard's Act rendered them illegal. Not until 1860 did they again become legal financial instruments.

Options are price insurance. The buyer of an option is the insured party, and the seller of the option basically acts as the insurance company. Therefore, when one buys an option, the only risk is the price of the option. However, when one sells an option, it is a different story. Risk is unlimited.

There are a number of ways in which options are traded. Over-the-counter options are similar to forward contracts. These are nonstandardized, principal-to-principal, off-exchange, agreements between two parties—the buyer and seller. Options also trade on futures exchanges. A number of important concepts are involved in trading these financial instruments:

- **Call options.** These grant the right, but not the obligation, to purchase an amount of an asset, in this case a commodity, at a specified price for a specified grade and during a specified time period.
- **Put options.** These grant the right, but not the obligation, to sell an asset, at a specified price and grade and during a specified time period.
- **Option premium.** This is the amount a buyer pays for an option and the amount the seller receives for granting (sometimes called *writing*) that option.
- **Option contract.** In the commodities world, contracts contain varying specified amounts. Crude oil, for example, is traded in lots of 1,000 barrels, and zinc is traded in lots of 25 (U.K.) tons on the LME.
- **Strike price.** This is the specified price for the commodity or the price level at which the insurance is granted.
- **The option grade.** This is the grade of the commodity that is required under the terms of the underlying futures contract.
- **Expiration date.** This denotes the specified time period of the option. Options on futures almost always expire prior to the delivery date of a futures contract.
- **Exercise.** The act of declaring the option and receiving a position (long or short) in a futures contract at expiration.

A put or call options value is calculated by using a variety of different mathematical models, the most popular of which is the Black-Scholes option-pricing model, developed in 1973 by economists Fischer Black and Myron Scholes. Black and Scholes won the Nobel Prize in economics for their work on options pricing, which led to a boom in options trading and provided mathematical and scientific credence to the activities of the Chicago Board Options Exchange and other options markets around the world.

Many different variables go into the pricing of options, including interest rates, the supply and demand of the options themselves, the number of buyers versus sellers, and the underlying price of the asset. However, the chief determinant of an option price is implied volatility. In Chapter 1, we discuss historical volatility, the measure of price fluctuation over time. Expressed as a percentage, this is the measure of a commodity futures past price range. However, implied volatility is the market's attempt to predict what lies ahead, and it is the market's perception of future volatility, or its future trading range, that ultimately determines the price of an option.

Option strike prices can be at any price level, and their intrinsic value denotes the options value at current prices. For example, a $2,000 put option in gold with the yellow metal trading at $1,800 an ounce has $200 of intrinsic value. An $80 call option on crude oil with crude oil currently at $100 a barrel would have $20 of intrinsic value.

There are three types of option strike prices:

- **Out of the money.** This is an option that has zero intrinsic value. A 30 cent sugar call option is out of the money if the current futures price for sugar is 28 cents. A $3 copper put option is out of the money if the current futures price for copper is $3.80.
- **In the money.** This is an option that has intrinsic value. A $30 silver call option is in the money with $5 of intrinsic value if the current futures price for silver is $35. A $2 coffee put option is in the money with 20 cents of intrinsic value if the futures price for coffee is $1.80.
- **At the money.** This is an option with a strike price equal to the current futures price. At-the-money options have no intrinsic value.

Buying a call option is a bullish trade, but the buyer is essentially insuring against higher future prices. By the same token, the buyer of a put option is insuring against lower future prices; this is a bearish trade. The purchase of an option is a limited-risk trade or investment, because only the premium paid for the option is at risk. While leverage in the futures market allows participants to control large amounts of a commodity for a small down payment, the purchase of an option provides the buyer with even more leverage. When purchasing an option, the buyer pays the seller immediately. Regardless of whether

the market moves up or down, there are never any margin requirements on the option buyer. Therefore, buyers of options can control
large long or short positions in commodities for just pennies on the
dollar.

The easiest way to understand options is to think of them as price
insurance. We insure our cars, our homes, and even our lives. We
really never want to collect on those policies, but we keep them just
in case. Options work the same way. Many investors buy options to
protect assets in their portfolios from disastrous losses. When it comes
to out-of-the-money options, the difference between the market price
of the underlying commodity and the strike price of the option is the
deductible. Where options differ from normal insurance is that investors and speculators often buy options to provide leverage when they
think a market is about to move up or down. Buying options can be a
limited-risk, high-reward investment tool.

EASY TIP

Buying or selling options depend upon the price level at which
they trade. As a guide, I like to compare historical volatility with
implied volatility. Many trading platforms offer these statistics
for traded assets. And as a rule, I consider an option cheap if
implied volatility on at-the-money options is below historical
volatility. In these cases, I am generally a better buyer of put or
call options.

However, there are also times when I buy options to protect
holdings of stocks, commodities, or other assets. And there are
times when I buy options because I think they are cheap, and my
technomental analysis indicates that a market can move sharply
in one direction or another.

Selling options is altogether a different game from buying options.
When you sell an option, you act as the insurance company. The
seller of an option immediately receives the premium for the option.
If the price moves against the seller, the losses can be unlimited.
Therefore, unlike buying options, futures exchanges require sellers to

post margin as a good-faith deposit of future performance against the option contract.

However, in spite of the risks, there are times when it makes a great deal of sense for investors to sell options. When you have a stock in your portfolio and you intend to sell it when it gets to a particular level, there are times when it is appropriate to sell a call option on that stock. Selling call options can generate income against an existing holding. If the price of the stock (or commodity) goes up, you will sell it at your desired level. Even if you don't sell, at least you can keep the premium from selling the call option. On the other hand, if there is a stock—or a commodity, like gold or silver—you want to buy, but you think the price may move lower, it is appropriate to sell put options at the desired level of purchase. If the price of the asset falls, you simply buy the asset at your intended level. However, if the price does not go lower and you sold a put option, you get to pocket the premium you received for selling the put option. This is often a great deal.

EASY TIP

When implied volatility on at-the-money options is much higher than historical volatility, I am a better seller of options. I generally look to sell put options on stocks, commodities, or assets that I want to buy at lower prices. Additionally, in this case I would look to sell call options on stocks, commodities, or assets I hold in my portfolio.

The best hedge for an option is another option on the same asset. Options on the same assets act similarly over time. While many investors buy and sell options and hedge their positions with the underlying commodities or stocks, this is a strategy best left to professionals.

Options are fantastic multidimensional trading tools. You can protect your portfolio at times by purchasing options. You can also turbocharge your investing with the leverage afforded you by purchasing options. Finally, selling options can provide a nice income stream for your nest egg when option premiums are attractive to sell.

ETFs AND ETNs

An ETF, or exchange-traded fund, is an investment fund that trades on the stock market. An ETN, or exchange-traded note, is a linked debt security issued by only one creditor, usually a bank. ETFs were first traded in 1989 on the American and Philadelphia Stock Exchanges and can hold any asset, including commodities. The first ETFs were a proxy for the S&P 500 index. Since then, however, ETFs have popped up all over the place. Today, an investor can choose from a wide variety of ETF products that attempt to replicate the daily market action of numerous individual assets. When the secular bull market in commodities began soon after 2000, commodity ETF products grew in popularity. For example, SPDR gold shares ETF (symbol GLD) began trading in November 2004 with the strategy, according to issuer State Street Advisors, "To replicate the performance, net of expenses, of the price of gold bullion." GLD in May 2012 had a massive market capitalization of more than $65 billion and has become an extremely popular proxy for holding gold. The ETF has performed as expected, moving higher (and lower at times) with the price of gold bullion, as Figure 2.1 confirms.

When GLD first began trading, it opened at $44.40 per share. In November 2004 active month gold futures opened at $429.50 per ounce. As of May 2012, the ETF had appreciated by 257 percent, while gold futures climbed by 280 percent. In this case, the ETF tracked the price of gold effectively. However, ETF products charge fees called *expense ratios* to those who use them as investment assets. In the case of GLD the expense ratio is 0.40 percent. In May 2012, prices of $158.70 for the ETF and $1,637 for gold would amount to 63.5 cents a share or $6.55 per ounce in fees. Nonetheless, GLD has been a successful proxy for the price of gold for investors.

When it comes to commodity-based ETFs, some do the trick and others do not. The United States Oil (USO) fund ETF, introduced in April 2006, is an ETF that has not worked. USO seeks to reflect the performance of West Texas Intermediate (WTI), the benchmark crude for NYMEX futures contracts. Because of poor performance, USO

Figure 2.1 **Monthly price chart gold futures versus SPDR GLD—ETF.**
Line chart = gold futures; candlestick chart = GOLD ETF.
Source: CQG, Inc. © 2012. All rights reserved worldwide.

had a market capitalization of just $1.3 billion in May 2012, around the time this book was written. However, the oil market is much larger than the gold market, and the performance of USO has failed to attract investment capital to the extent that GLD has.

As shown in Figure 2.2, when USO began trading, it opened at $68.25 and active month NYMEX crude oil futures stood at

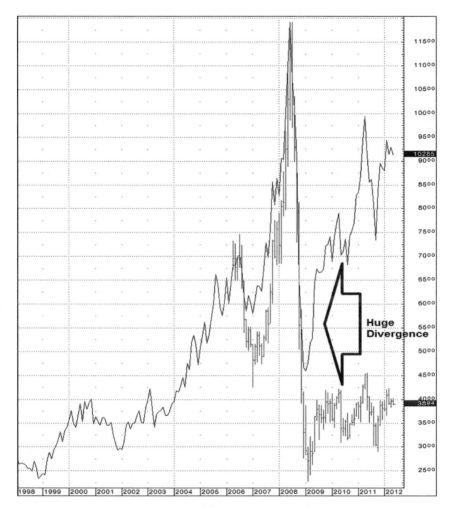

Figure 2.2 **Monthly price chart of oil futures versus USO oil ETF.**
Line chart = oil futures; bar chart = USO ETF.

$66.36 per barrel. The difference between the ETF and futures con-
tract was just 2.8 percent. As of May 2012, active month crude oil
futures were around $103 per barrel.

However, USO stood at $38.93. An investor in 2006 who pre-
dicted crude oil prices would climb higher and bought the ETF got
the market call correct but would have lost half the value on the USO

ETF. It's hard enough to make money in any investment market, but it is galling to get the market right and still lose money.

There are reasons why USO failed. The administrators who run the ETF buy active month crude oil futures. As delivery day approaches, they roll those contracts forward. In many cases, there is a cost for the contract roll. The price of USO reflects the cost of these rolls. We see in the next chapter how time spreads (sometimes called calendar spreads) between traded contract months in the same commodity are of paramount importance when understanding why commodity prices do what they do.

Caveat emptor, as the saying goes—buyer beware. The moral to the gold and oil ETF story is that some ETFs perform as intended and others perform poorly. Investors should always do their homework to make sure that the product reacted as they expected it to.

The latest development in the ETF world is the turboleveraged ETF, which invests in futures and/or options contracts to create leverage that boosts risk on several ETF products. For example, some products will pay $2 for every $1 move in gold. This type of ETF is gaining in popularity. Remember, any ETF that promises higher upside returns comes at the price of greater downside risk. If gold drops by $1 and the investor owns a long-leveraged ETF, a lot more that $1 can be lost.

Meanwhile, exchange-traded notes first traded in June 2006. These are exchange-traded instruments that perform like a typical forward contract. The issuers of an ETN does not hold the commodity (as do ETF administrators). Rather they generally have a financial hedge, such as a forward or swap, against the risk of granting the ETN.

ETNs are available for a number of different commodities, but it is crucial that investors understand and check the creditworthiness of the issuer; the investment strategy of the associated ETN; and the risks, fees, and charges.

ETFs and ETNs have made commodities more accessible to the ordinary investor. Many analysts believe that both have added liquidity to the commodity markets by bringing in new participants.

THE DIRTY "D" WORD

The word has become the equivalent of a swear word in many circles, particularly in the wake of the 2008 financial crisis. However, in spite of the negative connotations, every product discussed in this chapter so far, with the exception of physical spot commodity transactions, is a "derivative." The word means copied or adapted from others. In the commodity space, all the financial tools available to investors are derivatives. Pricing starts with the value of the physical commodity itself. Forwards, swaps, futures, options, ETFs, and ETNs are all derivatives of the physical commodity price.

Nonetheless, there is good reason that the term has a bad rap. In 1980, the infamous Hunt brothers lost a fortune speculating on silver futures, a derivative market. In 1995, Barings, the oldest British merchant bank, collapsed as the head derivatives trader in Singapore, Nick Leeson, took unauthorized derivatives positions that depleted all of the bank's capital. In 1998, Long Term Capital Management almost took down the entire global financial system with highly leveraged derivatives bets on emerging-market debt. In 2008, French banking giant Société Générale lost $7.2 billion on unauthorized derivatives trades. That same year, a Bear Stearns hedge fund lost $2 billion and put the company out of business with bad derivatives bets on mortgage-backed securities. In October 2011, MF Global, a 200-year-old sugar broker went bankrupt on leveraged derivatives positions on European debt. There are other cases in which derivatives have caused financial calamity. However, it was not the derivatives that caused these crises, but the way in which these financial instruments were used. Leverage can be a wonderful tool but, when misused, the leverage that derivatives afford a trader can bring about nightmares.

In 2002, Warren Buffett, perhaps the best-known investor of our time, called derivatives "toxic" and told his shareholders they were "time bombs." In 2003, he described derivatives as "financial weapons of mass destruction." However, the legendary investor has certainly not practiced what he preached. In April 2010, Barclays Capital reported that Buffett and his company, Berkshire Hathaway, had a derivatives portfolio valued at $63 billion. And in February 2011, it was reported that Berkshire Hathaway's earnings increased by a whopping 43 percent on the purchase of a railroad and derivative bets.

The brightest and most successful investors use derivatives to enhance their portfolios. Derivatives tools available in commodity markets provide a wealth of data, insight, and investment opportunities for every investor. Building a successful and robust nest egg for the future requires this important knowledge.

Commodities flow through many hands en route from production site to consumer. The forwards, swaps, futures, options, and derivatives markets provide liquidity and make the journey possible. The more information and data you have, the better armed you will be and the more money you will make, and save, from your investments.

CHAPTER 3

Commodity Market Structure

Risk comes from not knowing what you are doing..
—WARREN BUFFETT

In 1991, I met a man whom I consider to be one of the world's greatest traders. Back then, Andrew Hall was the head oil trader for Phibro Energy, a division of Salomon Brothers. At that time, Hall had already spent a decade at Phibro, and while he watched the global oil market, the global oil market also watched him. He had a great track record, and he made billions trading crude oil and associated products. When the oil price moved, traders first looked at the oil-producing nations and OPEC. But when that did not explain the move, focus shifted to Andy Hall. Traders, bankers, speculators, and financiers all assumed that from his quiet office in Connecticut, this British-born trader with a degree in chemistry from Oxford and training at British Petroleum was the muscle behind the price of oil.

Not only did I have the privilege of working for Andy Hall from 1991 to 1996, but during that period I sat and spoke with him on a daily basis. It is true that Andy bought and sold huge quantities of crude oil and other commodities. It is also true that he reaped massive returns. Andy gained a powerful reputation for making major calls on market direction and getting them right. However, few knew what lay behind Andy's massive market forays. He certainly did not flip a coin, and he certainly did not "push" markets one way or the other. On the contrary, it was the market that told Andy what to do. He liked to call the method his *investment calculus*. And for Andy, this meant an analysis of a market's structure.

While Andy Hall ran a global physical oil business, dabbled in refinery ownership, and made overseas investments in oil-producing properties, his big profits came from elsewhere—his analysis of the structure of the oil market. If he were to sit in a vacuum with a screen and market data, Andy would still make huge sums of money.

This chapter outlines what I learned from my association with this extraordinary trader. It explains and illustrates how to use information that is readily available to detect long-term market trends in commodity prices, which will increase your investment acumen.

BACKWARDATION AND CONTANGO

Backwardation and contango are perhaps the two most important words in a commodity trader's vocabulary:

- **Backwardation.** This is a market condition in which prices are lower in the future than they are in nearby delivery months. Other terms for backwardation are "negative carry" market and "premium" market. These are costs associated with holding commodities. These costs can include storage, insurance, and current interest rates. When future prices are lower than the current price, the cost of carry becomes negative. Just think of negative carry as the multiplication of two negatives equaling a positive. In a negative carry market (premium or backwardation), a holder of the commodity can sell today and buy in the future and make money.
- **Contango.** This exists when forward or futures prices are higher in distant delivery months than they are in nearby delivery months. Contango is also known as a "positive carry" market or a "normal" market.

Why do these situations occur? If there is a short-term supply shortage in a commodity market, chances are the market structure will tend toward backwardation. Higher nearby prices may serve to decrease demand because of elasticity of demand. Conversely, when there is a surplus in a commodity market, chances are that the market structure will tend toward contango. The theory behind contango is that abundant supplies nearby do not guarantee abundant supplies in the future. In fact, if nearby supplies are so abundant, producers may cut back on production. The surplus will then be consumed, and prices will rise. Additionally, abundant nearby supplies and falling prices may also increase short-term demand. Think of gasoline prices. If they began to drop because of increased supplies, wouldn't you put some extra miles on your car? Once again, it comes down to the elasticity of demand. In commodities, contango markets also exist because abundant supplies must be financed, stored, and insured, the cost of which is reflected in progressively higher future prices.

Let's look at a few examples, as shown in Figures 3.1 and 3.2:

Markets are not always in a straight backwardation or contango state for all future delivery periods. A market's price curve is the total picture of the future pricing structure for a commodity. There are

	Open	High	Low	Last	Net	Tick	Prev	Bid	Ask
GCEK2	16512	16522	16313	16367B	-167	41	16534	16367	16370
GCEM2	16540	16543	16313	16375A	-165	25673	16540	16374	16375
GCEN2	16500	16500	16339	16383B	-188	21	16551	16383	16386
GCEQ2	16563	16564	16336	16397A	-166	301	16563	16395	16397
GCEV2	16573	16573	16360	16417A	-167	48	16584	16416	16417
GCEZ2	16591	16591	16376	16437A	-167	140	16604	16435	16437
GCEG3	16578	16578	16429	16457A	167	2	16624	16455	16457
GCEJ3	16572	16572	16449	16477A	168	0	16645	16474	16477
GCEM3	16480	16480	16470	16498A	168	0	16666	16495	16498
GCEQ3	16492	16492	16492	16515B	174	0	16689	16515	16523
GCEV3	16515	16515	16515	16534B	178	0	16712	16534	16549
GCEZ3	16722	16722	16540	16561B	176	0	16737	16561	16574
GCEG4	16570	16570	16570	16616A	152	0	16768	16588	16616
GCEM4	16630	16630	16630	16649B	180	0	16829	16649	16675
GCEZ4	16735	16735	16735	16752B	184	0	16936	16752	16784
GCEM5	16850	16850	16850	16863B	190	0	17053	16863	16907
GCEZ5	16994	16994	16994	16930B	-269	0	17199	16930	17073
GCEM6	17142	17142	17142	17098B	-251	0	17349	17098	17307
GCEZ6	17316	17316	17316	17271B	-254	0	17525	17271	17413
GCEM7	17531	17531	17531	17452B	-288	0	17740	17452	17668
GCEZ7	17802	17802	17802	17655B	-356	0	18011	17655	17957

Figure 3.1 Contango market: COMEX gold futures.
All futures prices are progressively higher.

Source: CQG, Inc. © 2012. All rights reserved worldwide.

	Open	High	Low	Last	Net	Tick	Prev	Bid	Ask
ZSEK2						0	14606	14614	15066
ZSEN2				14730ᴀ	-4	0	14734	14730	14730
ZSEQ2						0	14524	14450	14556
ZSEU2						0	14000	13972	14400
ZSEX2				13676ᴀ	0	0	13676	13676	13676
ZSEF3						0	13622	13582	13636
ZSEH3						0	13362	13150	13400
ZSEK3						0	13210	13010	13236
ZSEN3						0	13224	12520	13300
ZSEQ3						0	12992		
ZSEU3						0	12640		
ZSEX3				12330ᴀ	0	0	12330	11650	12330
ZSEF4						0	12374		13000
ZSEH4						0	12364		13400
ZSEK4						0	12364		
ZSEN4						0	12410	12110	
ZSEQ4						0	12364		
ZSEU4						0	12266		
ZSEX4						0	12042	11720	12260
ZSEF5						0			
ZSEH5						0			
ZSEK5						0			
ZSEN5						0	12122		
ZSEQ5						0			
ZSEX5						0	11826	11800	12090

Figure 3.2 Backwardation market: CBOT soybeans. All futures prices are progressively lower (with minor exceptions).

Source: CQG, Inc. © 2012. All rights reserved worldwide.

times when a market is in states of both contango and backwardation at different times along the price curve. Seasonal factors such as weather and crop cycles as well as factors such as political events, elections, and economic cycles all contribute to the pricing structure of individual commodities.

Figure 3.3 shows a commodity that has both backwardation and contango in its forward price curve:

As you can see, the NYMEX crude oil market in this example starts off in a contango from June 2012 to January 2013, but then it flips into a state of backwardation from January 2013 all the way out to October 2015.

When you follow the structure of a commodities price curve day by day or week by week, you will notice changes, and the concepts of backwardation and contango are crucial. Markets often flip from contango to backwardation and vice versa. These movements are key because they are blueprints for what is occurring in the physical market, and they are also direct barometers of market psychology at any given point. An investor can see whether certain commodities are in short supply or surplus, whether the fundamentals of the pricing curve are changing, and whether market psychology is changing.

	Open	High	Low	Last	Net	Tick	Prev	Bid	Ask
CLEM2	10539	10542	10236	10258в	-264	30662	10522	10258	10260
CLEN2	10576	10577	10276	10296	-262	3797	10558	10296	10298
CLEQ2	10603	10603	10308	10325a	-258	1143	10583	10323	10325
CLEU2	10591	10610	1032?	10341в	-256	606	10597	10341	10344
CLEV2	10600	10600	1034?	10353в	-251	67	10604	10353	10357
CLEX2	10634	10634	1036?	10367в	-243	83	10610	10367	10370
CLEZ2	10624	10625	10367	10380в	-234	1157	10614	10380	10384
CLEF3	10580	10617	10379	10391?	-224	32	10615	10390	10395
CLEG3	10607	10607	10380	10389в	-214	8	10603	10389	10394
CLEH3	10570	10591	10384	10382a	-199	1	10581	10377	10382
CLEJ3	10508	10508	10325	10354в	-194	23	10548	10354	10361
CLEK3	10435	10436	10326	10316в	-188	1	10504	10316	10324
CLEM3	10449	10459	10250	10279в	-180	61	10459	10279	10283
CLEN3	10242	10242	10242	10242✓	-168	0	10410	9900	
CLEQ3	10201	10201	10201	10201✓	-164	0	10365		
CLEU3	10163	10163	10163	10163✓	-159	0	10322		
CLEV3	10130	10130	10130	10130✓	-154	0	10284		
CLEX3	10097	10097	10097	10097✓	-150	0	10247		
CLEZ3	10209	10215	10030	10061в	-152	192	10213	10061	10066
CLEF4	10021	10021	10021	10021✓	-139	0	10160		
CLEG4	9976	9976	9976	9976✓	-134	0	10110		
CLEH4	9930	9930	9930	9930✓	-129	0	10059		
CLEJ4	9888	9888	9888	9888✓	-122	0	10010		
CLEK4	9848	9848	9848	9848✓	-115	0	9963		
CLEM4	9810	9810	9810	9809a	-110	0	9919	9796	9809
CLEN4	9766	9766	9766	9766✓	-103	0	9869		
CLEQ4	9726	9726	9726	9726✓	-97	0	9823		
CLEU4	9692	9692	9692	9692✓	-91	0	9783		
CLEV4	9659	9659	9659	9659✓	-85	0	9744		
CLEX4	9635	9635	9635	9635✓	-78	0	9713		10100
CLEZ4	9665	9665	9550	9610a	-79	34	9689	9603	9610
CLEF5	9577	9577	9577	9577✓	-68	0	9645		
CLEG5	9539	9539	9539	9539✓	-64	0	9603		
CLEH5	9502	9502	9502	9502✓	-59	0	9561		
CLEJ5	9466	9466	9466	9466✓	-54	0	9520		
CLEK5	9432	9432	9432	9432✓	-49	0	9481		
CLEM5	9403	9403	9403	9403✓	-44	0	9447		
CLEN5	9377	9377	9377	9377✓	-39	0	9416		
CLEQ5	9351	9351	9351	9351✓	-34	0	9385		
CLEU5	9325	9325	9325	9325✓	-29	0	9354		
CLEV5	9299	9299	9299	9299✓	-25	0	9324		

◯ **Areas of contango**   ▢ **Areas of backwardation**

Figure 3.3 **Mixed bag of contango and backwardation: NYMEX crude oil futures**

Source: CQG, Inc. © 2012. All rights reserved worldwide.

EASY TIP

Understanding this price curve is one of the key lessons Andy Hall taught me. It was central to his investment calculus. The *Wall Street Journal* and other financial newspapers publish these price curves daily. The information is also available online, free of charge at numerous exchange websites. Following closing prices and the price curves for the commodities that affect the investments you hold is like looking into the future. Remember that a higher nearby price generally signals a shortage in that commodity. This means that a company will be forced to pay a higher price for these goods, and if you hold that company in your portfolio, this will likely impact negatively on your earnings. A lower nearby price will probably have the opposite effect and means that a company's share price will likely be unaffected because there are no current scarcity issues.

INTRACOMMODITY SPREADS

An *intracommodity spread* is the purchase of a futures contract and the simultaneous sale of another futures contract for a different month in the same commodity on the same exchange. Intracommodity spreads may also be referred to as *calendar* or *time spreads*.

Intracommodity spreads are the position of choice for professional traders and are often the vehicle with which they take advantage of commodities that swing from backwardation to contango and back again. My old boss, Andy Hall, traded these spreads more often than he traded flat-price long or short positions in the oil market.

In 1990, when Iraq invaded Kuwait, Andy had a huge intracommodity spread on crude oil. Andy called these trades "front to back" spreads. Back in 1990, he bought crude oil for nearby delivery and sold it for delivery farther out. He believed that all of the saber-rattling surrounding Iraq, a major oil producer and OPEC member, would result in a short-term supply squeeze in the crude oil market. The invasion began on the night of August 2, 1990. Andy entered into his "front to back" trade prior to the invasion when nearby crude oil contracts were trading at $20 a barrel. The price curve in oil was also fairly flat, which means that deferred contracts were also trading at around $20. On the evening of August 2, nearby crude oil futures doubled to $40 per barrel, but the deferred contract prices did not follow. Andy had been right.

Everyone knew the price of crude oil was soaring because of Saddam Hussein's invasion, but most people didn't know that the deferred crude oil contracts did not budge. They remained at $20 and in some cases, on the far-dated crude oil contract, actually fell. Why did that happen? The market believed that the invasion was a short-term political event that would cause short-term tightness in the oil price. War in the Middle East always causes supply concerns. That's why nearby crude jumped. The market also knew that the United States and the rest of the world would not put up with Iraqi aggression and that eventually normality would return. That's why the price of long-dated crude did not rise.

Andy won on both sides of the trade that night, and he pocketed more than a couple of hundred million dollars. He made money because he'd bought the nearby crude oil contracts and sold an equal number of deferred contracts. The price of the nearby crude oil doubled, and the deferred crude oil stayed the same or, on some contracts, fell.

The price volatility of a commodity is multidimensional. The financial press and news networks tend to pay attention only to nominal front month or physical prices. However, during the Iraq war, the structure of the oil market changed so rapidly and so dramatically that shares of oil companies, oil refining companies, natural gas companies, and all companies that use fuel moved in a big way.

Traders often use intracommodity spreads on markets that are trending toward backwardation or contango. A trader who is betting on backwardation will go long on the front contracts and short on the deferred contracts. A trader who is betting on contango will go short on the nearby contracts and long on the deferred contracts. Any investor watching commodity prices will understand that when backwardation occurs, it will be more expensive and more difficult to access a commodity that a company may require. Conversely, in a normal market or contango, it will be less problematic and often cheaper to access the necessary raw material.

The London Metals Exchange (LME) trades futures contracts on metals. LME futures act more like forward transactions than futures contracts. They trade for delivery 90 days from the date of a transaction. Every business day at the LME has the potential to be a delivery day. Consumers and producers not only use these markets to hedge, but also to make and take actual physical delivery of the metal. Base metals, including copper, aluminum, nickel, lead, zinc, and tin trade on the LME. What happens in the physical market for these metals directly impacts the action on the LME. As such, LME prices are the global benchmarks for base metals.

In the late winter of 1989, Philipp Brothers had a large contract with the Russian nickel producer, Norilsk Nickel, the largest producer in the world. Norilsk came to Philipp Brothers because at that time, cash was tight for that company. I entered into a pre-export financing arrangement with the Russian company. I paid for the nickel 90 days prior to delivery and made a nice profit margin for fronting the cash. The Russians probably would have loved to arrange for pre-export financing transactions far beyond 90 days, which would have yielded a huge profit margin, but they were a bad credit risk at the time. Once they delivered the metal to the LME warehouse in Rotterdam, in the Netherlands, I would then pull together another pre-export financed deal.

My job was negotiating the financing deal and to make sure that we hedged the price risk of the nickel. Once we agreed on the price, I sold 90-day forward nickel on the LME to lock in a healthy profit margin. The deal was a no-brainer—at least that's what I thought at the time. But 1989 turned out to be an extremely cold winter in Europe, and Norilsk is based in the northern-most part of Siberia, above the Arctic Circle. The plan was that Norilsk would ship the nickel via Dudinka, a port in Krasnoyarsk, Siberia. I had bought the 90 days forward nickel from the Russians and hedged by selling contracts on the LME. I had entered into what was essentially an intracommodity spread with the LME on one side and the Russians on the other.

I did not pay attention to the weather in this far away land. That was my first mistake. My second mistake was that I did not pay enough attention to the shipping schedule. I expected the Russians to send the shipping schedule indicating that the nickel was on its way, by ship, to Rotterdam. However, weeks went by, and the schedule did not arrive. Then nickel prices began to rise. I didn't worry because I had an intracommodity spread with a nice profit margin to boot. However, after six weeks of watching the LME nickel price rise, I decided to inquire about the arrival of my nickel in Rotterdam. I contacted my Russian counterpart and discovered that the metal was sitting in a warehouse in Dudinka because the ship could not get out of the frozen port where the ice was so thick that ice cutting ships could not clear the vessel's route from the harbor.

It took more than six weeks for the journey between Dudinka and Rotterdam, and the nickel was not even on the ship. Then nickel prices started to move even higher. However, I soon realized that I was not the only one who had struck this deal with the Russians. There were many other European commodity traders in the same frozen boat. We had all done the same deal, and we all lost a lot of money. I had a short position on the LME with no cover and no nickel coming in to deliver against that short position. My intracommodity spread was blowing up in front of my eyes.

That market moved from just under $6,000 per ton to almost $9,000 per ton in short order—a 50 percent move in 60 days. The action was happening in the nearby contracts. The nickel market was heading into a huge backwardation. Luckily for me, I saw this problem with six weeks to go, and I was able to cover my position for a loss—but that loss would have been much larger and more painful had I not acted when I did.

As you can see, intracommodity spreads can be extremely dangerous in commodity markets, and they can be more volatile than the nominal price of a commodity itself. But knowledge and awareness of these events can be useful information for an investor.

Imagine how the price of companies that produce or consume nickel moved during this period. An investor watching this situation would have seen everything unfold and would have had a wonderful opportunity to sell stock in a nickel producer during the short-term rally or buy the stock of a nickel consumer that may have slumped because of the sudden spike in the commodity price.

QUALITY AND LOCATION SPREADS

Andy Hall's crude oil trade in 1990 was a classic intracommodity spread. My nickel trade was a mixture of an intracommodity and a location spread, which involves the simultaneous purchase and sale of a commodity of the same or similar quality in two different locations. An example of a location spread would be the purchase of gold bullion in London and the simultaneous sale of gold bullion in New York. An investor who wishes to spread the geopolitical risk of holding an investment in gold, for example, could store gold in different locations. When analyzing commodity prices, investors need to understand that there are different prices for the same commodity in different locations. The differentials reflect transportation costs as well as the availability of the commodity. For example, natural gas may trade at $3 per thousand btu's in the United States, but in Asia it may trade at $12 per thousand btu's. An investor contemplating an investment in natural gas should not only understand the business of the companies involved but where they produce the commodity and where they sell it.

A quality spread is the exchange of one grade of a commodity for another. The purchase of North Sea Brent crude oil and the sale of West Texas crude oil would constitute a quality spread. The purchase of silver that is 99.99 percent pure and the sale of silver that is 95 percent pure is a quality spread. Often companies that consume commodities require a specific quality, which may differ from the deliverable grades traded on certain exchanges. For example, many food companies that buy wheat in the United States require a higher quality of wheat than is traded at the Chicago Board of Trade (CBOT). These companies may require wheat grades from the Kansas City or Minneapolis exchange. Different qualities command different prices. This knowledge can make an investor money. Pinpointing economic risk will uncover earnings potential.

Sometimes, as we saw with my nickel trade, location and quality spreads can occur at the same time. The nickel I was expecting was the wrong size and did not meet LME specifications. Cutting the nickel down into deliverable form was required before delivery against my short position on the LME. This type of spread offers invaluable information to investors doing their homework in various market sectors. Such was the case in the differential that occurred between wheat in Chicago and Kansas City in 2011.

The busiest futures contracts in the world for wheat are those that trade on the CBOT. This exchange trades soft red winter wheat. There are two other wheat futures exchanges in the United States: the Kansas City Board of Trade (KBOT), which trades hard red winter wheat, and the Minneapolis Board of Trade (MBOT) with its hard red spring wheat. While the world watches CBOT's wheat price, it is the KBOT wheat price many U.S. food processors use to price the wheat that goes into their manufactured products. In 2008, the price of wheat soared. After spending much of the previous 10 years below $4 a bushel, wheat on the CBOT traded up to almost $11 a bushel. Poor weather conditions in the United States, Australia, and Ukraine caused wheat crop yields to fall and prices to soar. Food manufacturers who rarely hedged prior to 2008 began to lock in prices for their wheat requirements. It turned out that many food processors in the United States priced their wheat purchases based on the KBOT price. As the food processors began to hedge, the spread between KBOT and CBOT wheat exploded.

Figure 3.4 illustrates the price spike as food manufacturers in the United States came into the futures market to hedge after the 2008 wheat price shock. Food consumers whose companies trade in the equity markets were hedging because they were fearful that wheat prices could rise again and that they might not be able to source wheat in the future. The food-consuming companies were feeling the potential for earnings pressures that would come if wheat continued to be more expensive. This was certainly valuable information for anyone with investments in food processing or agricultural companies that trade on the various stock markets around the world.

Quality and location spreads can paint an interesting picture when it comes to the risks that companies take or hedge against. An investor can monitor these spreads by looking at free data available from futures exchanges. All the data needed to truly understand commodity market structure are readily available to those who are interested.

PROCESSING SPREADS

Processing spreads signify the difference between two related commodities, where one is the product of another, for example, soybeans and soybean meal or soybean oil. Meanwhile, *crush spreads* reflect the cost of processing soybeans into the two products. For example, if crush spreads are wider than the cost of processing, the companies that do the crushing, such as Archer Daniels Midland (ADM), Bungee (BG), and other grain processors, will make a profit. If crush spreads are narrow or less than the processing cost, these companies lose money. The level of crush spreads can tell investors a lot about the future profitability of large food processors.

Investors who keep their eyes on processing spreads will have the power to make intelligent and educated investments. For example, in recent years, ethanol production around the world has increased dramatically. Brazilian factories process sugar cane into ethanol, and, in the United States companies like ADM, process corn into ethanol.

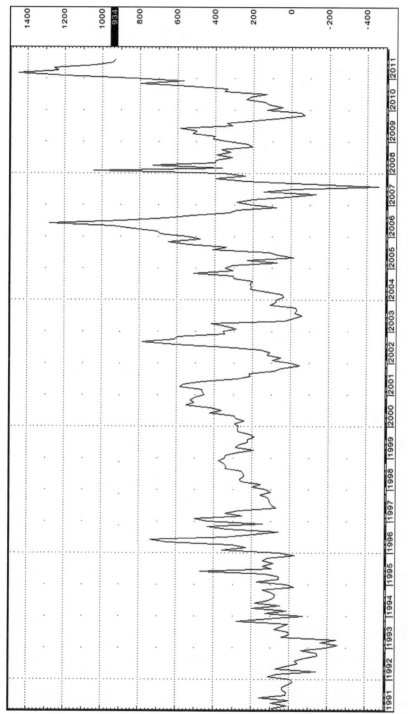

Figure 3.4 KBOT wheat versus CBOT wheat monthly chart. The premium for KBOT wheat over CBOT wheat, which averaged 20 cents per bushel for two decades, went to $1.40 per bushel in 2011.

Source: CQG, Inc. © 2012. All rights reserved worldwide.

Keeping an eye on corn and sugar prices compared with ethanol prices will give an investor important clues about the future direction of various investment opportunities.

Perhaps the most important processing spread for investors is the *crack spread*. Crack spreads reflect the economics of refining a barrel of crude oil into oil products. Crude oil is refined, or cracked, into gasoline, home heating oil, diesel fuel, jet fuel, and many other energy products. Crack spreads are key, because they determine how much you pay to fill up at the pump, or how much an airline stock might move. Understanding crack spreads will give an investor insight into the future profitability of oil refining companies much more so than will the nominal price of benchmark crude.

INTERCOMMODITY SPREADS

An *intercommodity spread* is the purchase of one commodity futures contract for a particular month and the simultaneous sale of a related commodity futures contract for exactly the same time period.

The price of one commodity can often affect the price of another, particularly when it comes to commodities that are interchangeable. Let's say that the price of one commodity becomes too expensive. People will adapt by switching to a cheaper product. This substitution is at the heart of intercommodity spreads. For example, in Brazil, the price of gasoline has skyrocketed over the past few years. So Brazilians decided to use their biggest export, sugar, to make ethanol and replace expensive gasoline with it. The use of sugar to make ethanol was driven by price and demand, but substitution can also occur on the supply side of the equation. If the price of corn skyrockets, farmers will plant more corn, because it's a cash crop. However, the more land that is used to grow corn, the less land is available for other crops, such as cotton or soybeans. The point here is that there is a finite amount of arable land on the earth. If a deficit occurs in cotton or soybeans, the price of those commodities will rise. If prices rise high enough, farmers may decide to plant cotton or soybeans in lieu of corn.

The logic behind intercommodity spreads is that consumers and producers make the best economic decisions, given the current prices for commodities at the time. That does not mean that things can't get out of whack for periods of time. When corn prices jumped in 2008 and farmers planted corn, cotton went into deficit and prices exploded by more than 500 percent in 2011. As you can see, intercommodity spreads can provide investors with a map of potential future scenarios and how they can directly affect an investment portfolio.

Intercommodity spreads highlight the potential for substitution. This information helps an investor look toward the future and determine how a company will switch gears during times of shortage or surplus and how those companies can control their price exposures, which directly impact the bottom line and a company's share price.

The pricing curve of a commodity, intracommodity spreads, quality and location spreads, processing spreads, and intercommodity spreads all work together to make up the market structure of each commodity. In 1991, Andy Hall told me that to make money in any market, I had to understand the calculus. That calculus is at your fingertips.

OPTION SPREADS

Option spreads are a different animal from those already discussed. As an instrument derived from futures contracts, the relative value of one option to another can serve to round out our foundation of knowledge. Many of the same issues raised about futures apply to options on futures, but there are a few more tricks of the trade involved.

Before using any option to invest or trade in a market, you must first analyze the volume traded in the particular option strike price you are considering. It is important to make sure that a critical mass and significant trading volume are present so that the option being considered is liquid. If there is little or no volume in a particular option, it becomes more expensive to execute purchase or sale transactions. Volume makes investing and trading easier because it is easy to get in, easy to get out, and easy to match buyers with sellers and vice versa. But options with no volume can be expensive traps.

The next step is to look at the open interest, the total number of short and long positions not yet closed out for a particular option and compare it with other option strike prices for the same commodity, stock, or asset. Open interest is the best way to gauge both liquidity and ease of trading an option. When open interest is small or non-existent, it means that there is little market interest in the option. When there is significant open interest, the option is more likely to trade often and with a tight bid/offer spread, which lowers the cost of execution and allows an investor or trader to quickly get in and out of positions.

Examining the open interest of options presents another important opportunity for investors. Option open interest is a clue to market psychology for a particular asset. If open interest is large around certain strike prices for both puts and calls, this tells you that the majority of market participants believes the price of the underlying asset will gravitate toward that strike price on expiration of the option. This is particularly helpful when you're looking at short-term options.

It also helps to examine the balance of bullish or bearish sentiment in a market by looking at the ratio of call to put options for the asset in question. For example, if the bulk of open interest in one-month options is around a certain strike price but there is much more open interest in calls than puts, you can surmise that market sentiment is more bullish at that moment. Let's take a look at this in practice, as shown in Figure 3.5.

Figure 3.5 is an example of a series of gold option premiums and open interest with 20 days left until expiration. You will notice that the vast majority of open interest is at the $1,650 strike price with gold futures trading at $1,643.90.

The $1,650 put option has more open interest (1.37 times) than the $1,650 call option, indicating a slightly bearish tone to the market. Other strike prices that have high open interest: the $1,500 puts have more than 13,000 contracts; the $1,600 puts have more than 9,000 contracts; the $1,700 calls have more than 5,000 contracts. You will notice that all of these options with large open interest are out of the money with zero intrinsic value. In all cases, the corresponding put options had little or no open interest. The out-of-the-money options had big open interest, and the in-the-money options had very small open interest. With 20 days until expiration I consider these options lotto tickets. They tend to be cheap to purchase, but the odds of a

GCE Gold Futures	JUN2 CALLS Current- 16439a Days til expir.- 20		JUN2 PUTS 16439a 20	
Strike Price	Premium	Open Interest	Premium	Open Interest
1495	15130✓	0	130▲	13
1500	14750▲	705	100ʙ	13075
1505	14260▲	0	140▲	139
1510	13770▲	0	110ʙ	130
1515	13280▲	0	120ʙ	1760
1520	12400ʙ	16	130ʙ	148
1525	11900ʙ	5	140ʙ	429
1530	11730▲	1	150ʙ	912
1535	11240▲	0	160ʙ	123
1540	10750▲	78	180ʙ	1311
1545	10260▲	0	200ʙ	188
1550	9780▲	1196	240▲	6011
1555	9010ʙ	0	240ʙ	104
1560	8830▲	197	300▲	619
1565	8070ʙ	0	330▲	226
1570	7890▲	102	360▲	713
1575	7150ʙ	1007	380ʙ	2422
1580	6970▲	80	450▲	634
1585	6520▲	0	470ʙ	177
1590	6080▲	16	560▲	1481
1595	5650▲	0	630▲	348
1600	5010ʙ	2576	710▲	9269
1605	4780▲	9	810▲	92
1610	4220ʙ	182	880ʙ	530
1615	4020▲	6	1040▲	325
1620	3650▲	375	1180▲	1443
1625	3170ʙ	393	1300ʙ	1423
1630	2950▲	555	1480ʙ	2413
1635	2570ʙ	2024	1730▲	1078
1640	2290ʙ	1842	1950▲	3001
1645	2030ʙ	269	2190▲	290
1650	1800ʙ	5594	2390ʙ	7680
1655	1640▲	242	2670ʙ	22
1660	1450▲	1482	2960ʙ	453
1665	1280▲	579	3270ʙ	608
1670	1120▲	2304	3610ʙ	474
1675	990▲	1911	4140▲	430
1680	870▲	2642	4320ʙ	1546
1685	720ʙ	791	4930▲	29
1690	660▲	879	5340▲	615
1695	590▲	284	5760▲	21
1700	510▲	5527	6200▲	2125
1705	460▲	189	6640▲	6
1710	370ʙ	1076	7100▲	207
1715	320ʙ	1198	7280ʙ	25
1720	280ʙ	1117	8020▲	318
1725	250ʙ	2066	8490▲	80
1730	220ʙ	640	8680ʙ	57
1735	200ʙ	159	9150ʙ	5
1740	190ʙ	392	9930▲	26
1745	170ʙ	838	10110ʙ	5

Figure 3.5 **In this case the gold futures price is $1,643.90 an ounce. The bulk of the open interest is in the $1,650 strike price with 5,594 call option contracts and 7,680 put option contracts—total open interest in the $1,650 strike = 13,274 contracts. There are 20 days to go in this option series. The $1,650 strike price has more open interest than any other strike price. There are 1.37 puts for every call in the $1,650 strike.**

Source: CQG, Inc. © 2012. All rights reserved worldwide.

big payoff are extremely low. Big rewards tend to come from taking big risks. Buying very short-term out-of-the-money options is a big gamble—the odds are stacked against the buyer who will usually wind up losing money.

I am particularly interested in the open interest around the current price and the open interest balance (or imbalance) of put options compared to call options. This is important for two reasons. First, it gives me a picture of market sentiment—bullish or bearish. Second, it can indicate where a market will go on expiration.

EASY TIP

With more than 30 years of watching option prices, I can tell you that futures markets, stock prices, and other asset prices more often than not will gravitate to the strike price with the largest and most balanced open interest.

For example, in the case of gold with 20 days to go until expiration, there is better than even money odds that the futures price will either gravitate to $1,650 over the next 20 days or go lower.

The technical reason for this gravitation toward a strike price with large open interest is that professional traders who own put options will be buyers of gold on prices below $1,650, and their ownership of the put option will protect their purchases of gold for 20 days. Meanwhile, traders who own call options will be sellers on prices above $1,650, and their ownership of the call option will protect their sales of gold for 20 days. Like two opposing sides exerting pressure—but it is worth remembering that there is more open interest in the put options than in the call options—the futures price will generally be pushed toward the strike price of the option series with the greatest and most balanced open interest. I call this phenomenon *strike price gravitation*. Other traders call it *pin risk*, because they are pinning the futures price to the strike price. This is the risk associated with being long or short on an at-the-money option (one with a strike price equal to the current futures price) on expiration day, because the long or short does not know if the option will be exercised until the final market price is known.

Looking at option prices and combing the market for directional clues will usually present an opportunity. There are times in which opportunities stick out like a sore thumb. Often, as expiration approaches, some options become cheap. It may cost only a few dollars to buy a put or a call option for a few days or a week.

If a market overshoots, either to the upside or downside, opportunities may present themselves for the agile investor. For example, the opportunity to buy a short-term call option in gold with only a week to run for $1 (or $100 a contract) will give the investor the chance to control more than $160,000 worth of gold for a week, with no risk other than the $100 contract price. If gold prices were to reverse and that option was to trade up to $2, the investor would pocket a 100 percent return. Monitoring and understanding option prices will open up a new world for investors. Options work the same way for all assets, but commodity options are particularly interesting because of the heavy volatility.

As I mentioned, while trading, I always monitor a market's historical volatility and compare it with the implied volatility of an option. This gives me a strong sense of whether the option is cheap or expensive. The comparison of the two volatility measures works particularly well with options that have strike prices in close proximity to where a market is currently trading.

Out-of-the money options generally trade at much higher levels of implied volatility. This usually occurs because of what I call the lotto theory of options investing. Speculators and investors love the thrill of controlling large amounts of an asset for pennies on the dollar, and sometimes it pays off big. Consider the investors who bought options on credit default swaps in 2007 and 2008 for pennies on the dollar. They made a killing. However, nine times out of ten, these out-of-the-money options die worthless at expiration. Because of the appetite for out-of-the-money options, they invariably trade at higher implied volatilities than at-the-money options. Therefore, the historical versus implied volatility analysis works best for options that are close to the price of the asset. The farther away from the current market a strike price is, the more it becomes a lotto ticket, and the more expensive it becomes.

THE CONCEPT OF THETA

The Greek letter theta denotes the rate of decline in the value of an option over time. Option values decline during their lifespan, and as they approach expiration, the rate of decline picks up rapidly. Sellers of options are big fans of theta—but to a buyer, theta is a curse.

To invest in an asset whose value you believe will appreciate, you can buy the asset directly or buy a call option. If you believe that the asset will decline in price, you can short it or you can buy a put option. In cases in which you choose to employ a long option strategy, you take a much smaller risk than going outright long or short, because you are risking only the premium you paid for the put or the call. However, less risk comes at a price. The option has a limited life span, and unless you are correct in your market view and act quickly, theta will simply eat your option value for lunch. So what happens when you think the price of an asset will do absolutely nothing? You can't go long or short. If you are correct, neither strategy will pay off. Selling options offers the solution. In this situation, theta is your best friend.

OTHER SIMPLE OPTION SPREADS AND ASSOCIATED IDEAS

When considering option strategies or spreads an investor must fully understand how an options strategy will respond if the market moves higher, lower, or goes nowhere at all. Options can be employed to express a bullish, bearish, or neutral market view.

- **Long call.** This is a bullish strategy you can use by purchasing a call option. The risk is limited to the cost of the premium. The best conditions for buying a call is when the implied volatility of the call option is at or below historical volatility for the same time period. The profit potential for a long call option is unlimited.
- **Short call.** This is a bearish strategy. However, the risk on a short call option trade can be unlimited, while the profit potential is limited to the premium received for selling the call option. The best conditions for call-option sales occur when the implied volatility of the option is above historical volatility for the same period. A covered call sale is the sale of a call option against a long asset held in a portfolio. Here the risk of loss is the loss of opportunity rather than an economic loss on the upside. A naked call sale is the sale of a call option with no asset held against it. Here the risk of loss is unlimited.

- **Long put.** This is a bearish strategy you use by purchasing a put option. Risk is limited to the premium paid. The best condition for a put purchase is when the implied volatility of the put option is at or below historical volatility for the same time period. The profit potential for a long put option is unlimited down to zero.
- **Short put.** This is a bullish strategy aimed at earning income by selling a put option on an asset. The risk here is unlimited. The profit potential is limited to the premium received for selling the put option. The best condition for put sales is when implied volatility of the option is above historical volatility.
- **Straddle.** This is a combination strategy involving the purchase or sale of both a put option and a call option with the same strike price and same expiration date. It was made infamous in 1995 by options trader Nick Leeson, whose actions resulted in the collapse of the 233-year-old Barings Bank. Nonetheless, it is useful if a big price movement is expected, but the investor is not sure about the direction. The purchase of a straddle is a long volatility trade, and the sale of a straddle is a short volatility trade. Risk is limited to the premium paid for the buyer and unlimited for the seller of a straddle. However, the profit potential is unlimited for the buyer and limited to the premium received for the seller. Those who believe a market will not move but remain in a tight trading range until expiration are sellers of straddles.
- **Strangle.** This is the purchase or sale of both an out-of-the-money put option and an out-of-the-money call option with the same expiration date. Risk is limited to the premium paid for the buyer and unlimited for the seller of a strangle. The profit potential is unlimited for the buyer of a strangle and limited to the premium received for the seller. The purchase of a strangle is a long volatility trade. The buyer of a strangle believes a big price movement will occur before expiration but is unsure of the direction. The sale of a strangle is a short volatility trade. Those who believe a market will

not move, but will remain in a tight trading range until expiration are strangle sellers.

- **Bull vertical call spread.** This is a bullish strategy that involves the simultaneous sale and purchase of two calls with the same expiration but different strike prices. Risk is limited to the premium paid for the buyer of the spread. Vertical spreads work best when option premiums are expensive (implied volatility is much greater than historical volatility). The vertical spread offers the bullish investor an opportunity to offset the purchase of an expensive call option with the sale of an expensive call option, thus limiting risk.

- **Bear call spread.** This is a strategy aimed at profiting from the falling price of an asset, stock, or commodity. It involves the sale of a call option that is closer to the current market price against the simultaneous purchase of a call option that is farther away from the market price. The options have the same expiration period. Risk is limited to the difference in the strike prices and the premium received for selling the spread. The profit potential is limited to the premium for selling the spread.

- **Bear put spread.** This is a strategy also aimed at profiting from the falling price of an asset, stock, or commodity. It involves the purchase of a put option that is closer to the current market price against the simultaneous sale of a put option that is farther away from the market price. The options have the same expiration period. Risk is limited to the premium paid for the spread. The profit potential is limited to the difference in the strike prices and the premium paid.

- **Bull put spread.** This is a strategy aimed at profiting when a price is expected to rise moderately. It involves the sale of a put option that is closer to the current market price against the simultaneous purchase of a put option that is farther away from the current market price. The expiration periods are the same. Risk is limited to the difference in the strike prices and the premium received for selling the spread. The profit potential is limited to the premium received for selling the spread. The vertical spread offers the bullish investor an opportunity to offset the sale of an expensive put option with the purchase of an expensive put option, thus limiting risk.

- **Time spreads.** Sometimes called *calendar spreads*, these are a derivative of front-to-back spreads or time spreads (calendar spreads) in futures. An options time spread involves the simultaneous purchase or sale of a call or put option for one futures month and the opposite position in the same strike price for a different futures month. Option time spreads are a way of positioning for anticipated movements in contango and backwardation.

There are also a number of other complicated options spreads, such as cap and collars, butterflies, condors, boxes, ratio spreads, and synthetic futures. These are used by professionals who trade volatility.

UNDERSTANDING OPTIONS

Options are a chess game. Those proficient in trading them generally put on spreads and trade around them. One spread can become another over the life of an option trade. Professional option traders run a "book," which can contains thousands of positions. Quantitative computer-driven models will measure and assess all the risks of the options in the book. And there are many different risks, including the price of the underlying asset, interest rates, and the volatility of the underlying asset for different periods of time, the intracommodity spread risk, and sometimes the intercommodity spread risk. Nonetheless, options are one of the most versatile tools available to investors, and they are the only tools that allow investors to profit even when a price remains the same.

Most importantly, the information gleaned by those who understand how options work is another variable in the great equation of investment calculus. Even if you never trade an option, make sure you understand what the option markets are telling you about the assets in your portfolio.

All trading platforms provide option prices, as do many exchanges. Many platforms also offer pricing models and information on historical and implied volatility, as well as volume and open interest data on options to customers. The information is free and often compelling!

CHAPTER 4

Energy

THE FUEL
OF SOCIETY

My formula for success is rise early, work late, and strike oil.

—J. PAUL GETTY

Energy markets affect our lives every day. We fill our gas tanks, heat and cool our homes, and prepare our meals with products from energy markets. Trucks, railcars, ocean-going vessels, and airplanes bring the goods we purchase to local markets. For the investor, energy prices affect the cost of goods sold for almost every company on earth. Energy is a volatile commodity, and its price is perhaps the key variable that affects company earnings. This, in turn, has a direct impact on your nest egg, your portfolio, and your future.

OIL AND OIL PRODUCTS

Although we probably do not often think of it, crude oil is a fixture in our lives, much like our monthly rent or mortgage payment. And we are all involved in the crude oil market in one way or another. This is what makes this commodity such an important investment vehicle, perhaps the most important investment vehicle. As a society we are addicted to crude oil, and as investors we can use our everyday knowledge and experience of it to enhance our portfolios.

Reducing our dependence on foreign crude oil has been the stated energy policy of the United States and Western Europe since the 1970s. I got my first car in 1976. It was a 1967 Buick LeSabre, and it was a gas guzzler. Gasoline was around 80 cents a gallon back then, and it cost around $15 to fill the tank. Today, that same gas tank would cost more than $80 to fill. More than 40 years of political argument and promises have done nothing to reduce our dependence on foreign oil. The fact is that population growth and increasing wealth in the emerging markets, such as China and the rest of Asia, has made competition for oil all the more fierce and has increased prices dramatically. The decreasing value of the U.S. dollar has not helped matters either.

The amount of oil in the world is constantly debated. It seems that the more the demand for oil rises, the more oil is discovered. The higher the price of crude oil climbs, the more economical it becomes to explore and drill for oil that is increasingly expensive to produce. It is easy and cheap to produce oil in some areas of the world. For example, crude oil will flow in Saudi Arabia simply by turning a spigot.

In other places like the North Sea, the Gulf of Mexico, and other offshore sites, underwater drilling is expensive. Producing oil from the tar sands in Canada is extremely expensive. The production level of oil depends not only on the reserves of the commodity but also on the environmental policy of the countries where the reserves are located. Environmental policy in the United States and Europe often conflicts with the need to produce crude oil. In Russia and the Middle East, environmental policy is rarely a factor. To complicate this sector further, many oil-producing countries do not have stable governmental systems, and corruption in a number of major oil-producing countries is rampant.

Since 1960, the price of crude oil has been under the influence of a powerful cartel—the Organization of Petroleum Exporting Countries, or OPEC. The stated mission of OPEC is to "coordinate and unify petroleum policies among member countries, in order to secure fair and stable prices for petroleum producers; an efficient, economic and regular supply of petroleum to consuming nations; and a fair return on capital to those investing in the industry." OPEC's members include Algeria, Angola, Ecuador, Iran, Iraq, Kuwait, Libya, Nigeria, Qatar, Saudi Arabia, the United Arab Emirates, and Venezuela. As of 2010, OPEC members held roughly 79 percent of the world's crude oil reserves and 44 percent of the world's crude oil production. OPEC, therefore, wields considerable influence. It establishes quotas and seeks to control global crude oil prices. The cartel's influence coupled with rising and addictive global demand has made crude oil the most political commodity on the planet. With 79 percent of the world's reserves, any new discovery or production of oil can be met with a decrease in OPEC's production in order to keep prices attractive for its members.

There is always hoopla surrounding OPEC meetings. The question is usually the same: Will the cartel raise or lower production? The group's decisions often determine the future price of the commodity because OPEC controls a bulk of the available supply to consumers all over the world. Before each meeting or during it, analysts speculate on OPEC's production decision. If the decision is in line with predictions, there is generally a muted response. However, if the decision runs counter to expectations (as it often does), oil and oil products markets tend to move violently. At the same time, OPEC members, such as Iran and Venezuela, often use these decisions to further their political agendas.

Often when there is political turmoil or the threat of war in the Middle East, the global price for oil contains a risk premium, which takes into account the potential for supply disruptions. The fact is that many important oil-producing nations with significant production are not members of OPEC.

In 2011, there were 87.5 million barrels of crude oil produced each day. The Arab League is by far the largest producer of oil with 24.171 million barrels produced per day. The largest single oil-producing country was Russia, with 10.54 million barrels of production a day. The United States was third with 7.8 million barrels per day (bbl/day). China produced almost 4 million bbl/day, and Canada 3.3 million bbl/day. Mexico and Brazil are also top-tier oil producers. Of the top 10 oil-producing nations in 2011, only four were OPEC members.

Oil demand has continued to rise over the past decades. The fastest rate of growth has come from Asia. The top oil consumers in the world are the United States (19.2 million bbl/day), China (9.4 million bbl/day), Japan (4.4 million bbl/day), and India (3.12 million bbl/day). The United States consumes about two and a half times more crude oil than it produces, and so it is heavily dependent on foreign crude. Some analysts say that the United States is addicted to foreign crude. In addition to keeping an eye on OPEC, there is another way to monitor crude oil fundamentals. Each week, the U.S. Department of Energy and the American Petroleum Institute issue reports on the level of crude oil and oil product stockpiles. These reports also include U.S. demand data. Analysts also issue consensus estimates of stock levels and demand prior to the release of reports. Various news services publish these estimates free of charge. If the reports deviate from the consensus estimates, crude oil prices rise or fall, sometimes dramatically.

Meanwhile, China consumes three times more oil than it produces. The Arab states, Russia, Nigeria, Venezuela, and some other producers export the crude oil the world depends on. These countries consume less than they produce; therefore, they are net exporters of the commodity, which is why crude oil prices are volatile and sensitive to geopolitical events such as conflict and international policy disagreements. But at the same time, crude oil demand has surged with the growth of Asia.

I first traveled to China in the mid–1980s. I remember traveling from the airport to my hotel in Beijing on a beautiful new superhighway. I laughed to myself during that trip because I was being driven in the only automobile on that road. Everyone else on the highway pedaled bicycles. I thought to myself, why did the Chinese spend all this money on a superhighway for bicycles? I found the answer on the same highway 10 years later. The trip that took 30 minutes in the 1980s took two and a half hours in the 1990s. The superhighway was the scene of a super traffic jam. All those Chinese cyclists were now in cars.

During the 1980s and 1990s the price of crude oil ranged from between $10/bbl and $40/bbl. Since the turn of the new millennium, things have changed. In 2008, crude oil prices traded at historic highs of $147/bbl. The world has slowly adapted to higher crude oil prices. At the time of writing this book, crude oil prices were hovering at around $100/bbl. As Figure 4.1 illustrates, the price of crude oil reached a new high at above $40 in 2004 and never looked back. Demand has increased, particularly from Asian consumers. Today, that trip to Beijing from the airport might take five hours or more!

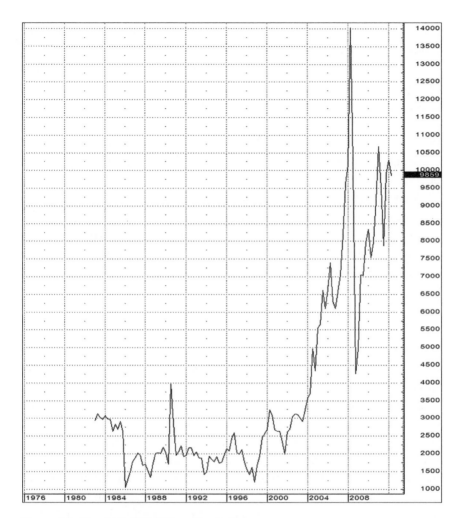

Figure 4.1 **Quarterly NYMEX crude oil chart**
Source: CQG, Inc. © 2012. All rights reserved worldwide.

There are different grades of physical crude oil. The most popular traded grades are Brent crude oil and West Texas Intermediate (WTI).

Brent refers to oil that is produced from the Brent oil field and other sites in the North Sea. Its oil price is the benchmark for European, African, and the Middle Eastern crude that flows west. The pricing mechanism for Brent crude values roughly two-thirds of the world's oil supplies. Brent is "sweet" crude, which means it has a sulfur content of below 0.5 percent. Brent's sulfur content is around

0.37 percent. The lower the sulfur content, the easier and cheaper crude is to refine into products, such as gasoline.

WTI, the benchmark crude for North America, is sweeter than Brent. It has a sulfur content of around 0.24 percent. While WTI is a better grade of crude oil for the production of gasoline, Brent oil favors the production of diesel. NYMEX (New York Mercantile Exchange) lists futures contracts on WTI. Delivery for WTI crude occurs in Cushing, Oklahoma. Asian countries use both the Brent and WTI benchmarks to price their crude oil. Meanwhile, Brent crude futures trade on the Intercontinental Exchange (ICE).

WTI costs about $3–$4 per barrel to ship from Europe to the United States. There are also some differences in costs related to storage in oil-trading hubs in Europe and the United States. In a normal market the spread between these two locations hovers at around $2.50–$4, with the WTI crude trading at a premium to Brent, historically—although this has not always been the case.

Sometimes, as a result of world events, the spread between these two low-sulfur crudes can move violently for long periods of time. At the start of 2011, the Brent-WTI spread was around flat. The spread widened during 2011 with Brent trading at a premium to WTI throughout the year. The Suez Canal is a key passage route for crude oil. As violence in the Middle East flared and the Arab Spring in Egypt got under way in February 2011, the spread between Brent and WTI widened thanks to a perceived shortage of Brent as a result of a potential closure of the Suez Canal. As tensions eased, so did the spread. However, later in 2011, Iranian threats to close the Strait of Hormuz (through which 20 percent of the world's crude oil flows each day) caused the WTI-Brent spread to remain at historically high levels. (See Figure 4.2.)

As we saw in the previous chapters, the nominal price of crude oil is just one factor involved in the understanding of how oil prices affect your portfolio. The spread between Brent and WTI is a perfect example of how quality and location spreads affect the structure and pricing of the crude oil market.

There are times when crude oil prices and the share price of companies operating within the oil sector get out of whack. These are the times when investors need to pay close attention. Often the share prices of related companies will tell you something about the price

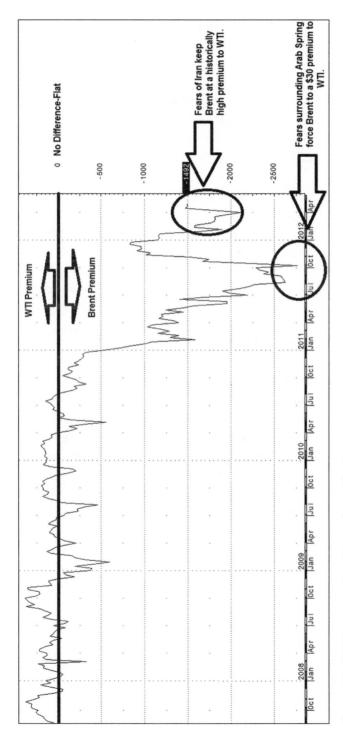

Figure 4.2 WTI-Brent crude oil spread weekly chart

of oil, and sometimes the price of crude will provide important investment clues about the price of stocks in your portfolio. Let's take a look
at some examples:

The price of Baker Hughes stock and the price of oil are highly
correlated, but notice the circled areas in Figure 4.3 where the stock
and crude price disconnected for a period of time.

As Figure 4.4 illustrates, a similar pattern occurs when tracking
the historical relationship between the price of oil and Halliburton
stock.

Figure 4.5 again presents a similar pattern of the divergence of
Schlumberger stock and crude oil prices.

Schlumberger (SLB), a top-tier oil-services company is highly
dependent on the price of oil, as are the two other companies—Baker
Hughes (BHI) and Halliburton (HAL)—charted below. When crude
prices move higher, the share prices of these companies tend to rise.
and conversely when crude oil dips, so do these companies' stock
market value. On each chart, I have circled periods where these stocks
diverged or disconnected from the price of oil. As you can see, in 1997,
2006–2007 and 2011–2012, the gap between the companies' share
prices and the price of crude was at its widest. For the investor, these
charts illustrate when the stocks are cheap or too expensive relative to
the oil price. An investor, with knowledge of the crude oil market, can
profit from situations in which companies like these diverge from the
price of the commodity that defines their underlying businesses.

In 1997, the value of all three stocks got ahead of crude oil prices.
History shows that it was not a great idea to hold them in your portfolio during 1998. However, in 2005, the value of all three stocks traded
close to the oil prices, which meant that they were valued fairly and, in
some cases, cheaply. But then in 2008, they became expensive, relative
to the crude price, as the spread widened.

Understanding the ins and outs of the oil market could have produced a handsome profit for a clued-in investor in these three stocks. As
I write this book, I see that the price of the three stocks have dropped
over the past weeks. A divergence is occurring before my eyes. A situation like this is a call to action to the informed investor. (As it turned
out, the prices of the stocks were signaling a fall in the price of crude
oil, which plummeted to below $80 a barrel for a short time as the book
was being edited.)

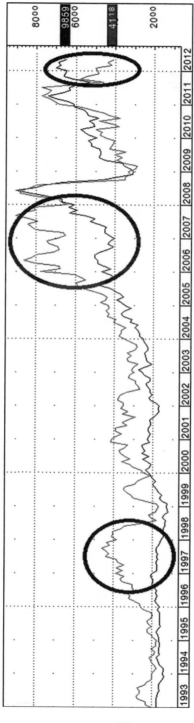

Figure 4.3   Baker Hughes (BHI versus WTI crude oil monthly chart)

101

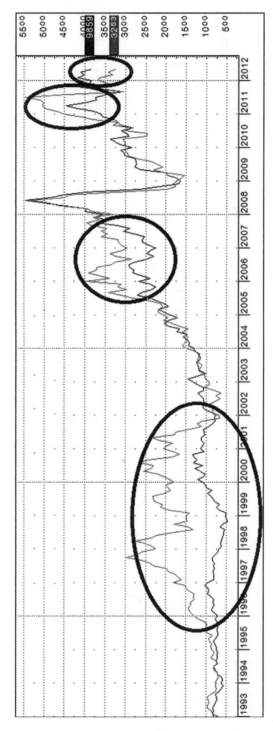

Figure 4.4 Halliburton stock (HAL) versus NYMEX crude oil monthly chart

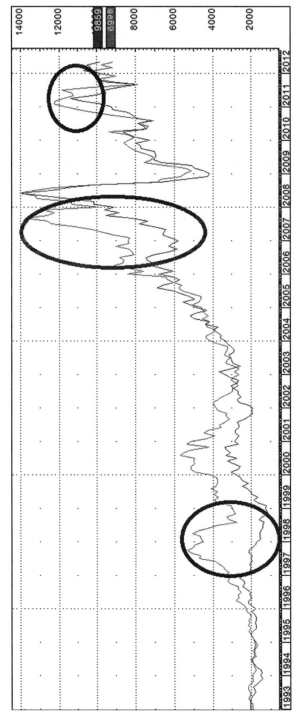

Figure 4.5 Schlumberger stock (SLB) versus NYMEX crude oil monthly chart

Source: CQG, Inc. © 2012. All rights reserved worldwide.

EASY TIP

Keep an eye on equities that are directly related to the price of certain commodities. A divergence in price can yield extraordinary profit potential.

There is an interesting correlation between equity prices and crude oil prices that investors ignore at their peril. Demand for crude oil increases in direct proportion to global growth. Conversely, during periods of contraction, demand for crude abates. But things can also get out of whack when price shocks occur. While increased economic activity often benefits both the equity and oil markets, there are times when spikes in the crude price can adversely affect a company's earnings, sending its stock price lower (see Figure 4.6). Both markets react poorly to economic crises.

There are times when gasoline prices at the pump are sky high and crude oil prices are static. For example, during the first quarter of 2012, NYMEX crude prices rose by 3.9 percent, but gasoline prices jumped by more than 26 percent and heating oil prices climbed by 9.3 percent. This apparent anomaly was caused by changes in refining costs, which skewed the differential between the market price for refined oil products and the market price for crude oil. These differentials are known as *refining* (or *crack*) *spreads*.

The refining business has always been volatile for oil companies from a revenue-generating perspective. However, the wider the crack spread, the more money the refinery makes. The higher the price of gasoline and heating oil, relative to the price of crude, the more profits refiners generate. Nonetheless, refineries require huge sums of capital to cover their operating costs. If crack spreads fall below a refinery's breakeven point, the business can very quickly become a losing proposition.

Futures exchanges offer contracts on crack spreads. Crack spreads are often actually more volatile than the underlying price of crude oil. Let's take a look at the Reformulated Blendstock for Oxygenate Blending (more commonly referred to as RBOB) gasoline crack spread in Figure 4.7, which is traded on NYMEX.

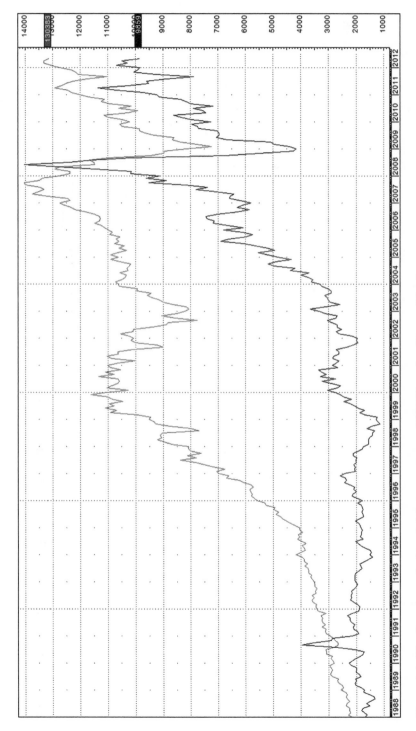

Figure 4.6 The Dow Jones Industrial Average versus NYMEX crude oil monthly chart

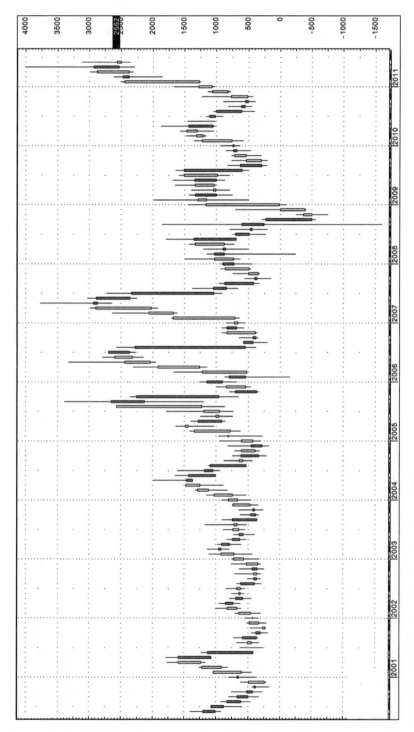

Figure 4.7 Monthly chart of NYMEX gasoline crack spread

Source: CQG, Inc. © 2012. All rights reserved worldwide.

As you can see, the average historical level for the gasoline crack spread is around $10–$15 per barrel. However, there have been times when the crack has traded up to $40 per barrel (oil refiners make a lot of money at this level) or down to a $15 discount per barrel (oil refiners lose a lot of money at this level).

EASY TIP

A study of the gasoline crack spread provides hints concerning where the price of underlying crude oil might be heading as well as highlighting warning signals of changing fuel costs for companies that are held in investment portfolios.

The same is true with the NYMEX-traded crack spread for heating oil, which is often a proxy for the price of diesel fuel. Indeed, many consumers of diesel fuel use NYMEX heating oil contracts to hedge their needs or to lock in future prices.

Gasoline and heating oil are seasonal products, and crack spreads display a high degree of seasonality. Since the United States is the world's biggest consumer of oil, gasoline tends to rally toward the summer months, so much so that this is sometimes called "driving season." Heating oil tends to rally during the winter months, or "heating season." The hedging activity using heating oil as a proxy for diesel fuel always adds a small premium to the heating oil crack during the off-season summer months. Gasoline cracks tend to trade at higher levels as driving season approaches.

So, let's put this all together, as shown in Figure 4.8.

This chart shows the relationship between the crude oil price and the two crack spreads. Sometimes, crack spreads lead the crude price; sometimes, it's the other way around. Once again: refining spreads often give important clues to the future direction of crude oil prices and thus the future profit levels of certain companies. Investors ignore crack spreads at their peril. A case in point is Exxon Mobil (XOM), the largest U.S. oil-refining company.

Figure 4.9 illustrates how the gasoline crack spread has affected Exxon's share price. The long-term trend of higher refining margins

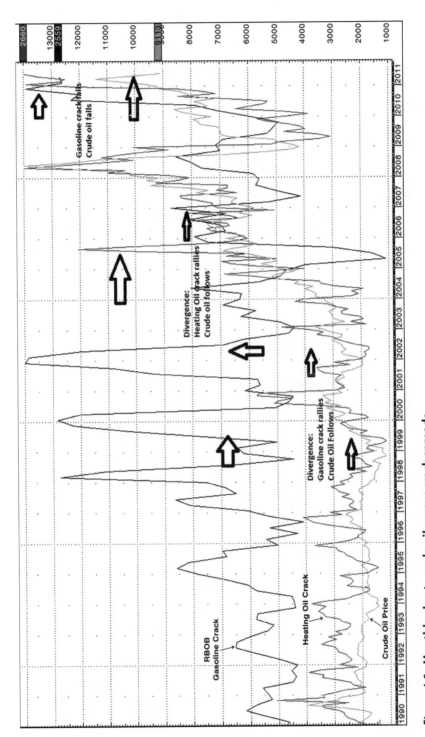

Figure 4.8 Monthly chart, crude oil versus crack spreads

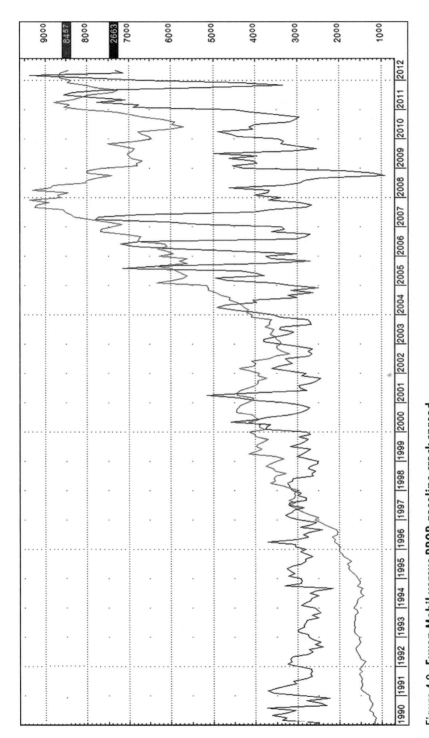

Figure 4.9 Exxon Mobil versus RBOB gasoline crack spread

Source: CQG, Inc. © 2012. All rights reserved worldwide.

has acted as a support for Exxon's rising stock market value. However, notice also that in late 2008, weaker refining margins caused the stock to fall—all the result of the correlation between the price of crude oil and oil products.

Another example is international shipping and logistics manager FedEx (FDX), which consumes huge amounts of oil-based fuel. (See Figure 4.10.) As oil prices rose slowly and steadily between 2001 and 2007, FedEx was able to pass its increasing costs along to its customers. However, in 2008, oil prices shot up to $147 a barrel. The move was so sharp that FedEx was unable to raise prices quickly enough, which had an immediate and dramatic impact on the company's earnings. As a result, its share price plummeted.

The box in Figure 4.10 illustrates the time period where the price of oil rose slowly and FedEx was able to adjust to and pass on higher fuel costs. The oval illustrates the sharp short-term price volatility in oil prices that had an immediate effect on the price of FedEx stock—the earnings of the company were affected in terms of higher costs eating into profits and causing earnings to plunge.

In 2008, I spotted an incredible short-term buying opportunity in an airline stock as oil prices skyrocketed. The airlines, which are huge consumers of jet fuel, another oil product, came under incredible pressure. Airline earnings have a negative correlation with the price of oil. The higher crude rises, the greater the cost to the airline, which cannot simply pass the cost along to the consumer, because when the airlines raise ticket prices, sales fall. I was looking at domestic airline JetBlue (JBLU), and, as oil made new all-time highs in 2008, the carrier's shares were dirt cheap. (See Figure 4.11.)

When the price of crude oil fell, there was a short-term correction in JetBlue's price—it shot up by more than 100 percent in six months. This is just one of many examples of how awareness and knowledge can lead to profits in your portfolio.

THE IMPORTANCE OF TECHNICAL INDICATORS IN THE CRUDE OIL MARKET

Technical indicators are like searchlights that illuminate what influential traders and investors are doing in the crude oil market, or any commodity market for that matter.

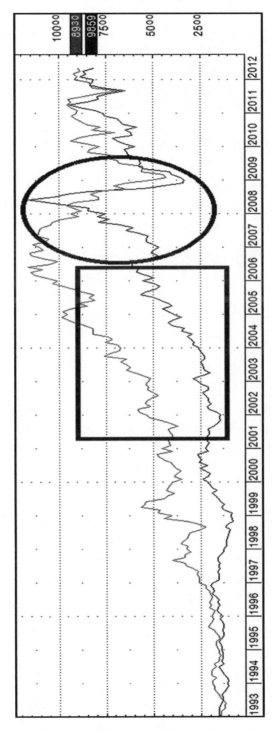

Figure 4.10 FedEx stock (FDX) versus NYMEX crude oil

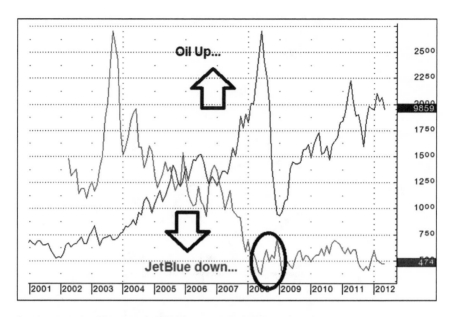

Figure 4.11 JetBlue stock (JBLU) versus NYMEX crude oil

Figure 4.12, a daily chart of crude oil, illustrates the importance of technical levels. Notice how the period between February 18 and June 17 formed a key support level at $95. However, once this level was broken, the oil price moved sharply lower, and the $95 support became resistance. These levels provide an investor with a good idea of the short-term range.

Support and resistance levels are great guidance for where other market participants will be buyers or sellers. Also, notice that the market held the all-important 200-day moving average for a very long time. Once this level was broken on June 15, the crude oil market headed south. For the conservative investor, there are many equities that are highly correlated and sensitive to the price of crude oil and associated oil products. Global stock exchanges trade stocks on oil producers, exploration companies, drillers, refining companies, and equipment suppliers. All these companies are guided by the price of crude oil, and its price provides the basis for earnings.

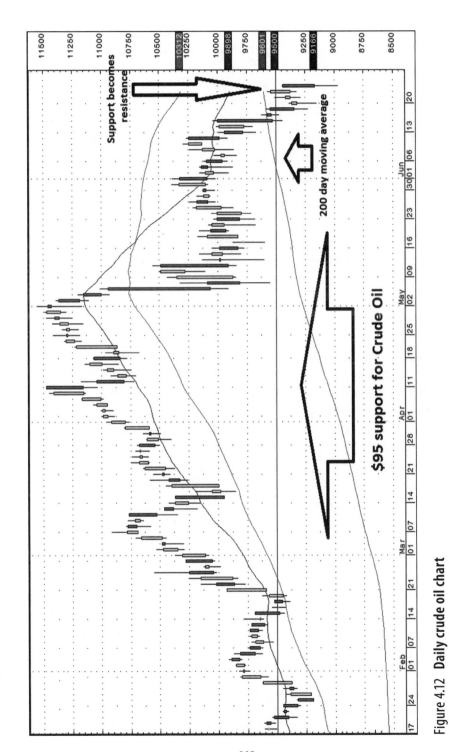

Figure 4.12 Daily crude oil chart

113

EASY TIP

Many investors make the mistake of buying into any oil-related company when prices start to move. It is important to pick wisely. Exploration, drilling, and services companies do best in a bull market for oil. However, in a bull market for crack spreads, oil-refining companies perform best. Understanding a market's structure will minimize mistakes and enhance opportunities.

Some ETFs and ETNs also take their directions from the crude oil price. These present less conservative methods of participating in oil-price movements. However, the less conservative the vehicle, the more the potential reward for the right bet on the price direction of this commodity.

There are even more aggressive ways to play the oil market. For example, long options—calls and puts—on futures are limited-risk instruments with limited time horizons that can provide huge returns for a small investment. Call options on futures are especially useful for capturing a quickly rising crude oil or oil-product market, and put options on futures can be used to capture returns from a falling market. Meanwhile, combinations of calls and puts, straddles and strangles, can be used to take advantage of high volatility, even when you are not sure which way the market is about to move. Short options offer a much higher level of risk, but a seller of options can profit from periods of little or no volatility. Historically, the crude oil price tends to rise over long periods of time and crash over short periods. When crude oil heads low, both historic and implied volatility tends to spike higher. This tends to make options expensive during down moves.

Finally, futures markets offer investors a leveraged way to participate in the daily movements of crude oil markets. The impact of a position in the futures markets can be huge because of the leverage futures provide, and price movement can happen quickly. A professional commodity trader I know likens day-trading crude oil futures to watching a slot machine, because the price moves so quickly. It is important to remember that futures offer high rewards, but they come with a great deal of risk—they are not for the faint of heart. Constant monitoring is necessary because these markets trade and move 24 hours a day.

Whether you use a crude oil trading vehicle or not, an education in this market can only make you a better and more-informed investor, helping you hone your investment skills and change how you look at energy use throughout the world.

Every government, whether it is from a consuming or producing nation, pays a great deal of attention to the international price of crude oil. The chairman of the U.S. Federal Reserve rarely gives a speech or makes a comment without referring to the international oil price. And protecting oil interests has caused more than a few wars and international conflicts. The world's spotlight is on crude oil, and it will always affect your portfolio.

NATURAL GAS

The story of natural gas goes back to around 1400 BC, when an unsuspecting goat herdsman came across what he believed was a "burning spring." What he saw was a flame rising from a crack in the rock at the top of Mount Parnassus. The Greeks believed the flame to be divine and built a temple over it. This temple eventually became home to the Oracle of Delphi—where it was said heaven met earth. It was also probably history's first reference to natural gas. Back in those days, people didn't know how to use it, and they certainly didn't know how to invest in it. It was not until 500 BC that people in China used the natural-gas flames to boil sea water, separating the salt from the water. Since then, this gas has been finely tuned, regulated, and used in various ways.

Coal and oil remain the most common fuels in the United States. In fact, the entire world is addicted to oil, yet it pollutes the environment as it burns. Many politicians, scientists, and businesspeople believe that natural gas is the answer to the problem. I believe natural gas is the fuel of the future. It is cleaner than crude oil, and there are abundant resources around the world. However, in the world of markets and investment, natural gas is the most volatile commodity traded.

In spite of the fact that it is raising increasing environmental concerns and higher oil prices, natural gas has become increasingly popular, slowly proving itself to be a wonderful fossil fuel after all—more efficient, safer, and cleaner than its brethren. Today, natural gas is one of the cleanest and most versatile energy sources available. It can heat and cool your home. Just a few of its uses include cooking, lighting, and transportation, as well as the manufacture of plastics, fertilizers, and antifreeze. Perhaps most importantly, it can also be used to power vehicles cheaply and is already an alternative to gasoline and diesel. Along with its abundance, this commodity's low cost is expanding daily use as the world seeks alternative energy sources.

In 2011, the United States and Russia were by far the world's largest producers of natural gas. (See Figure 4.13.)

In terms of reserves, however, Russia leads the world, followed by Iran, Qatar, Saudi Arabia, and the United States. Current global estimates stand at 6.7 quadrillion cubic feet, which is enough natural gas to provide nearly 65 years of global energy output at current rates. New discoveries are also continually adding to reserve estimates. The Marcellus Shale, which runs through the states of New York, Pennsylvania, Ohio, Maryland, West Virginia, Virginia, New Jersey, Kentucky, and Tennessee, contains more than 100 years of natural gas supplies for the United States. While the total extent of the reserves in this region is subject to debate, there is one certainty: the more we explore for natural gas reserves around the world, the more

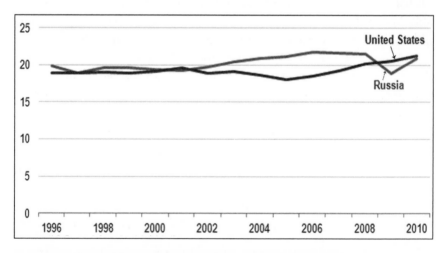

Figure 4.13 **Annual dry natural gas production: United States and Russia, 1996–2010, trillion cubic feet per year**
Source: U.S. Energy Information Administration.

we find. Since 2010, further reserves have been uncovered in Israel, Mozambique, Colombia, Cyprus, and Poland to name but a few. Asian countries are minor producers of natural gas, and so they are net importers of the commodity.

Nonetheless, exploration and production of natural gas in the United States faces a number of problems, chief among them is *fracking*. This is the process of mining shale gas by injecting water, sand, and chemicals into rocks to release the commodity from rock formations in the earth. Environmentalists contend that the fracking process contaminates water supplies and causes other damage to the environment. In recent years in the United States, various conservation lobby groups have succeeded in slowing down production. Fracking promises to be a hot-button political issue in the United States for years to come. In other gas-producing countries, such as Russia, however, environmental concerns are rarely considered.

The largest consumer of natural gas in the world is the United States, followed by Russia, which has roughly one-third the population of the United States. However, the United States uses more of its natural gas production domestically, while Russia is a bigger exporter. Asian nations rank among the top 10 consuming countries. With higher crude oil prices and increasing demand for energy in Asia, the demand for natural gas there is growing rapidly. Japan ranks fifth and China eighth in the world in demand. India, which ranks fifteenth, has experienced skyrocketing demand since 2001. With both supply and demand growing, natural gas is shaping up to be a key future energy market.

As of the middle of 2012, the natural gas market in the United States has experienced a multiyear bear market. While most other commodity prices have moved higher, natural gas prices have been falling steadily since 2008. Increasing reserves and production of the commodity have stayed well ahead of demand. In the United States, natural gas stockpiles are abundant, and prices have tumbled. The price of the commodity has spiked higher three times since the turn of the millennium. In 2000, the price spike was the result of a perceived supply shortage. Then, in 2005, Hurricane Katrina damaged natural gas infrastructure in the Gulf of Mexico, and prices surged above $15.50 on the active month NYMEX futures contract. Similarly, Hurricane Ike in 2008 caused infrastructure damage and resulted in another spike.

Historical volatility, on a monthly basis, is dramatic for natural gas. The commodity typically trades at more than 50 percent historical volatility—in other words an extremely wide range. In spite of its recent bearish performance, open interest and volume have risen, indicating that the natural gas market has grown in size. Given the historical volatility of the commodity, producers, consumers, and other market participants use the futures markets to hedge and speculate on the price of this commodity. Seasonal factors affect natural gas prices. An unusually cold winter or a scorching hot summer will increase demand and cause stockpiles to diminish and prices to move sharply higher. A mild winter or summer season will result in increased stockpiles, causing prices to fall. Natural gas is so volatile that in recent years it has attracted increasing numbers of speculators who have made and lost fortunes trading the commodity. In September 2006, Connecticut-based hedge fund Amaranth lost more than $6.5 billion on a natural gas futures position that went horribly wrong. The hedge fund bought natural gas futures in the wake of Hurricane Katrina, and when prices collapsed, the fund went belly up, marking one of the largest trading losses in history.

Natural gas prices often move so violently that huge profits or in this case losses result.

As I write this, natural gas prices in the NYMEX active month are trading at around $2.20, while prices three years into the future are trading at double that level—a huge contango for any commodity. When natural gas prices spike higher on an event, such as a hurricane, the price curve tends toward backwardation.

Natural gas also trades at different premiums or discounts, depending on where delivery takes place in the United States or abroad. The NYMEX futures contract calls for delivery at Henry Hub, which is a pipeline located in Erath, Louisiana. Of course, natural gas trades all over the United States. Premiums or discounts (location swaps) are based on both delivery charges and available supplies at particular locations. Stockpiles also affect the price of U.S. domestic natural gas. The U.S. Energy Information Administration releases weekly reports on natural gas stockpiles. The commodity's futures market tends to move dramatically when these reports deviate from analysts' estimates.

Natural gas prices were so low that in 2012 they traded below production cost for many producers, thus rendering the process uneconomical. Over a period of time, production cuts are bound to lead to higher prices, assuming that demand remains stable. Conversely, when prices rise, demand tends to decrease, and this causes prices to fall. Commodity markets are extremely efficient.

Natural gas also trades elsewhere in the world. While U.S. prices languished at around $2 per thousand btu's in 2012, the commodity traded as high as $16 per thousand btu's in parts of Asia, home to the commodity's most vibrant demand. In 2009, China was the eighth largest natural gas consumer in the world. That year, the country used 87.08 billion cubic meters of the commodity. In 2011 China's consumption grew to 129 billion cubic meters. In 2012, the country is expected to consume 164.4 billion cubic meters, an increase of 27.4 percent from 2011.

Natural gas consumption is also growing throughout the rest of Asia. While Japan's consumption of natural gas grew 6 percent from 2009 to 2011, South Korea's grew 26 percent, India's grew 26.7 percent, and Malaysia's grew 36 percent. These are amazing growth rates for the use of a commodity so inexpensive in the United States.

The Fukushima Daiichi nuclear disaster in 2011 resulted in record Japanese imports of natural gas as the country moved to replace nuclear power. A 27 percent leap in China's first-half purchases of natural gas, sent Asian prices even higher. While U.S. prices are plummeting, prices in Asia are soaring.

Companies in the business of producing natural gas in the United States, of course, have a high correlation with the price of the commodity itself. Many natural gas producers also produce other energy commodities, such as crude oil. However, let's take a look at Williams Energy (WMB), which is pretty close to a pure natural gas play, as shown in Figure 4.14.

As you can see, Williams Energy correlated nicely with the price of natural gas futures. However, there can also be times of dramatic divergence. In 1999, a Williams Energy share price move preceded higher natural gas prices. As divergences occurred over the years between 2000 and 2011, there were opportunities in both the stock and the commodity itself. In 2012, a wide divergence also emerged,

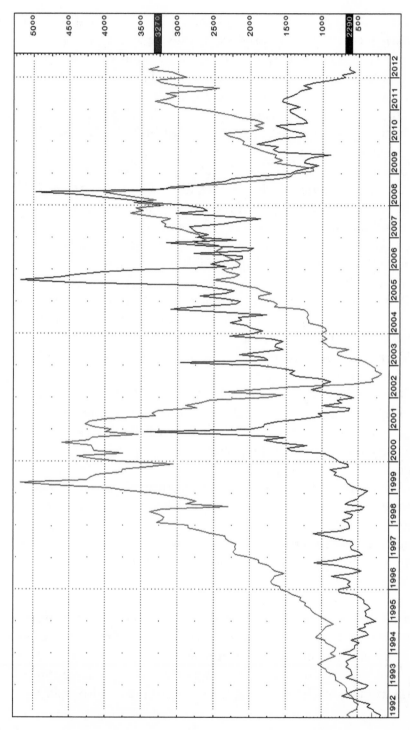

Figure 4.14 Williams Energy (WMB) versus NYMEX natural gas monthly chart

telling us that either the price of Williams Energy was too high or that the price of natural gas was too low.

The United States Natural Gas Fund (UNG) is an ETF based on the price of natural gas futures. As shown in Figure 4.15, it seems to be highly correlated with the price of the commodity, unlike the USO, the oil ETF, which we looked at earlier.

You will notice divergence between this ETF and the price of natural gas at the time of writing. This divergence signals that either UNG is too low or that the price of natural gas will rally from levels shown on the chart. In either case this ETF should come back into line with natural gas prices at some point in the future.

Finally, let's look at a company whose business is influenced by natural gas prices. Potash (POT), a fertilizer manufacturer, uses a tremendous amount of the commodity in its fertilizer production process. As Figure 4.16 shows, Potash's share price has climbed as the price of natural gas, one of its key production ingredients, has fallen. The stock has had a negative correlation with the price of natural gas since 2008. While natural gas is not the only factor that determines the earnings of Potash, the commodity is a major cost factor and affects the price of goods sold for the company's products. The current price divergence and recent weakness in Potash stock could be telling us something about natural gas prices.

So what is the investor to do with this wild and crazy commodity? There are futures contracts that trade on the NYMEX, and there are options contracts as well. Natural gas options can be an effective way to invest directly in the commodity. When natural gas prices start moving, options become very expensive to trade. There are also natural gas producers and consumers, as well as ETFs that trade on equity exchanges.

And don't forget to keep your eyes on technical indicators in natural gas. We have already noted the growth in open interest and volume. That means that speculators and investors are in there playing. Natural gas prices tend to move when resistance or support levels are breached, and this could have a direct impact on the stocks in your portfolio.

Natural gas is one of the most interesting commodities out there. Oversupply has pushed the market price below production costs. However, market efficiency will eventually remedy this condition. Second,

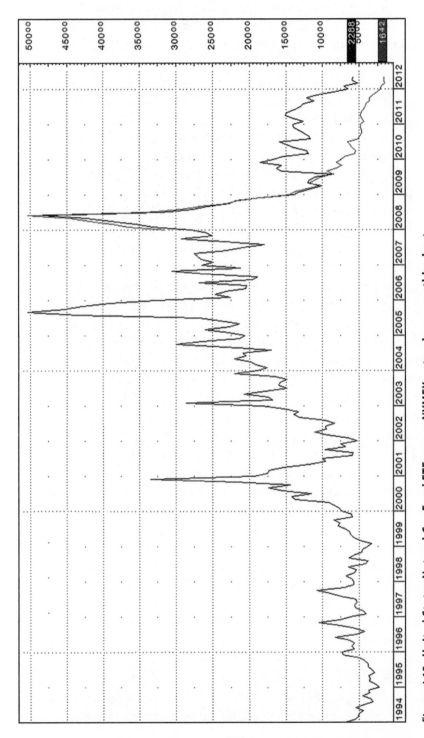

Figure 4.15 United States Natural Gas Fund ETF versus NYMEX natural gas monthly chart

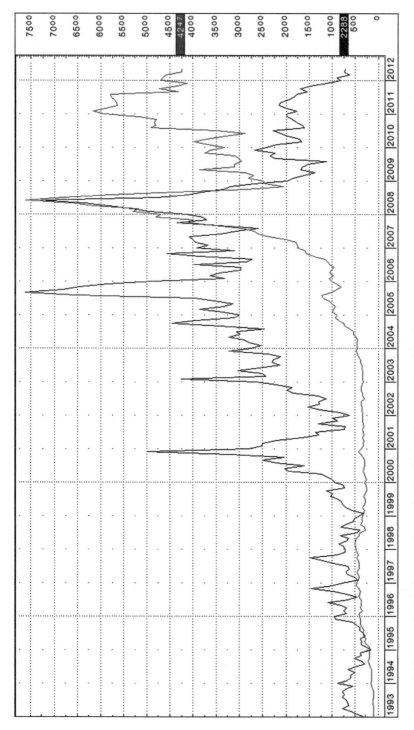

Figure 4.16 Potash (POT) versus NYMEX natural gas futures monthly chart

demand for the commodity is growing globally at an accelerated pace. Meanwhile, public policy seems to be shifting toward the use of natural gas—chiefly because the commodity is cheap.

And this leads me to my next investment tip. Try to look ahead and use your noodle to see the future. Natural gas infrastructure companies are popping up all over the place these days. Some companies are developing natural gas engines; others are in the process of developing, manufacturing, and bringing to market natural gas filling stations for cars and trucks that may one day run on this cheap and clean fuel. Companies are developing conversion kits for traditional gasoline-driven motor vehicles. There is also ongoing development of technology to liquefy natural gas, so it can be shipped to lucrative markets around the world. It costs only a few bucks to send the commodity by ocean vessel in liquefied form from U.S. shores or by pipeline from Russia to Asia. Natural gas infrastructure promises to be an extremely exciting area for investment over the coming years.

Natural gas will continue to be a volatile commodity—but volatility means opportunity.

ELECTRICITY, COAL, AND OTHERS

Crude oil, oil products, and natural gas are the most liquid of the traded energy commodities. These markets will always provide investors with a myriad of potential opportunities. However, the energy space also contains a number of other important fuel sources. Since the cost of energy affects all your investments, awareness of these other sources are important variables in your investment calculus.

Electricity

Electricity itself trades on the NYMEX commodity exchange, but there are very few speculators and investors in this market because contract volume is low and trading is anemic. Electricity futures offered by the NYMEX are cash-settled financial futures, and trading physical electricity is a difficult business. It is one of the few commodities that can fall to a price of zero or below. If buyers of physical electricity do not use it, they lose it—but they still have to pay for transport or transmission through the grids.

Power plants produce electricity, and cogeneration uses natural gas, coal, or oil to produce electricity. (Cogeneration is the simultaneous production of power or electricity, hot water and/or steam from one fuel.) Electricity can also be produced using nuclear power, solar power, wind power, and biofuels. When trading electricity, the most important component is not the production of the energy but its transmission via power lines.

A number of states in the United States deregulated electricity in the 1990s, that is to say the government reduced its role in the market. During those years, I worked for a large commodity broker that conducted transactions between buyers and sellers of commodities. One of those commodities was electricity. I was involved in the attempted creation of a clearinghouse for physical and future electricity among power companies, traders, and energy users around the United States.

Huge companies like AEP, Duke Energy, Florida Power and Light, Con Edison, and others were involved in the project. I believed a clearinghouse would eliminate credit risk and facilitate smooth trading and hedging activities. At the time, the most powerful trading house in the electricity sector was the now infamous Enron Corporation. Enron took a lead in the meetings. We were never able to establish a clearinghouse for electricity because Enron insisted that it control the market and the clearing mechanism to which the other power companies would submit. Enron's bankruptcy ended that attempt to create an electricity clearinghouse.

Electricity prices can be very volatile. In 2000 and 2001, Enron and several other electricity traders purposely created a shortage of electricity by taking power plants offline to boost prices and thus caused huge blackouts in California. The U.S. Federal Energy Regulatory Commission (FERC) investigated the market manipulation and, ever since, electricity traders have been on a short leash. Electricity trading never reached the potential initially envisioned.

Coal

Coal is a physical market. The United States, Russia, and China have the largest coal reserves in the world. China and the United States are both the largest producers and consumers. Both countries use coal to produce a bulk of their electricity. The price of coal historically has been lower and more stable than prices for crude oil and natural gas.

However, burning coal and other fossil fuels emits carbon dioxide, sulfur dioxide, arsenic, lead, and other harmful toxins. A system of emission allowances has been set up in an attempt to curtail the global-warming activities of companies. Power plants, for example, burning coal are limited to a certain amount of emissions each year. An active market for trading emission allowances has also developed. If a company does not use all of its allowances because it produces less greenhouse gases than the limit permits, it can sell its remaining allowances. By the same token, a company that overemits can purchase extra allowances.

A number of companies now use technology to capture or reduce greenhouse gases produced from burning coal by creating cleaner coal. There are also innovative methods of liquefying coal to make it cleaner. Because of availability and cost, coal has been a dominant energy source in the United States (and globally) for many years, but this will not be the case for long. New environmental legislation in the United States aims to decrease the use of coal in the future. The EPA has recently passed new regulations, that limit heat-trapping pollution from new power plants. These limits will decrease the demand for coal.

The new standard requires that new coal-fired power plants capture and store carbon pollution underground or inject it to extract more natural gas. This type of technology is not yet fully developed, but it holds promise for the future.

Nonetheless, stringent new standards will create more demand for natural gas among power plants and less demand for coal in the years to come. America is energy-hungry, and so is the rest of the world. Exxon Mobil has reported that by the year 2030 global energy usage will increase by 30 percent.

Power plants aren't the only ones scrapping coal usage for natural gas. Some steel companies have figured out that they can save hundreds of millions of dollars a year by switching to natural gas for power production and operation. These savings also allow them to sell their steel piping to gas drilling companies at a lower price, thereby increasing demand.

NYMEX trades coal futures, but the futures contracts are not liquid. ICE also offers coal futures. The exchanges and the U.S. Department of Energy website provide prices and data for coal.

Others

Significant investments have been made to find new forms of alternative energy. Wind turbines that turn wind into electricity and energy are in use throughout the world. Solar power has grown in popularity as a source of energy, but the current technology has proven to be too expensive to use on a grand scale. The power of water, hydropower, a source of alternative energy, and biofuels have gained in popularity around the world.

Given the increasing thirst for energy on a global scale, we have seen more investment in technologies centered on alternative energy sources; wind, hydropower, solar power, and biofuels.

Today wind turbines creating energy pepper the countryside in the United States and abroad.

China and India have been investing heavily in hydroelectric projects in order to reduce their reliance on fossil fuels. In June 2012 Jindal Power Limited, a unit of India's largest steel maker, announced plans to invest $7.7 billion in new hydroelectric projects over the next decade.

Perhaps the most publicized solar power venture—Solyndra, a manufacturer of solar panels—was the recipient of loan guarantees from the U.S. government. The failure of Solyndra in 2011 caused political jawboning and finger-pointing between parties in the United States. There have been many companies born over the last decade competing to find the Holy Grail when it comes to harnessing solar power (and other alternative sources of energy) in a cost-effective manner to provide alternative energy solutions.

Ethanol added to gasoline has long been a method of decreasing reliance on fossil fuels and hydrocarbons. In the United States gasoline for use in automobiles is a blend of petroleum-based gasoline and 10 percent ethanol. Ethanol has been added to gasoline in the United States since the oil crisis of the late 1970s. Ethanol is a product of corn. The drought in the spring and summer of 2012 caused a corn harvest that was far below expectations. This resulted in higher prices for gasoline at the pump because the 10 percent blend of ethanol was mandated by the U.S. government—as corn prices shot up, so did gasoline prices. In Brazil, the world's largest sugar producer, sugar is used to make ethanol. Many cars in Brazil are run with sugar-based fuel. Corn and sugar are both biofuels. As you can see, increasing worldwide demand for energy is causing a rush for alternative technologies to replace traditional energy sources.

All these types of energies have their positives and negatives. Human beings are amazingly adaptive creatures. Given the finite nature of resources and energy, new technologies will be born to fuel our planet in the decades to come. As these new forms of energy emerge, a need to trade and hedge their prices will certainly also arise.

CHAPTER 5

Precious Metals

HARD MONEY, THE BAROMETER OF GLOBAL FISCAL HEALTH

When we have gold, we are in fear; when we have none, we are in danger.

—ENGLISH PROVERB

Some metals are considered precious because of their extreme rarity. Many of these are traded intensely and held closely for generations.

All precious metals are mined. Some of them are by-products in the production of other metals, such as lead, copper, nickel, molybdenum, zinc, and others. Some precious metals are mined as primary production. Certain precious metals can affect the cost of goods sold for industries, such as automobile manufacturing. Precious metals are the easiest commodities for investors to directly own. They have value and can generally be stored in vaults, safe-deposit boxes, or even kept at home. There are three types of demand for precious metals: industrial demand, investment demand, and fabricated demand (fabricated demand generally refers to the manufacture of jewelry). Knowledge of precious-metal markets is key to understanding investments in mining stocks, fixed-income assets, the movement of currencies, and the state of the overall global economy.

GOLD

Gold is the perfect place to begin learning about the world of precious metals. It has amazing properties. The metal is soft, dense, lustrous, brilliant, ductile, and malleable. Gold enjoyed its first role in prehistory. The Neolithic period, some 12,000 years ago, marked the first discovery of gold in its natural form in river beds. Gold ornaments, mostly ring-shaped amulets, made of hammered sheet metal have been dated to the Stone Age.

The Bible tells of how the Israelites at the foot of Mount Sinai more than 3,000 years ago grew weary of waiting for Moses to return and "feasted and danced around the golden calf." Homer in the *Iliad* and *Odyssey* refers repeatedly to the metal. Menes, founder of the first Egyptian dynasty around 3100 BC, first documented the relationship of gold to silver in his code, marking the first intercommodity spread in history. The Incas called gold the tears of the sun. Around 700 BC, Lydian merchants operating in what is now western Turkey produced the first known gold coins from electrum. These early coins were stamped lumps of the compound, containing 67 percent gold and 23 percent silver.

The value, myth, and importance of gold have survived across millennia. Even today, gold remains the ultimate prize. A competitor who finishes in first place receives a gold medal. A heart of gold belongs to a kind person. A gold credit card has more status than an ordinary card. The exchange of gold bands symbolizes love and marriage in many societies. This metal is the ultimate symbol of the pinnacle of human achievement, and its value today is a psychological barometer of market sentiment.

Gold is a rare metal. By 2009, only 165,000 tons of it in total have been mined in the history of the world. That's about 5.3 billion ounces, worth just under $9 trillion at the price of $1,640 an ounce. Gold is not consumed in the traditional sense, but remains long after those who discovered and coveted the metal are gone. In that sense, gold is held and hoarded only temporarily. It never disappears. It is a constant.

There are two schools of thought when it comes to the value of gold. There are those who believe that gold is a barbarous relic of days gone by, and others who believe that gold is the ultimate symbol of wealth. Those who fall into the first group believe that owning gold is like worshipping an idol. However, others believe that true value lies in productive assets that yield dividends and growth. The second group believes that gold is the ultimate asset and the ultimate currency.

Historically, gold has been the most versatile commodity to have been used as a means of exchange. Societies have used salt and cattle to barter for other goods. Native Americans sold the island of Manhattan for wampum. During World War Two, cigarettes served as currency. And in the 1980s in Russia, I witnessed Levis, alcohol, cigarettes, and condoms being used as currency. However, only gold has survived as a form of exchange from the ancient world. Doug Casey, the economist and professional investor, has said, "Gold is money" (see http://casey-research.com/cwc/doug-casey-gold). Like the ancient Greek philosopher, Aristotle, Casey believes that gold is durable, divisible, consistent, and convenient, and that it possesses value itself. Precious metals have all of these qualities.

Central banks and governments around the world are gold bugs (people or institutions that believe gold is real money). As of 2010, central banks, governments, and supranational institutions held around 30,800 tons of gold as reserves. Government vaults hold 19 percent of all the gold ever mined. But why do governments hold gold? It is a part of national foreign exchange reserves. In other words, governments view gold as a currency. Many people also consider gold the ultimate currency. A government can print as much paper money as it wishes, and the faith and credit of a government stands behind this paper currency. But when it comes to gold, governments cannot control value. Thus an individual government could never dilute the value of its gold reserves. It has the power only to sell gold or buy more.

The debate over the value of gold continues. One school of thought is that the only way to ensure fiscal responsibility is to back paper currency with gold, like the gold standard that existed for many years. Under a gold standard, paper currency must be backed by a requisite amount of gold that the government holds in reserve. A gold standard prevents governments from printing currency when no gold exists to give the currency value. However, given current levels of government debt, this would require an astronomical price of gold—many multiples of the all-time high struck in 2011 at just over $1,900 an ounce.

The United States holds more gold than any other country in the world. It reports its holdings at 8,133.5 tons, or around 26 percent of global governmental holdings, which is 5 percent of all the gold ever mined. The U.S. gold reserves represent 76.6 percent of U.S. national foreign exchange reserves. Germany is second with almost 4,000 tons, and the International Monetary Fund is third with 2,814 tons, followed by Italy, France, and China. Indeed, China holds just 1.8 percent of its foreign exchange reserves in gold, which makes it potentially a huge buyer of gold bullion. In 2011 central banks purchased around 16 percent of all new gold production from mines, and China was one of the buyers. China has also added to reserves by virtue of its own increasing domestic production.

Meanwhile, a multiyear bull market in gold has sparked huge activity in gold-based ETFs and physical bullion funds. These instruments purport to hold gold against interests in futures contracts and gold bullion. As of May 2011, they held over 2,150 tons which would make the gold held against these contracts number five on the list of bulk gold holdings, between France and China, reflecting the huge investment demand for gold today.

In 2011, there was a total of 2,800 metric tons of gold produced. For many years, the largest and most influential gold producer in the world was South Africa. However, in 2007, China became the world's number one gold producer and is followed by Australia, the United States, South Africa, Russia, Peru, Indonesia, Canada, Ghana, and Uzbekistan.

Gold demand in 2011 outpaced supply, and the price rose by 10.23 percent. In 2011, demand was 4,067.1 tons, the majority of which came from India, China, and Europe. Central banks bought 440 tons or 16 percent of annual mine supplies. Fabricated demand for jewelry production absorbed around 50 percent, investment demand took 40 percent, and industrial users, including the electronics, dentistry, and medical sectors, absorbed 10 percent of annual mine supply.

There are quality differences in gold: 24-carat gold is 100 percent pure (or fine). Pure gold is malleable. Standard Good London Delivery gold bars are minimum 99.5 percent pure or 23.88 carat. Industrial users generally purchase gold that is at minimum 99.99 percent pure or 23.9976 carat. The industry term for this gold is "four nines" gold.

London is the hub of the international physical gold market. However, the dominant futures exchange for gold is based at COMEX in New York City. Zurich and Hong Kong also operate as physical gold-trading market hubs.

Size matters in the gold market as well. Good London Delivery bars are generally 400 fine troy ounce bars. (There are 12 troy ounces per troy pound, rather than the 16 ounces per pound found in the more common avoirdupois system.) Central banks tend to hold these bars as reserves. Good delivery COMEX bars are 100 fine troy ounces in size. Each futures contract also represents 100 troy ounces of gold. Industry generally uses kilo bars, which weigh 32.15074 fine troy ounces. Half and quarter kilo bars are also available. Investment gold can range from 400-ounce bars to fractional ounce bars. Coins come in denominations of one ounce, one-half ounce, one-quarter ounce, and one-tenth ounce. Bars weighing 5, 10, 20, 50, 100, and 200 grams are acceptable for delivery in London. However, the Indian market trades 10 tola bars, which weigh around 3.75 ounces. The Chinese market trades taels (five taels weigh around six ounces). There are also gold wafers in smaller sizes. The London Bullion Market Association approves the refineries that produce these bars. Only bullion bars produced by approved refineries are good for delivery in the London market, and London market approved vaults store these bars.

Worth Its Weight …

The gold standard, a monetary system in which the standard economic currency unit is a fixed weight of gold, began in Great Britain in1821. It wasn't until more than half a century later in the 1870s that the rest of Europe followed suit. However, the Great Depression in the 1930s marked the end of the U.S. export of gold bullion, and the United Kingdom abandoned the gold standard in 1931. By the mid-twentieth century, the U.S. dollar had replaced gold in international trade.

Nonetheless, the benchmark price for gold bullion is still set at the daily London gold fixing session. For many years, the fixings took place at the offices of N. M. Rothschild and Sons (the merchant bank begun by Nathan Mayer Rothschild in 1811), and included the five fixing members of the London bullion market. The Rothschilds made a fortune trading government bonds and were the most powerful bankers in the world during the nineteenth century. The first gold fixing took place on September 12, 1919. The original fixing members were N. M. Rothschild & Sons, Samuel Montagu, Mocatta & Goldschmidt, Pixley & Abel, and Sharps Wilkins, all bullion brokers. Today, the fixing members are Bank of Nova Scotia (Scotia-Mocatta), Barclays Bank, Deutsche Bank, HSBC, and Société Générale.

Central banks and other influential market participants tend to buy and sell big quantities of physical gold bullion based on the fixings. Each member brings orders to the fixing each business day at 10:30 a.m. and 3 p.m. GMT. Buyers and sellers must match against each other at the same price to fix the price. The members state how much gold they wish to buy or sell for customers in units of 400-ounce Good London Delivery bars.

The goal of the fixing is to find the equilibrium price where buyers and sellers can transact business. Sometimes fixing, which is made in three currencies (U.S. dollars, U.K. pounds, and euros) can take time. The record for the longest fixing was set on Black Monday, October 19, 1987, and took two hours and fifteen minutes. There is a good reason the physical market for gold uses a fixing mechanism. Often central banks and gold producers utilize the fixing to buy and sell gold bullion. Using the fixing to transact business eliminates all potential for accusations of speculation by these market participants.

Gold delivery in the London market can be either physical or unallocated. Physical delivery entails the actual allocation of gold bars with specific serial numbers and weights at a London delivery vault. In the case of physical delivery, storage and insurance charges are a consideration. Unallocated delivery entails a book transfer or credit/debit system of gold bought and sold. Approved vaults hold physical metal against unallocated balances. The holder of an unallocated balance can take physical delivery at any time on request, and often there are charges for allocation. The London bullion market is regulated by the United Kingdom's Financial Services Authority in conjunction with the Bank of England.

Meanwhile, in New York, the futures exchange trades gold futures around the clock. The electronic market for gold futures trading opens at 6 p.m. EST and closes at 5:15 p.m. the following day. The market opens Sunday night and closes Friday afternoon, but is also closed on certain holidays. There is an active arbitrage market—the practice of taking advantage of a price difference between markets—for COMEX and the London gold market.

Most people believe that professional gold traders make money from handling customer orders and from being long or short on gold. This is usually not the case. Professional bullion dealers make money from time spreads and arbitrage. Many are market makers. They show prices where they are willing to buy and sell gold at the same time. A customer then decides whether he wishes to buy or sell based on the market maker's price. I worked in London as a bullion dealer between 1988 and 1991. I once made the mistake of calling a customer a client. One of my colleagues set me straight. He told me, "Bullion dealers have customers; prostitutes have clients." I never repeated the mistake.

The business of trading gold is all about arbitrage and time spreads, and the gold market is almost always in a contango. The price for future delivery is always higher than the price for nearby delivery because gold is a currency, and currencies always have an interest rate attached.

Central banks sit on huge amounts of gold. Creditworthy professional bullion dealers and banks borrow this gold from central banks for a fee, which provides the banks with a small yield on their gold holdings. Dealers then use central bank gold to fund long-term producer hedges, which are forward transactions.

This is an example of how the process works:

1. Producer sells gold for delivery next year to a bullion dealer.
2. Bullion dealer needs something to sell to lock in the price.
3. Bullion dealer borrows gold from a central bank usually for three months at a time.
4. Bullion dealer sells the central bank gold, thus hedging price risk.

5. Bullion dealer must now reborrow the gold three more times (for three-month periods) until the producer delivers gold or buys back the hedge.
6. When the producer delivers the gold, the dealer will return the central bank gold or enter into another forward transaction using the same central bank gold.

In essence, dealers borrow short term from the central banks and lend longer term to the producers. This is called *liquidity funding*.

The average price paid to a central bank for borrowing gold over the past 40 years is around 0.3 percent per year. If the bullion dealer prices the forward bought from the producer at 1.30 percent under the forward price, the bullion dealer will pocket 1 percent on the deal. At a price of $1,640 an ounce for gold, that is $16.40 per ounce profit a year. On a one-year forward hedge of 100,000 ounces, the dealer will make $1.64 million. Naturally, the dealer is taking the credit risk that the producers will deliver the gold when promised—although, they usually do. This is a very profitable business for gold bullion traders. There are 2,700 tons of gold a year produced by mines. If 10 percent is hedged, it amounts to 8.7 million ounces.

That hedging is worth close to $150 million in profits to the bullion dealers at a 1 percent margin. Often, profit margins are higher. The bullion-dealing community is small, so there are plenty of profits to go around. Keep in mind that producers will often hedge production further into the future, so this business is a cash cow for professional bullion dealers. In addition to producer hedges, bullion dealers also use the central bank bullion they borrow for arbitrage against the futures exchange. Gold arbitrage is a form of time spread, which can also be a very profitable venture. However, it is worth noting that professional traders make money from the intracommodity time spreads, not from speculating on the price of gold.

As a bullion dealer in the 1980s and 1990s, I had the opportunity to conduct business with many of the world's central banks. I borrowed their gold and arranged a variety of transactions with them. The central banks of financially robust nations loaned gold for three-month periods, and were very conservative. Collateral instruments, such as letters of credit, were required by some countries against the gold loans. However, these instruments came at a cost. Posting collateral created a secured gold loan. Other central banks simply lent gold on an unsecured basis. This was the best type of transaction for my business, because it allowed me to create cash.

My precious-metals business was self-funding because of the unsecured gold loans. Central banks of other countries used their gold to create cash. Countries like France or Denmark had no need for cash, but for nations like Hungary, Romania, and Poland it was a different story. These countries used whatever gold they had to take short-term loans. Instead of lending the gold for a fee, they would sell their gold and buy it back in the future. This would raise immediate funds and create short-term funding support. Other countries would add to or sell from reserves through bullion dealers like me. In 1988, I traveled to Taiwan, following a rumor that the country was preparing to buy gold and increase its reserves.

A central bank of Taiwan official in Taipei suggested I would need a local agent to do business with the bank. As I interviewed an agent, I was told there would have to be a cash payment made to the agent (and shared with the central bank officials) to get the business. I will never forget how the agent, a former central bank official who had retired, explained the process and reasoning to me. At a meeting in a restaurant, we dined on a Taiwanese delicacy, fried baby birds. As the agent sucked the eyeballs from the birds, he explained that the central bank did indeed plan to buy gold and add to reserves, but added that I could have the order if I gave him $1 million in cash. In the United States there is a law called the Foreign Corrupt Business Practices Act, which prevents U.S. businesses from paying off current and former foreign government officials to receive business. I explained this to the agent, but he expressed the view that I was crazy.

The business was worth tens of millions of dollars to my firm. Why wouldn't I be willing to pay him a measly one million bucks? After all, that was the way the government had arranged to take care of him in his retirement. Of course, I did not pay the agent and did not go forward with the deal.

Many bullion dealers keep gold deposits on an unallocated basis for those holding gold accounts with them. Customers can call for physical delivery at any time, but they rarely do. Bullion dealers maintain fractional reserves for physical delivery and lend the rest out. It all functions like the traditional banking deposit business. Banks

fund loans with cash from depositors and central banks. Bullion dealers do the same except with gold. A producer hedge is a long-term gold
loan. The London Bullion Market Association (LBMA) website provides a wealth of juicy and enormously helpful data for understanding
the machinations of the physical international gold and silver markets.
Additionally, COMEX also has a great website. All these data are freely
available to the public.

Gold is a barometer for inflation: the higher the price, the
greater the potential for future inflation. Gold prices tend to rally in
low interest-rate environments. Because gold is a contango market,
higher interest rates mean more cost to carry gold bullion. Therefore,
lower interest rates make gold more attractive to investors. There are
times when interest rates lead gold and times when gold leads interest
rates. This is another reason investors with fixed income portfolios
should keep their eyes on the gold market. From the early 1980s, high
interest rates depressed gold prices for 20 years.

Gold is not really a commodity, at least not as we understand
the term. Unlike commodities, gold is rarely volatile. The quarterly historical volatility for gold at the time this book was written
stands at 9.76 percent. Compare that with 27.23 percent for crude oil,
33.61 percent for corn, 32.54 percent for copper, or 45.1 percent for
sugar. Volatility is 9.09 percent for the dollar. Gold is currency, which
is why central banks hold it as a foreign exchange reserve. Is gold the
ultimate reserve currency? It certainly has all the characteristics of a
currency. Professional gold traders operate within a framework akin
to the traditional banking business. Moreover, this precious metal
reacts to fear on a global scale, and it is generally correct. When the
gold market becomes volatile, it is a warning signal.

Between 1999 and 2001, gold traded mostly below $300 an ounce.
During those years Gordon Brown, the former U.K. prime minister,
at the time the chancellor of the exchequer, subscribed to the school
of thought that gold was nothing more than a barbarous relic. Gold
had spent almost 20 years in a quiet market that ranged from $300 to
$400 an ounce, with the exception of a brief spike to $800 in 1980.
Gordon Brown thought that gold's heyday was over and, at prices
below $300 an ounce, he sold off 60 percent of the Bank of England's
gold reserves or 395 tons of gold in three years. Traders often quip that
the British made him prime minister in 2007 because they would have

done anything to get him away from the country's checkbook. As I write this book, gold has come down to $1,640 an ounce. At this price, Mr. Brown's golden sell-off lost more than $17 billion for the United Kingdom. Quite fittingly, London gold dealers refer to the price at which he sold, $275 an ounce, as the "Brown bottom."

How Gold Knowledge Can Make, and Save, You a Fortune

The gold market contains important lessons for your portfolio. The price of the gold has risen dramatically since it broke above the $450 resistance level in 2005. The breach was a signal that the global economy was in a heap of trouble. Those who were paying attention could have taken advantage of the situation simply by buying gold for themselves. As it turned out, gold was responding to the long-term bear market in the U.S. dollar. The following year, it reacted to the mounting debt levels of governments and individuals in the West, particularly in the United States and Europe. A lustrous metal, gold reflects global economic health. It is also sensitive to the movement of the U.S. dollar in comparison to other currencies. In 2008, after a brief dip, gold exploded to more than $1,900 an ounce, levels never before seen. Why? Mounting deficits on both sides of the Atlantic, coupled with forced policies of government-supported low interest rates—a perfect economic storm for gold prices to continue their upward momentum.

As I write this, the U.S. deficit is fast approaching $16 trillion. At the same time, sovereign debt in Europe continues to plague the global economy. There is no quick and easy solution to these problems. Only fiscal austerity on a global basis will return gold to lower levels. Actually, gold has held its value from 2005 to 2012. The problem is that other assets, except for government bonds, controlled by a policy of monetary easing, have weakened. According to the gold barometer, the fear index in 2012 is flashing signs of high-level danger ahead.

Owning Gold

The simplest and most correlated method of owning gold is to buy physical bars, coins, or wafers. But investors should buy only gold that has well-known refinery stamps. The London Bullion Market Association website is a great resource for identifying acceptable gold refiners.

There have been many reports of fraudulent gold ingots. Hollowed-out bars filled with other less expensive metals, such as tungsten, turn up from time to time. Larger bars are at more risk of fraud. Investors who wish to purchase physical gold should always buy the metal from reputable dealers. Buying physical gold is the only direct investment in the metal.

Gold ETFs have historically tracked the price of gold well. As we saw in Chapter 2, the ETF, SPDR Gold (GLD) has performed with a positive correlation over time. But be sure to check the correlation of any ETF or ETN product with the underlying market results that you are trying to replicate in your portfolio. ETFs could at times disconnect from their underlying assets in wild markets. Remember that when you invest in ETFs or ETNs, you are not investing in the underlying commodity, only in the investment vehicle, which carries its own set of risks.

COMEX gold futures and options markets are extremely liquid, but they can be volatile over short periods. Gold futures are for traders, not investors. However, there are times when long options strategies are appropriate for some investors because they carry limited risk. Gold options are cheap, compared with other commodities, because gold trades like a currency with low volatility.

Owning Gold Mines

A favorite instrument of investors is the purchase of gold mining companies that trade on stock exchanges. Gold stocks have their pluses and minuses. On the positive side, gold mining companies make money and have earnings. They take gold out of the ground and sell it at the market price. The average production cost of gold in 2011 was between $600 and $700 an ounce, depending on the producer. Of course, these production costs vary among companies. With gold prices above $1,600, gold mining is a profitable business these days. Theoretically, the higher the gold price, the more the mining companies earn. Theoretically, gold mining stocks should move in step with the gold price.

Gold mining companies are businesses, and some have good management and some don't. An investment in gold protects against inflation and economic disaster. However, gold mining companies are always at risk of rising production costs as a result of runaway inflation. They are also at risk from falling levels of production. Many gold miners produce in countries around the world and some take political risks when they produce in certain regions. For example, in 2011, Hugo Chavez the president of Venezuela, nationalized his country's gold mines, which was a major blow to mining companies that invested in mines and mining operations. When there is a flood in a mine or a project does not yield expected results, the stock's share price will suffer. These are extraneous factors that have nothing to do with the price of gold. To mitigate these risks for investors, there are indexes that represent baskets of gold mining stocks. I find these baskets extremely useful in determining whether gold stocks are cheap or not, relative to the price of gold bullion.

Figure 5.1 shows one of the most popular baskets of gold mining stocks, the Philadelphia Gold and Silver Index, which contains some of the largest gold-producing companies in the world. Clearly, there are times when gold stocks signal moves in the gold price. Throughout the 1990s, gold mining businesses were better investments than gold itself. However, in 2002, gold stocks began to signal the rally. Since 2008, gold has been a much better investment than gold mining equities, but the divergence has moved so dramatically that by 2012 many wondered if the gap was too wide.

In 2012, gold mining shares signaled that gold was too high or that gold mining shares were too low or that there is something fundamentally wrong with the gold mining business itself.

Gold is an enigma. It is both a commodity and a currency. Mystery, myth, and emotion all play into its price. Gold is the most psychological of all commodities, but it is a barometer all investors must watch.

SILVER

Many people regard silver as gold's little brother, but it is a commodity with a dual role. Silver is both a precious metal and an industrial metal, and it is this duality that causes its price to react differently to macro-economic market events than does gold metal at times. When gold is currency, silver is the change. Like gold, silver meets all of Aristotle and Doug Casey's stipulations for hard money. And like gold, silver has a long history as money. Ancient civilizations found deposits of silver on or near the surface of the earth. More than 5,000 years ago, when Pharaoh Menes stated that, "One part of gold equals two and one half parts silver in value," he established the gold-silver relationship that remains today.

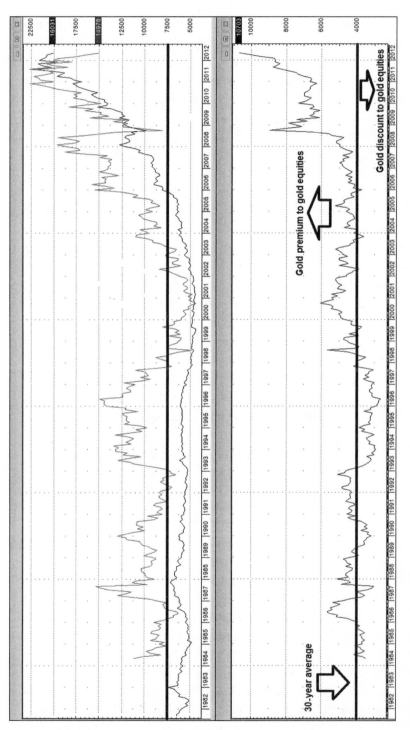

Figure 5.1 (Top) XAU (basket of gold and silver stocks) versus COMEX gold futures; (bottom) COMEX gold divided by XAU

Source: CQG, Inc. © 2012. All rights reserved worldwide.

Silver ornaments, utensils, and coins have documented the metal's uses throughout history. Electrum, a naturally occurring alloy of both gold and silver, was a currency unit used by seventh-century merchants from Lydia. Lydian coins were made up of 23 percent silver. The Lydians were the first people believed to have used coins as currency. The Romans also used silver as currency. In 1792, the U.S. Congress based the fledgling nation's currency on silver and its relationship to gold. Some 250 years earlier in the mid-sixteenth century, Spanish explorers discovered a mountain of silver in Peru that yielded 45,000 tons of the metal and turned Spain into the richest country in the world.

Before the discovery of Cerro Rico, or "Rich Hill", at Potasi, in Peru, silver prices were extremely high. In the early fifteenth century the price surpassed $1,200 per ounce in 2011 dollars. Thanks to basic economic forces of supply and demand, which at the time were undocumented in the Old World, these Peruvian silver discoveries and others in the New World caused silver prices to plummet.

Physically, silver has many similar properties to gold, but it is a harder metal. Both have luster and shine. Silver tarnishes, but its shine returns when it is polished. During World War Two, the U.S. government loaned silver from its strategic stockpile for industrial uses because of a shortage of copper, nickel, and tin, which were being used as part of the war effort. Silver often became a substitute for these industrial, nonferrous base metals. However, that substitution also served to highlight silver's industrial qualities as an extraordinary conductor of electricity. Today, wiring, electronics, batteries, bearings, catalysts, and solder soak up a great deal of the annual supply of the metal. There are also industrial applications in automobile manufacturing and other sectors.

The lion's share of modern-day silver production comes as a byproduct of other metals. The ores of copper, lead, and zinc contain silver. In 2011, some 23,689 tons (761.6 million ounces) of silver were mined. And the Silver Institute that year reported demand of 876.1 million ounces, with half of that demand coming from industry. The largest producer in the world is Mexico, followed by Peru, China, Australia, Chile, Poland, Russia, and Bolivia. The United States and Argentina are also significant silver producers.

The silver price shot up to a high of more than $49 an ounce in 2011 before tumbling. There is much more to the price of silver than just annual supply and demand. Global silver stockpiles are a key ingredient, but their true levels are difficult to establish. Analyst CPM Group estimated total global government holdings in 2004 at around 125 million ounces. I tend to discount these numbers because large silver-producing countries like Russia and China will probably never reveal their true total stocks. Other silver stockpiles are transparent. For example, COMEX warehouses hold around 140 million ounces. Despite this transparency, even outside of countries like China and Russia, the amount of silver stocks in many places, such as London, is widely disputed.

I have always believed that total silver stocks held by the London bullion market to be around 200 million ounces—but that is an educated guess. Meanwhile, the total amount of silver-backed ETF instruments is close to 500 million ounces. The ETF market in gold and silver has added a new dimension of liquidity, making these precious metals increasingly available to everyday investors. Silver is also held in vaults, in homes, and in individual stockpiles around the world. During periods in which the silver price rises, increased amounts of the metal will come back to the market. Individual holders sell silver hordes, which are then refined into bars to satisfy demand.

The estimate of total global silver stocks ranges between 1 billion and 1.5 billion ounces. Estimates of total worldwide silver production (throughout history) range between 40 billion and 60 billion ounces. The question is: Where is it all? Individuals hold the bulk of the world's mined silver. Whether it is silverware in your drawer, ornamental silver, coins, bars, or artwork, silver is found in millions of households around the world.

Meanwhile, the physical silver market is the object of considerable conjecture. Some conspiracy theorists believe that there is not enough silver to satisfy all the holders of paper silver, which backs ETFs, unallocated silver held in London vaults, and open interest in derivative markets. I don't believe anyone really knows the answer, but if all the holders of paper silver called for delivery at the same time, it would create quite a problem.

The Silver Market

The silver market operates in the same fashion as the gold market. At noon each business day, the silver price is fixed by the Bank of

Nova-Scotia, Deutsche Bank, and HSBC. I remember that my old boss always used to ask why precious metals were fixed in London when they weren't broken in the first place? Our British colleagues thought he was an idiot, but he wasn't. COMEX silver bars as well as those in London weigh 1,000 ounces. Good Delivery silver is 99.9 percent pure or *three-nines fine*. In addition, 99.99 percent pure silver is available, and this *four-nines fine* silver is required for many industrial applications.

While gold trades more like a currency; silver, because of its industrial nature, trades like a commodity and only occasionally takes on a financial role. (See Figure 5.2.)

Silver has seen some amazing price spikes over the past few decades. In 1979 and 1980, the white metal traded up to $50 an ounce when two brothers, Nelson and Bunker Hunt, attempted to manipulate physical silver and silver futures contracts. In the end, the brothers made a small fortune from a large one. U.S. regulators shut the operation down. The Hunts purportedly owned 200 million ounces of silver but were forced to sell their position when they could no longer finance it, and the exchange ordered a liquidation-only rule. The pair lost hundreds of millions of dollars on their silver foray.

As with any commodity, silver experiences periods of tightness, which means it can also experience periods of backwardation, where nearby prices are higher than those that are deferred. However, professional bullion dealers do much less long-term hedging and swapping in silver than they do in gold. As a by-product of other ores, there is less primary production of silver. Therefore, there is less demand for long-term hedging in this metal. Unlike gold, postproduction sales in silver are the norm.

Investing and trading in gold's little brother has for many years been a wild ride. Fortunes have been made and lost in this volatile market. Horace Tabor, a U.S. senator and legendary silver prospector, also known as the Bonanza King of Leadville, made and lost a fortune after the repeal of the Sherman Silver Purchase Act in 1893, which had enforced an increase in the monthly government purchase of silver. The repeal, however, resulted in Tabor's financial demise.

In the late 1970s and early 1980s, the Hunt brothers saw huge profits turn into massive losses after the price of silver plunged from $50 to $15 over a few short months.

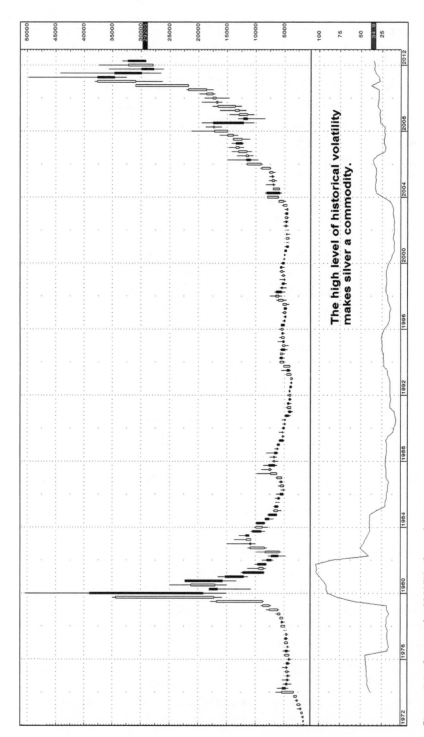

Figure 5.2 Quarterly COMEX silver chart

In 1995, I tested my own luck in the silver market. Together with three other traders at the Phibro division of Salomon Brothers, I took a substantial position in the white metal. The price of silver had been languishing below $5 in late 1994 when we decided to buy the metal as a strategic position for the firm. By the time we were finished, we had purchased more than 250 million ounces, worth $1 billion-plus, a bigger position than the Hunt brothers took back in 1979.

At that time, I knew there were between 100 and 150 million ounces in COMEX warehouses. And I had estimated that the London bullion market held between 150 and 200 million ounces. We had decided to buy the silver for one simple reason—it was too cheap. Over a six-month period, we bought silver and then sold it on the instructions of the Commodity Futures Trading Commission (CFTC), the regulators, which apparently believed that the position was too large and that we were attempting to manipulate the market. We had no intention of manipulating anything—we just thought it was cheap.

Unlike Horace Tabor or the Hunt brothers, we did not lose a fortune. However, we didn't make a fortune either. But I learned something interesting about the silver market. Half of our position was in futures, while the other half, some 125 million ounces, was composed of silver bars held in private warehouses in London and New York. When our total position surpassed 200 million ounces, we decided not to lend our unallocated silver into the London market. The time spreads in London started to move toward backwardation, with prices lower in the future than in nearby delivery months. I suddenly realized that there was not much silver available in the London market after all. That day, when silver spreads moved into a backwardation for the first time, a Bank of England official called and asked kindly if I could lend silver into the market. We had no legal obligation to do so, but we lent the silver at their request. Time spreads quickly normalized and returned to contango.

Conspiracy theorists believe that London does not have enough physical silver to deliver against unallocated silver holders. However, while I believe London is not as short as some believe, it is much shorter than it would like the market to believe. My experience in April 1995 has led me to believe there are not a lot of silver stockpiles in London. In other words, there would be a run on the bank if everyone showed up at the same time and demanded delivery of their silver. This situation was confirmed in 1997 when another investor, Warren Buffett, stuck his toe in the silver market.

Buffett bought only 130 million ounces of the commodity, but he still managed to drive silver into a backwardation. When Buffett loaned silver, he did so by selling nearby and buying slightly farther out. Each time he traded, the market paid him because he sold at higher prices than he bought back. For me, that was proof that the London silver market is not particularly liquid and that the bullion banks do not hold significant stockpiles. Unlike Tabor, the Hunts, and my foray at Phibro, Buffett pocketed several hundred million dollars on his silver trade.

EASY TIP

I often use vertical option spreads to trade silver. This way, when I have to pay high option premiums, at least I recoup some money by selling options at the same time.

Silver is a speculative market because at times it can be extremely volatile. The metal began a wild ride in 2004 when it was trading at less than $6 an ounce. By 2011, silver peaked at $49. The most recent ride up from 2004 through 2011 was different. The rally was longer, and many more investors came along for the ride. The liquidity of new products, such as ETFs, made silver available to increasing numbers of investors who had not had a way to participate previously. At the same time, the silver market is always rife with rumor. In 2011, Mexican billionaire Carlos Slim was rumored to be a big buyer. As I write this, silver is trading at around $29.50. While I believe silver's rise is justified, no one knows for sure where silver will go this time. I am only sure that silver's volatility will continue.

Silver-Gold Relationship

Just as quarters, dimes, nickels, and pennies are change for the dollar, silver is change for gold. The relationship is as strong today as it was during the time of Menes. There are many who trade the gold-silver ratio today. It is an intercommodity spread worth watching. Figure 5.3 illustrates the gold-silver ratio that existed between 1975 and 2012.

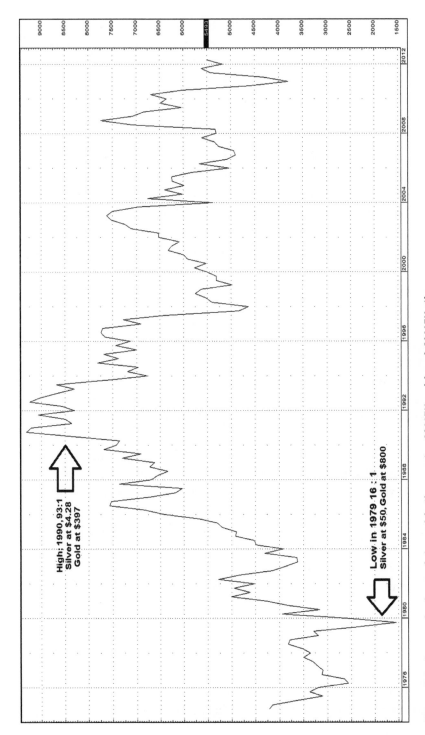

Figure 5.3 Quarterly chart of the gold-silver ratio, COMEX gold and COMEX silver

149

In the days of the pharaoh Menes, two and a half ounces of silver equaled one ounce of gold. That ratio of 2.5:1 is generous by today's standards. In late 1979, during the height of the Hunt brothers' activities, the ratio stood at 16:1. In 1990 it was 93:1 With the Hunt debacle only a decade old and the pain of silver's precipitous fall still fresh in the minds of traders, speculators, and investors, no one wanted to invest in silver. At 93:1 silver was truly a poor man's gold, and it was a steal.

As I write, the gold-silver ratio is around 55:1. Many people say that it is still too high. However, it is exactly in the middle of the trading range for my 30-plus year career. I regard the current price as fair value. The gold-silver ratio is also an excellent way to watch the value of hard money.

The wise investor keeps a close eye on technical indicators in the silver market. Because it is so speculative and volatile, many technical traders love to play silver. When key supports or resistance levels are broken, silver tends to follow through in a big way. A wealth of fundamental data is available on silver from the Silver Institute. Market data are available from the LBMA website and COMEX.

Investors can trade silver in various forms. Physical silver is available, but unlike gold it is heavy and clumsy. Each 1,000-ounce bar of silver weighs almost 70 pounds. ETFs track the price of silver nicely. However, if silver ever really starts to rise, I wonder whether the silver that backs those instruments is really there? Dedicated silver mining equities are available, but there are not many. As a by-product of other ores, dedicated silver mining is the exception, not the rule.

Futures and options on futures can be traded on the COMEX. However, futures in silver are not for the faint of heart. Each silver futures contract represents 5,000 ounces of the commodity. It is not unusual to see silver move $1 in a day, which means that the value of each contract can move $5,000 in one day. Opportunity always means risk. Options on futures contracts tend to be expensive, thus reflecting silver's volatility.

EASY TIP

The silver market can tell you a lot about the gold market. While the gold market is the barometer of global financial health, its little brother reflects the industrial health of the economy.

PLATINUM GROUP METALS

Platinum group metals (PGMs) are rarer than gold. The group comprises two subgroups: palladium group-platinum group elements (PPGEs) and iridium group-platinum group elements (IPGEs). The first group consists of platinum, palladium, and rhodium; the second consists of iridium, osmium, and ruthenium. All are highly resistant to heat, do not tarnish, are resistant to chemical attack, and are top-notch electricity conductors. PGMs also have excellent catalytic properties. Platinum was first discovered around 700 BC; the other PGMs didn't make their way onto the scene until the nineteenth century.

Automobile manufacturers are the largest industrial users of PGMs, which are used in the production of catalytic converters. Catalysts that refine crude oil into oil products require PGMs, as do various forms of chemotherapy and other medical applications. Molds for the production of fiberglass are made with these rare metals, and there is a large demand for certain PGMs for fine jewelry and coinage. The trading market for platinum and palladium is highly active.

Platinum

Platinum is more than 10 times rarer than gold. In 2011, the total mine supply of platinum was around 250 tons. The vast majority of platinum production comes from two countries: South Africa, which produces 80 percent of the global annual supply, and Russia, which produces 15 percent. Russian platinum is a by-product of nickel production. No other country is a major producer of this commodity, although there is minor production of the metal in the United States, Canada, and Zimbabwe.

Platinum production will not increase in coming years, according to industry analysts. In South Africa three companies, Anglo Platinum, Impala Platinum, and Lonmin, account for all the country's mine supplies. South African producers have already mined the platinum that is close to the earth's surface, and today producers must dig deeper for the metal. Deeper mining means higher production costs and less production of the commodity. In 2011, the average production cost for platinum was reportedly more than $900 an ounce.

In some areas, production costs are closer to $1,500 an ounce. Moreover, while there are stockpiles of platinum in Zurich, they are not significant. There are few strategic platinum stockpiles in the world. In 2011, ETFs contained approximately 1.4 million ounces of platinum. Some platinum is reclaimed and recycled from industry each year because of its high value. Two decades ago, Russia had a strategic stockpile of platinum and PGMs, but I believe today that stockpile is far smaller.

Three quarters of the annual mine supply of platinum is claimed by industrial consumers. As demand for automobiles increases, the price of platinum tends to follow. Platinum demand and prices are highly correlated to global automotive production. Japan is a major automobile manufacturer, and the price of platinum dipped in 2011 as the country was struck by a major earthquake and tsunami. However, as new-car sales increase in Asia, demand for platinum will follow.

Platinum is, in many ways, rich people's gold. There is a high demand for platinum for jewelry and other adornments. Traditionally, the Japanese prefer platinum jewelry to its gold counterpart. Platinum coins are also popular with investors. At the same time, PGMs also meet Doug Casey's hard-money requirements.

While London is the hub for precious-metal trading, delivery takes place in Zurich, Switzerland. Fixings occur for platinum and palladium twice daily at the London Platinum Palladium Market (LPPM), the trade association that designates rules for the market. The LPPM is also a great information resource for platinum and palladium, trading data, and physical requirements for these markets.

NYMEX trades futures contracts on platinum and palladium. These contracts are less liquid than gold and silver futures because the markets for PGMs are much smaller. No options are offered on platinum or palladium futures contracts. The Tokyo Commodity Exchange also trades futures contracts for platinum and palladium.

A smart equity investor views platinum and palladium prices as an indicator of what automobile manufacturers are thinking and doing. The better the car business, the more of this precious metal manufacturers will require, and the higher prices will rise. For investors, platinum and palladium prices can signal investment opportunities galore.

As Figure 5.4 illustrates, platinum is a volatile commodity. It rises and falls with global industrial conditions. Throughout the 1990s, platinum prices were depressed because Russia sold its strategic stockpiles for cash. Platinum prices peaked at $2,300 an ounce in 2008 before the global economic crisis.

Investors can directly invest in platinum through physical purchases of bars, coins, platinum jewelry, EFTs, and even equities in some of the South African platinum producers. Platinum is a commodity that can provide insight into various industrial companies. Watching

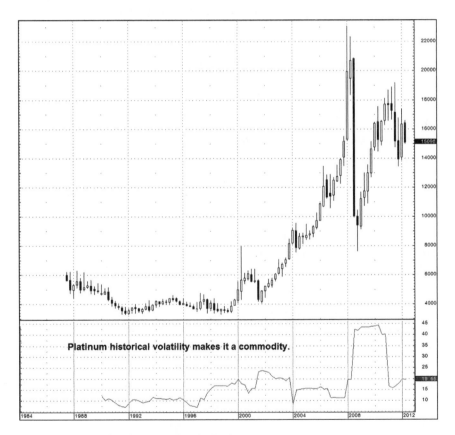

Figure 5.4 **NYMEX platinum quarterly chart**

platinum and comparing it to industrial equities gives investors special insight into growth or contraction in the industrial sector.

Palladium

Palladium is the most commonly occurring PGM. In 2011, the total mining supply of palladium was approximately 230 tons, with the vast majority of production coming from Russia and South Africa. Russian palladium is a by-product of nickel production. The United States is also a producer of the rare metal, accounting for 14 percent of the annual global supply. Two companies, North American Palladium and Stillwater Mining, produce primary palladium. Palladium production will not increase in coming years according to many industry analysts. Since the majority of palladium production comes as a by-product, it is difficult to assess annual production costs.

Zurich holds some strategic stockpiles of palladium, but they are not significant. The Russians also maintain a small strategic stockpile. ETFs accounted for approximately 2.2 million ounces of palladium in 2011. Around 60 percent of the annual mine supply goes to the automobile sector. As demand for automobiles increases, particularly in emerging markets like China, the price of palladium will likely follow. Like platinum, palladium demand and prices are highly correlated to global automotive production. The electronics industry consumes around 20 percent of the metal's annual production. Jewelry demand, mostly from China, as well as dentistry, accounts for a further 20 percent. Palladium coins are also available to investors. In 2011 total palladium demand was around 8 million ounces, with demand only slightly more than supply.

The trading characteristics of palladium are the same as those for platinum. Most professional traders trade the two metals under the same terms, conditions, and market structure. Neither has a liquid forward market. Time spreads are generally within one year, and only professional PGM dealers trade these spreads to manage risk. Location spreads for both metals are a function of transportation and insurance costs.

As Figure 5.5 illustrates, palladium is even more volatile than platinum, reflecting global industrial conditions. Market perception in the 1990s was that the Russians had depleted vast stockpiles of

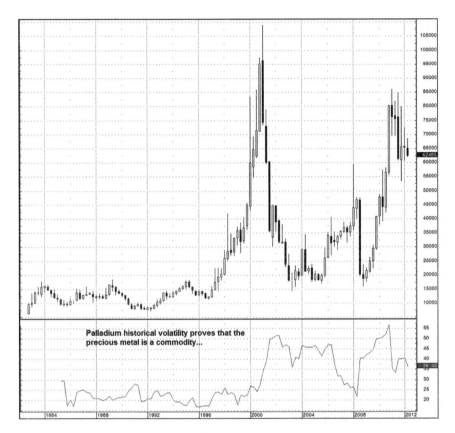

Figure 5.5 **Quarterly NYMEX palladium futures chart**

palladium. Between 1990 and late 1992, palladium traded between $80 and $100 an ounce. I spent a great deal of time in Russia back then. Now, as I write this, palladium prices stand at just over $600 an ounce. However, the metal's price peaked in 2000 at $1,090 an ounce, after an increase in economic activity.

Back in 1991, I ran the global precious-metals trading business for Salomon Brothers. My desk was responsible for trading gold, silver, and PGMs. I had always maintained a great relationship with the Russians, and I did a lot of business with them in those days, including setting up a joint venture with Almazjuvilirexport, the Russian government agency responsible for the global marketing of platinum group metals. We named the joint venture Salmaz, a nod to both companies involved. As part of the agreement, three senior Russians from the agency came to work at the headquarters of Salomon Brothers in New York.

Before our joint venture, industry purchased PGMs from either the Russians or from traders, who acted as intermediaries. Now Salmaz was *the* source of the majority of PGMs destined for industrial users in the United States. Salmaz was the source for automobile companies, fiberglass manufacturers, oil companies, and others that needed these metals. This joint venture cut out all of the other intermediaries.

Salmaz soon became the dominant force in physical PGM markets. During this period, I saw a bulk of the flows of PGMs from the former Soviet Union. Russia was actively selling these metals, but they were pushing palladium in particular, and I witnessed the liquidation of a great deal of Russian stockpiles. Russia sold at between $80 and $100 an ounce, a price so low that it sparked significant buying from around the world. Russia probably holds some palladium today, but nothing like the levels of stocks they held back in 1990.

Today, investors can directly invest in palladium through physical purchases of bars, coins, jewelry, EFTs, or even equities in some of the U.S. producers. Like platinum, watching palladium in relation to industrial equities can provide an investor with special insights that others ignore.

Other PGMs

Rhodium, osmium, ruthenium, and iridium are IPGEs and trade only in the physical market. All these metals have important industrial applications. The problem with them is that it is difficult to monitor their prices and flows. These metals are volatile and illiquid, and their bid-offer spreads are often extremely wide.

None of these metals is produced in large quantities. All are rare and are produced in the same regions as platinum and palladium. Only supply and demand fundamentals determine the price. There is very little, if any, speculative interest or trading in these minor metals—except for rhodium. My former boss, Andy Hall, loved to play the rhodium market. The price of rhodium has ranged from less than $1,000 an ounce to more than $10,000. These metals follow cyclical trading patterns, and when they become too cheap, fierce rallies tend to follow.

There are precious-metal dealers who specialize in these metals, and it pays to watch for bargain-basement prices when you decide to dip a toe into these interesting and volatile commodities.

Intercommodity Spreads

PGM traders monitor the spread between platinum and palladium. The automobile industry uses both metals (and even some rhodium) to manufacture catalytic converters. If the price of palladium rises faster than the price of platinum, as it did in 2000, carmakers will use more platinum than palladium. If the opposite occurs, carmakers use more palladium. If the price of rhodium drops, they may even switch to this metal. The relationship among the prices of platinum, palladium, and rhodium is an important indicator of the future direction of PGM prices because of the potential for substitution. Major divergences often signal opportunity.

It is beneficial to watch the relationship between gold and platinum—the most liquid precious metal versus the most liquid PGM. Historically, both metals are hard money and have all the characteristics of real money. As illustrated in Figure 5.6, gold has a low historical volatility, less than 10 percent. Platinum's historical volatility of 19.78 percent is certainly on the lower end of the scale for commodities. Most commodities have historical volatility levels well north of 20 percent.

As you can see, platinum has spent much of the time between 1986 and 2012 trading at a premium to gold. Only three times has the price of platinum traded below the price of gold during this period. As I write, platinum is sitting at a significant discount to gold. However, platinum is signaling that global industry is in a slowdown, and gold is signaling global economic trouble. The industrial index (platinum) is low, and the fear index (gold) is high. This is a great way to monitor market perception.

Even if you never trade, own, or even believe in precious metals as an investment, it is incumbent upon you to understand and monitor

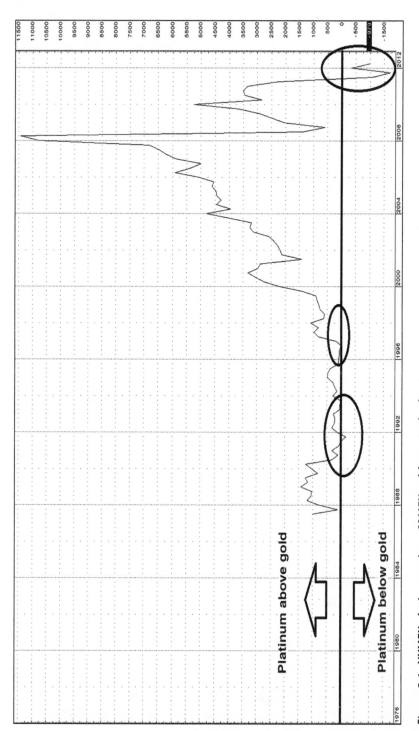

Figure 5.6 NYMEX platinum minus COMEX gold quarterly chart

their prices. Precious metals measure different aspects of global industrial and financial health, and they provide a wealth of clues on trends
in both equity and fixed income investments. When you feel sick, you
take your temperature to check for a fever. Similarly, precious metals
are thermometers for your portfolio.

CHAPTER 6

Base Metals

THE BUILDING BLOCKS
OF SOCIETY

A nickel ain't worth a dime anymore.

—YOGI BERRA

Base metals are nonferrous metals—those that do not contain iron. This group includes copper, aluminum, nickel, lead, zinc, and tin; all are elements on the periodic table. Base metals trade on the London Metal Exchange (LME). Futures contracts for copper are traded on COMEX. While market trading occurs in London, physical trading of these metals takes place around the world. These days, Asia, specifically China, is the demand side of the equation for base metals. Throughout history, however, demand has shifted to high-growth regions around the globe. Supply, on the other hand, tends to remain localized.

Base metals are the building blocks of society. Price movements often signal global economic growth or contraction. Investors who do not observe these movements are ignoring key signals of economic trends and incredible investment opportunities. The equities or funds that make up your portfolio will certainly contain companies that produce and/or consume these strategic metals. There are times when base metals prices lead equity and fixed-income markets, and other times when they follow.

THE LME

Leadenhall Street in London is the hub of global base-metal trading. International trade in metals in this part of the world dates back to 43 AD, when the Romans invaded Britain and extracted copper and tin from Cornwall and Wales. The Romans needed these metals to produce bronze, an alloy of copper and tin.

Commodity traders began meeting in London on a regular basis in the late 1500s. The Royal Exchange opened in 1571. At first, traders dealt with only physical metals for the domestic market. However, as Britain became a major exporter of metals, European traders arrived to join in the trading activities. In the early 1800s, so many traders, ship charterers, and financiers were on the scene that it became difficult to do business, so the action moved to a nearby coffee house, where the term "ring" was born. Sellers drew a ring in sawdust on the floor of the coffee house and called out "change," at which point the buyers would gather around and call out their bids. The LME has been an institution since 1877. Open outcry commodity trading in the U.S. exchange occurs in a pit; in the United Kingdom it still takes place in a ring.

Great Britain was self-sufficient in copper and tin until the industrial revolution changed everything. Britain became the most advanced country in the world as its empire expanded. The need to import large tonnages of metals meant that the method of trading also needed to change. Demand for metals grew, and traders began importing ores and concentrates from mines in South America and Asia. The problem was that the traders did not know the value of the metals once they arrived at British smelters and refineries. Buying abroad entailed a high degree of financial risk, not to mention the problems and costs associated with shipping and delivery to local markets. However, with the advent of telegraphs, it became possible to communicate estimates for the arrival of ships and cargos. Communication also enabled traders to lock in prices and remove some risk from importing and exporting commodities.

The LME trades metals for spot, or cash delivery, but the most active trading occurs in the 90-day forward contracts, although there are also contracts with much longer duration than 90 days. The exchange, which lists more than 450 brands of metals from more than 60 countries as acceptable for delivery, also has rules that standardize grades of quality and delivery locations. The metal stored in any of the 600 LME warehouses, located at 37 sites around the globe, must be of an approved brand and conform to specifications covering quality, shape, and weight. A diverse group of companies own these LME warehouses, such as Goldman Sachs, J.P. Morgan, Glencore International, and even Coca-Cola. Interestingly, none of these warehouses is located in China, the world's top consumer of base metals. At the time of this writing, China's Securities Regulatory Commission has banned foreign exchanges from using mainland warehouses for futures-contract–related deliveries of commodities. Perhaps the Chinese wish to continue to keep strategic stockpiles of commodities a state secret.

Different locations trade at premiums (or discounts) different from official prices, depending upon available supplies and transport costs. The amount of each metal that is on warrant, or depository receipt, is transparent and reported by the LME, which is regulated by the Financial Services Authority (FSA), the U.K. market watchdog. The FSA cooperates with regulatory agencies around the world, such as the CFTC because the market for LME-traded products is global.

Twice each day, for periods of five minutes per commodity, trading occurs in the ring, and this is where benchmark prices are established. After the ring, the curb is the 25-minute period of trading after official prices are established. Like other futures exchanges, the LME operates a clearinghouse to guarantee contracts.

The LME is a delivery point of last resort. Consumers who buy and producers who sell here are guaranteed a contract partner. The exchange's effective mechanism for physical delivery also guarantees price convergence between futures and physical prices. This means that as futures contracts approach expiration dates, the price of the futures and the price of the physical cash commodities (i.e., copper, aluminum, and the other base metals) converge. On delivery day the price of the expiring contract will equal the physical cash price for the commodity at the LME delivery location.

The exchange approves its members and conveys trading privileges upon them. Members can trade the listed products 24 hours a day. There are different levels of membership at the LME:

- Category 1 members, the highest level of membership at the LME, can trade at all times. They are ring dealing members.
- Category 2 members cannot trade in the rings. Otherwise they have all the privileges of category 1 members. Category 2 members must give their ring orders to category 1 members. They are associate broker clearing members.
- Category 3 members may not trade in the ring and cannot issue client contracts. They are associate trade members.
- Category 1, 2, and 3 members are clearing members of the LME.
- Category 4 members may issue customer contracts. They are associate broker members.
- Finally, category 5 members have no trading rights except as clients. They are associate trade members.

The LME trades futures and swaps. It operates an index based on the six base metals contracts, as well as options and traded average price options (TAPOs), average-priced options based on monthly average settlement prices. The LME also trades minicontracts in copper, aluminum, and zinc. The currency used for all LME contracts is the U.S. dollar.

Meanwhile, the exchange operates three trading platforms side by side. Ring dealing operates from 11:45 a.m to 5 p.m. GMT. The electronic trading platform operates from 1 p.m. to 7 p.m. GMT. And telephone trading operates 24 hours a day. In addition to the base metals, the LME also offers contracts in minor metals (cobalt and molybdenum) and steel.

Steeped in a grand tradition, the LME remains one of the most active trading exchanges in the world. The mechanisms that guarantee convergence, the movement in the price of a futures contract toward the price of the underlying commodity cash price, are very important. The LME is the benchmark market for trading in copper, aluminum, aluminum alloy, nickel, lead, zinc, and tin.

Base metals are complex and volatile markets, swinging back and forth between contango and backwardation over time. One of the questions on one of the tests required to become a broker of commodity futures asks true or false: "A time or calendar spread is less volatile than an outright price." The answer is false. As we have learned, spreads can be more volatile than nominal prices in many commodity markets, and they also paint a useful picture for investors.

While each metal has its own characteristics, the base metals sector is connected and correlated to global industrial growth.

DOCTOR COPPER

Copper is an economic bellwether commodity. Many traders and analysts refer to this base metal as *Doctor Copper*, because it provides a diagnosis of the global economic climate. Its price climbs during periods of global growth and falls when the worldwide economy contracts. Moreover, moves in copper often precede moves in other industrial markets. Therefore, it is important to watch the price and market structure of copper for important clues about the future of global economic conditions. It is also the bellwether commodity for China, which requires it to build its infrastructure. Indeed, Chinese consumption of copper today accounts for the ultimate price direction of the metal and is a great measure of Chinese growth. China alone accounts for 22 percent of the world's copper demand. It has been estimated that copper demand is increasing by 575,000 tons every year.

This metal's use dates back to earliest humans and was probably first discovered in Persia (now Iran), where the ore is abundant. Copper sources were very close to ground level in those days. Copper is easy to mold by melting and hammering, and thus ornaments, weapons, tools, and objects of art were fashioned from the metal. The Romans used copper as a form of currency, and only in 1982 did the United States stop using copper to produce pennies.

Copper production begins by taking sulfide and oxide ores out of the earth in walnut-sized chunks. These days, it is processed using electrowinning and smelting, which also extracts precious metal byproducts from the ore. (Electrowinning is the electrodeposition of metals from their ores that have been put in a solution or liquefied.) Copper has numerous beneficial qualities. It does not corrode and is a superconductor of electricity. Construction, piping, refrigeration and air conditioning, cookware, computers, and medicine all require copper. The metal's main alloy is brass, which is used in the production of musical instruments, construction materials, jewelry, and pieces of artwork.

Annual global production of copper is approximately 15 million tons. The largest producer by far is Chile, which produces one-third of the world's supply. The United States, Peru, China, Australia, Indonesia, Russia, Zambia, Canada, Poland, and Kazakhstan are also significant producers. LME and COMEX warehouses provide data on copper stockpiles. However, the total global level of strategic stockpiles is harder to establish, because countries like China and Russia do not report their holdings.

Between 1972 and early 2004, copper traded in a $0.45 to $1.60 per pound range. In 2005, the price broke out to the upside and traded as high as $4.65 in January 2011. However, in the trading world, copper is a volatile commodity. Long-term historical volatility for this base metal is more than 30 percent. During the financial crisis in 2008, copper prices plunged from $4.22 to $1.25 in just seven months (see Figure 6.1).

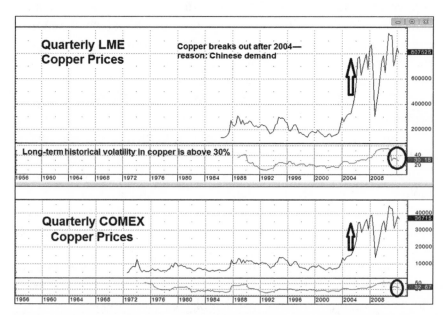

Figure 6.1 **Quarterly copper chart. (Top) LME copper prices. (Bottom) COMEX copper prices.**

Source: CQG, Inc. © 2012. All rights reserved worldwide.

Back in the mid-1990s, the copper market was ground zero for a major international scandal in the commodity markets. For many years, the most influential copper trader in the world was Yasuo Hamanaka at global trading giant Sumitomo Corporation. His nickname was "Mr. Five Percent" because his dominant and aggressive trading in copper led him to control 5 percent of the global annual supply of the commodity. Back in the 1980s and 1990s, I was never able to figure out what he was doing, but I respected the influence he wielded. Controlling 5 percent of the annual global supply of any traded commodity places that party in a position to influence price.

Hamanaka was a trading legend. When he traveled from Tokyo to trading centers in London and New York, he was wined and dined. Everyone in the commodity market wanted to know what Hamanaka was doing and why he was doing it. I believed his influence came from a special relationship with the Chinese, the ultimate buyer of copper. Then came a major surprise. On June 13, 1996, Sumitomo reported a $1.8 billion loss and blamed it on unauthorized copper trading by Hamanaka. In September of that year Sumitomo revealed that those losses were significantly understated and should have been reported at some $2.6 billion. It turned out that Hamanaka was always long copper and had to finance a massive cache. He used some creative accounting to hide the losses, hoping the copper price would rise and bail him out of a losing long position. From 1985 to 1996 copper traded in a range between just under 54 cents to $1.60 a pound. Hamanaka wound up serving seven years in prison in Japan for his financial crimes.

Upon his release in 2005, he was shocked to find that copper had rallied. It was trading at $1.70 a pound just above the highest level that he had seen over the course of his career. And by 2006, copper more than doubled in price to more than $3.40 a pound. Hamanaka's bullish view on copper had been correct. He was just too early and had perpetuated a fraud to cover his losses while he waited for the price to move higher.

However, the greatest base metal trader I had ever witnessed was Manfred Koppelman, an employee at Philipp Brothers during the 1970s and 1980s. One year, when he was telling me about my bonus after a profitable year of trading commodity options, he said: "Remember, all that matters to me is sourcing and placing physical units of copper."

Koppelman, a man with steely blue eyes and a heavy German accent, was acerbic and impatient. Company legend had it that one year when the chairman of Salomon Brothers asked for business plans from department chiefs, Koppelman's was the only one accepted. Other department heads presented their plans, chock full of supply-and-demand data, volume projections, and profitability targets. However, Koppelman's plan was handwritten on a single sheet of paper, which contained the simple statement: "When I like it, I buy it; when I don't like it, I sell it."

He knew the copper market inside and out, and he made things happen. Koppelman liked to call his method "tampering with the mechanism." When he "liked it," he bought a lot of copper, sometimes up to 100,000 tons or more. He would take the copper he bought on the LME off warrant. (Taking copper off warrant means that Koppelman would take delivery of the physical copper and cancel the warehouse receipt representing the metal. Taking copper off warrant results in the copper disappearing from warehouse stock data which results in a decrease in visible supplies.) His physical traders would then try to sell the copper to consumers. As they sold, he would buy more copper on the LME. When Koppelman "liked it," many industrial consumers who depended on this copper guru for advice would buy on his advice. The appearance of a drop in the reported copper stocks would frequently cause the price to rise. Often, copper was simply moved from one side of an LME warehouse to the other when it was taken off warrant. This would give the appearance of falling stocks and rising demand to those who watched the market's daily machinations. Often other base metal prices would follow, as demand for copper signaled growing demand for base metals in general. Koppelman knew how to use the market's perception to his benefit, and he would load up on other base metals at the same time to enhance his profitability. Today "tampering with the mechanism" would almost certainly result in a charge of market manipulation, but in those days it was a kosher and profitable business practice.

Investors can study Doctor Copper's price movements via free information published by COMEX in the United States and the LME in London. Both of these markets offer futures contracts and options on futures. There are many copper mining stocks and copper consuming companies that trade on U.S. and international stock exchanges.

At the same time, ETFs that rise and fall with the copper and other base-metal prices are available to investors.

ALUMINUM

While Doctor Copper is the most important base metal, aluminum is perhaps the most liquid, and its market trades huge volumes. Aluminum is the third most abundant element in the earth's crust. Its existence was discovered in 1807 by Sir Humphrey Davy, but it took years to find an efficient method of extracting the metal from its ores and even longer to find practical uses for it. Today, it is prized by numerous industries as a lightweight and versatile metal. It is found in automobiles, motorcycles, airplane parts, license plates, roofs, gutters, window frames, paint, cans, trays, foils, bottle caps, gum and candy wrappers, lightbulbs, phone and power lines, sports equipment, food additives, and even aspirin, to name just a few.

Annual aluminum production exceeds 40 million tons. The largest producer in the world is China, which produces more than 40 percent of the world's primary supply. Russia, Canada, and the United States round out the top four aluminum producers. Countries building infrastructures demand the metal. China is the world's largest aluminum consumer, with the rest of Asia not far behind. The United States produces more than $40 billion worth of aluminum products each year. The United States consumes aluminum and exports it to foreign markets. A tremendous amount of the metal is recycled each year. Recycling rates in Brazil and Japan are well over 80 percent.

Aluminum is the most stable of all base metals that trade on the LME. Because of the huge annual production and consumption, the volumes of aluminum traded daily are enormous. The quarterly historical volatility for aluminum is just over 20 percent, which is low for any commodity, especially for a base metal.

I traded options on aluminum back in the middle 1980s. During that period, I visited brewing giant Anheuser-Busch, the maker of Budweiser beer, in St. Louis, Missouri. Besides getting a lesson in the art of beer making and seeing the Clydesdale horses, I learned that this company was one of the largest consumers of aluminum in the United States. It probably still is today. But back then Busch had a problem.

The company initially bought beer can stock from aluminum smelters around the world, but the investment was high. The company struggled until the advent of recycling, and the market in used beverage cans (UBCs) lowered its costs. Buying UBCs from recycling centers meant that instead of paying 100 percent for can stock, the company paid a fraction of that cost.

Busch wanted to buy call options on UBCs to lock in prices for many years into the future. It would have been an amazing deal for the company I worked for. The volume and profit margin would have been enormous. The problem was that I had Busch as a buyer, but I could not find a seller anywhere in the world. The aluminum smelters would not sell the options because they could get a guaranteed flow of UBC volume from recycling centers. The recyclers were too small to meet the volumes demanded by Busch, and the ultimate suppliers of these recycled cans were the beer drinkers themselves, who could not be relied upon to turn in their empty cans. I would have made a lot of money if I could have found a way to pool the nation's beer drinkers.

The price of aluminum tends to follow copper and other base metals. In 2004, when base metal prices surged, the price of aluminum doubled. As with other commodities, there are periods when shortages and oversupply occur in the aluminum market. Like all base metals, aluminum time spreads move around and can see periods of backwardation and contango. Aluminum spreads are less volatile than the commodity's price itself, but these spreads move around over time. Aluminum premiums reflect certain location and quality spreads in the physical market. Available supplies (or demand) in particular markets play a role in localized premiums. Premiums reflect not only transportation costs, storage, and insurance, but also costs associated with the production of aluminum products, such as billets and ingots required for particular industries and markets. (See Figure 6.2.)

There are many companies that use aluminum to produce and package products, and all of them are at risk of a rise in the commodity's price. Anheuser-Busch is just one example of the many companies that depend on the metal. A sudden price spike will negatively affect earnings, just as a sudden price dip might increase earnings.

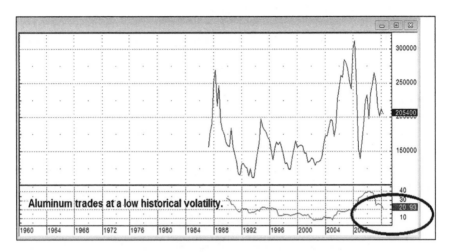

Figure 6.2   Quarterly LME aluminum prices and historical volatility
Source: CQG, Inc. © 2012. All rights reserved worldwide.

EASY TIP

When you look at your portfolio or consider future investments, make sure you understand the sensitivity of the investment to the underlying commodity. Keep an eye on the commodity's price and stockpiles. A sudden spike in the price of electricity, for example, might cause aluminum prices to jump because of the impact on smelting and other production costs.

There are many companies that produce aluminum directly. The price of aluminum has a direct effect on the price of the traded equities in these companies.

Both aluminum and aluminum alloy trade on the LME, where you can also find a wealth of information on the metal. There are also ETFs that reflect the price of aluminum. As the base metal commodity with the greatest market liquidity and lowest historical volatility, aluminum's price gives an investor important clues. For example, China, currently the world's biggest aluminum consumer, is self-sufficient in aluminum, which probably explains why the price is so stable.

But if China ever needs to import the metal (or if it decides to export it), watch out. Aluminum might then become as volatile as many other base metals.

NICKEL

Nickel, a silvery white, lustrous metal with a slight golden glow, is one of the least liquid and more volatile base metals. Archeologists date nickel use back to 3500 BC. Swedish mineralogist and chemist Axel Fredrik Cronstedt first classified the metal as an element in 1751. The word *nickel* comes from the German, *kupfernickel*, meaning devil's copper. Certainly nickel prices can be so volatile that those on the wrong side of a move have been slaughtered to such an extent they might believe demonic forces were at play.

One of nickel's key properties is that it is resistant to corrosion. As such, it is the perfect plating metal for iron and brass. Nickel is also ferromagnetic. While strong magnets require iron and rare earth metals, magnets of intermediate strength utilize nickel. Coinage, glass production, rechargeable batteries, and bulletproof safes also use nickel.

Nickel ore is extracted from the earth via open-cast and deep-shaft mines. Smelting separates the nickel from the ore. Worldwide nickel production stands at approximately 1 million tons per year. The largest producers in 2010 were China and Russia, accounting for about 50 percent of world production. Other significant nickel producing countries include Japan, Canada, Australia, and Norway. Cuba is also a producer of nickel. China and Russia hold strategic stockpiles. However, there was evidence of Russian stockpile selling in the early 1990s.

China is the world's dominant consumer of nickel. Stainless steel and alloys account for almost 87 percent of annual nickel demand. China is a major force in all base metal markets because of the country's infrastructure-building needs.

The price of nickel moves around significantly. Long-term historical volatility for the metal is around 35 percent. However, from 2007 through 2009, prices fell from more than $40,000 a ton to $10,000 a ton, and that's after the metal rallied from $15,000 to $45,000 two years previously (see Figure 6.3). Since then, the price has calmed down a bit. Nonetheless, nickel has always been a volatile commodity. Back in the winter of 1989, a time spread cost me more than $1 million as

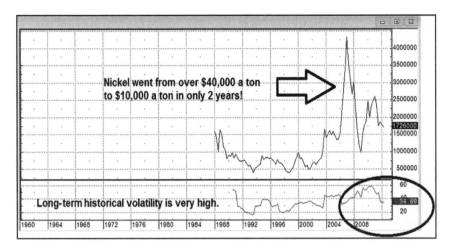

Figure 6.3   Quarterly LME nickel chart
Source: CQG, Inc. © 2012. All rights reserved worldwide.

physical nickel jumped from $6,000 a ton to more than $9,000 in just a few weeks. That type of move is not particularly exceptional in the nickel market, as I painfully learned. It was an expensive lesson early in my career.

The stakes when trading nickel now are much higher than they were in 1989, because the nominal price of the metal is now much higher. The move back in 1989 was a 50 percent price rise, and it cost those holding short positions $3,000 for each ton they were short. As I write this, nickel trades at around $17,000 a ton. A 50 percent move today would cost $8,500 to those on the wrong side of the move. Of course, there is both risk and potential reward. Watching the price of nickel and identifying those companies that will benefit from dramatic price moves in the commodity will create profitable opportunities for investors. When a commodity like nickel makes a big move, the market is either over long or over short. When the nickel market moves, many traders and market participants experience a great deal of financial upheaval—but their pain can be your gain, if you keep your eye on the market.

It pays to watch the nickel price when you're contemplating an investment in a steel company. And nickel can often signal moves in other base metals, which in turn can signal more macromarket information. As one of the most illiquid and treacherous base metal markets, nickel is often the one that moves first. Like other metals, the LME provides data on nickel prices and warehouse stocks. The free information is out there. Access it!

LEAD

Lead was one of the earliest metals discovered by humans. A lead statue found in Turkey has been dated back to 6500 BC. The Romans used lead for many purposes, including pipes, bathtub linings, cosmetics and paints, and for food and wine vessels. The Romans thought that lead added flavor to food that was cooked in lead pots. Almost 100 recipes in the fifth century Roman Apician cookbook included lead as an ingredient. Of course, lead is toxic, and its toxins accumulate in the body over time causing numerous health problems. Many members of the Roman aristocracy suffered from lead poisoning. Indeed, the prevalence of lead poisoning at the time has led some historians to believe that the consumption of lead aided the decline of the Roman Empire.

Today, the single most common use of lead is in the manufacture of batteries, but it is also used for a number of alloys as well as in nuclear reactors, some artistic paints, and certain types of ammunition. Lead was a component in the production of gasoline for many years for its antiknock properties in engines, but it is now banned in many countries, including the United States.

The production of lead involves mining lead ore and then concentrating it by removing the metal from the waste rock. The lead concentrates are then floated, filtered, roasted, and put in a blast furnace. Gold and silver are present in lead concentrates and are extracted during the refining phase. Annual lead production is approximately 3 million tons. The largest producers are China, Australia, Peru, the United States, Canada, and Mexico, which between them produce 80 percent of the world's annual lead supply. Lead is also recycled from scrap.

Traditionally, lead prices have been less volatile than many of the other nonferrous metals. However, the bull market in base metals (and commodities in general) caused lead prices to soar between 2004 and 2008, rising from $750 per ton to a peak of $3,870 per ton. This rise was sparked by shortages and increased demand for batteries in China (see Figure 6.4).

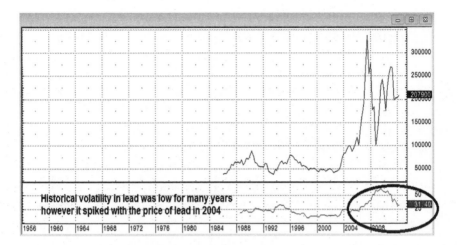

Figure 6.4 **Quarterly chart of LME lead prices**
Source: CQG, Inc. © 2012. All rights reserved worldwide.

I remember the huge number of scrap yards I saw during my travels through China and Taiwan. There was no Environmental Protection Agency, and these toxic yards filled with lead were scattered across both countries, often in residential areas of towns and villages. I was told by contractors and agents that life expectancy in many of these areas was much lower than the national average.

Lead is an important commodity for many companies that need backup battery power systems, and investors should keep that in mind when they're buying a utility stock.

Lead trades on the LME, where lead futures and options are available, along with a wealth of data on stocks and prices.

ZINC

Zinc is the third most actively traded commodity on the LME, behind aluminum and copper. Its market is liquid. Centuries before zinc was discovered as a metal, its ores produced brass and zinc compounds, many of which are still used as medicinal agents for soothing wounds and sore eyes.

Zinc was the eighth metal known to humans. From the twelfth to the sixteenth century, India produced zinc ores and zinc oxide.

It was discovered in Europe during the sixteenth century. The first zinc smelter opened in the United Kingdom in Bristol in 1743.

Annual production of zinc exceeds 11 million tons, around 55 percent of which goes into galvanizing steel as a protection against corrosion. A further 12 percent goes to produce brass and bronze, with the remainder used for zinc-based alloys to supply the die-casting industry and rolled zinc applications, such as gutters, roofing and pipes, and coinage, as well as the production of compounds.

China is the world's largest producer of zinc today, followed by Peru, Australia, the United States, Canada, and India. These six countries account for over 70 percent of annual global zinc production. China is also the world's top zinc consumer; it consumes 30 percent of annual global production, three times more than the United States, the world's second-largest consumer.

Like other base metals, zinc plays a part in the multiyear commodities bull market. Zinc spent a lot of time in the 1990s trading within a range of low volatility. Volatility returned to the zinc market during the first few years of the millennium, and prices climbed more than 400 percent between 2003 and 2007. The zinc market is fairly liquid, and its spreads trade in good volume on the LME, which also offers a minicontract in zinc.

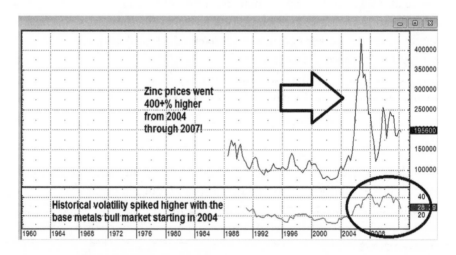

Figure 6.5 **Quarterly LME zinc prices**

Source: CQG, Inc. © 2012. All rights reserved worldwide.

In 2001, I worked for a hedge fund located in lower Manhattan. The price of zinc at the time was around $800 a ton. I believed that was far too low. I believed infrastructure growth in China would increase and so would the demand for metals, including galvanized steel. I also suspected that there would be production cuts, because low prices rendered zinc production uneconomical. The low price meant that many smelters and miners operated at a loss. There were plenty of zinc stocks around in 2001, but I did not believe they would last long. A couple of years later zinc stocks fell, but it took longer than I expected.

At the hedge fund, I entered into a long position in zinc using long-dated call options. Although I got that market call right in the long run (zinc went from $700 to $4,000 over the next seven years) the short-term results were quite different. The events of September 11, 2001, caused a macroeconomic shock around the world and caused commodity prices to plunge. Zinc was just one of the casualties as prices dropped from $800 to $700 for a brief period. I had to close out my position, and I lost money. Zinc was in a contango, and it cost me money to hold a long position. I simply could not afford to finance the position any longer. In commodity markets, timing is everything.

EASY TIP

Sometimes it is not that hard to predict the future. When a commodity price drops far below production cost, it will only be a matter of time before stockpiles become exhausted and producers curtail production. This is the time to look for opportunities on the long side. Timing is everything. Conversely, when the price of a commodity climbs too high, human beings will adapt and find a substitute, thus decreasing demand and causing prices to correct themselves. Human beings and markets are adaptable and efficient.

TIN

Tin, one of the oldest metals known, is the most illiquid or thinly traded nonferrous metal on the LME. It is also one of the most volatile commodity markets. Its uses go far back in history. Copper and tin are the ingredients used to make brass, which was used to make utensils and other products as far back as 3500 BC. The fourteenth century saw the development of tinned iron, and tinned steel came along in the seventeenth century.

This metal has many uses. Electroplating requires a coat of tin applied to copper, aluminum, steel, or other metals. Countless household applications require tin, as well as pharmaceutical solutions, capacitors in electrodes, fuse wires, ammunition, fungicides and pesticides, solder, and pewter. Even toothpastes require tin fluoride as a key manufacturing component.

Annual production of tin is 350,000 tons. China is the world's largest producer followed by Indonesia, Peru, Bolivia, and Brazil. Malaysia has the second-largest tin reserves in the world, and the Malaysian state of Penang is the center of massive tin mining and refining operations. I traveled to Penang to buy tin from several small tin companies in the 1990s and saw smelters dump their toxic wastes directly into the ocean and drinking water supplies. As is true in many other nations, environmental protection came second to cash flow at that time in Malaysia. However, because the metal itself is nonharmful, tin has replaced lead and other toxic elements in the manufacture of a number of goods, such as electronics and ammunition.

Historically, the United States, Japan, the former Soviet Union, and Germany have been the largest consumers of tin, but Chinese demand is growing precipitously. Strategic stockpiles of tin are held by a number of governments around the world, but their extent is not known.

Tin is the most volatile of all LME-traded nonferrous metals. Its historical volatility is high at over 35 percent. Tin prices increased by a multiple of six between 2003 and 2010 (see Figure 6.6). The market structure is just as volatile as the price. The tin market has a delicate supply-demand balance and tends to swing back and forth between contango and backwardation. As with all base metals traded on the LME, futures and options are available. LME data on the commodity and information on related stocks are useful for investors.

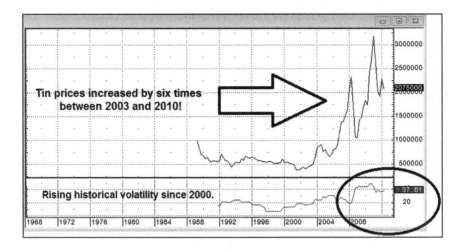

Figure 6.6 **Quarterly LME tin chart**
Source: CQG, Inc. © 2012. All rights reserved worldwide.

BASE METALS COINAGE CONTAINS REAL VALUE

In March 2011, it was reported that a sharp rise in cotton prices had caused the U.S. Government Accountability Office (GAO) to reconsider printing currency on paper bills. The GAO's plan was to replace the paper bills with coins. Reportedly, it cost 9.6 cents to print a dollar bill, compared with 6.4 cents in 2008. The GAO was worried about the price of cotton, the chief ingredient in the U.S. paper currency, which had rallied from 50 cents in 2008 to $2.27 a pound in March 2011. Metal coins are significantly more durable than paper bills and remain in the market far longer.

The same thing happened with the penny a number of years ago. Pennies were made of copper until the price of the metal began to soar and the government mint switched to zinc. Today, as I write, it costs about 1.79 cents to make a penny from zinc. Nickels are made of a copper-nickel alloy—but not long ago they contained pure nickel. Using the alloy, nickels now cost around 4.4 cents each to make, significantly less than the cost of pure nickel nickels. It seems that the use of base metals for coinage is providing the coinage with real and intrinsic value. Coins have the implicit value of the metal they contain. The price of paper is what implicitly backs bills or notes, rather than the full faith and credit of the government that prints that paper currency.

The U.S. mint still has its plan to switch from paper bills to coins. But which metal will it use—copper, aluminum, nickel, lead, zinc, tin, steel? Prices of all these metals have jumped since the early part of the millennium. Whatever metal the GAO chooses may simply result in another strain on the already tight global supply-demand equation for base metals. For the investor, this story is another reason why an understanding of base metal prices is so important. Not only are these commodities connected to the value of your portfolio, but base metals also reflect the value of the change in your pocket.

CHAPTER 7

Agriculture

FEEDING THE WORLD

Farming looks mighty easy when your plow is a pencil and you're a thousand miles from the cornfield.

—DWIGHT D. EISENHOWER

During the tenth millennium BC, when humans began to widely practice agriculture with domesticated wheat in Southwest Asia and the Nile Delta, the total population of planet earth stood at fewer than 10 million. Fast forward 10 thousand years to 1 AD, and the world's population had reached 200 million. From there, it took only 1,500 years to more than double to 450 million, and just another 300 years to hit 1 billion people.

Then the number exploded. By 1927, the world's population doubled again, and by 1999 there were 6 billion people on earth. According to U.N. estimates, the planet's human population will hit 8 billion by 2025 and 10 billion by 2083. (See Table 7.1.)

The world is getting smaller, and it is also getting hungrier. The population is growing fastest in Asia, but it is also growing quickly in Africa and the Middle East. As the population rises, there is an ever-increasing need to grow more crops for food. The world is eating more

Table 7.1 **Population Growth and Estimates of Future Growth**

Year	Global Population
1	200 million
1500	450 million
1804	1 billion
1927	2 billion
1975	4 billion
1999	6 billion
2011	7 billion
2025*	8 billion
2043	9 billion
2083	10 billion

*Projected future figures are in italics.

and stockpiling less. Moreover, growing more crops requires more arable land. However, the amount of arable land in the world is finite. The potential for food shortages has become greater than ever before in history, which has put considerable strain on the supply-and-demand equation.

At the same time, the amount of clean water on earth is in crisis. With rapid population growth, water is becoming a scarce commodity. Agriculture requires clean water—some 67 percent of the water used by human beings is for agricultural purposes. Ironically, China and India, which have the world's fastest population growth rates, are also facing some of the most severe water shortages.

Meanwhile, the trend of organic farming in the United States and Europe has disturbed the tenuous efficiency of agriculture. Organic farming requires more water and land; in other words, organic farming produces less food per acre than do traditional farming methods. An April 25, 2012, *Scientific American* article, "Will Organic Food Fail to Feed the World?" by David Biello, published findings by environmental scientists at McGill University. Verena Seufert, the lead author of the study, said they "found that, overall organic yields are considerably lower than conventional yields. But, this yield difference varies across different conditions. When farmers apply best management practices, organic systems, for example, perform relatively better." So although we have the potential of eating healthier, it may be a luxury we can't afford globally.

A 1999 report titled "Global Land Resources & Population Supporting Capacity," published by the U.S. Department of Agriculture concluded that, at the time, there was enough arable land to grow crops to feed the world. The report is alarming, however, when you consider population growth and shifting demographics, particularly since 1999. Only 12.6 percent of the land on earth is well-suited to growing crops, and at the highest level of output this land can feed roughly 7.5 billion people. We are almost there today with more than 7 billion people in the world. As I write this, in mid–2012, we are almost at our maximum capacity for feeding the world. Figure 7.1 clearly shows that increasing population has resulted in less harvested land per person. Land is finite, and the population keeps growing.

Meanwhile, another demographic factor is putting added strain on global food supply—increasing wealth and the burgeoning middle classes

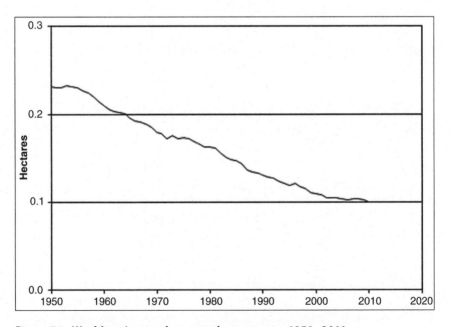

Figure 7.1 **World grain area harvested per person, 1950–2011**

Source: U.S. Department of Agriculture, UNPop, Earth Policy Institute (www.earth-policy.org).

worldwide, particularly in Asia. The first thing populations do after climbing up from the bottom rung of the ladder is to improve their diet.

As wealth grows in places like China, a rice-staple diet has given way to rising demand for animal protein foods, such as steak, chicken, turkey, and pork. In turn, a rising animal population requires a greater supply of grains, such as corn and soybean meal, to feed them. Moreover, animal protein requires more land per calorie than do grains. David Pimentel, an ecology professor at Cornell University's College of Agriculture and Life Sciences, noted in 1997: "Animal protein production requires more than eight times as much fossil-fuel energy as production of plant protein, while yielding animal protein that is only 1.4 times more nutritious for humans than the comparable amount of plant protein." In other words, eating grain is more efficient than eating meat, but the world continues to desire more meat in its diet.

Also, as a direct result of greater human competition for less available food per person, the price of food must rise. The increased value of food can be seen clearly in the contrast between U.S. residential housing prices and the value of farmland since 2008. (See Figure 7.2.)

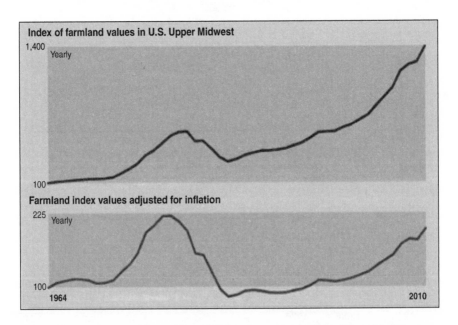

Figure 7.2 **Inflation-adjusted farmland values, 1964–2010 from the Chicago Federal Reserve District**

Source: Bloomberg.

While the housing market was battered during the financial crisis, farmland values continued to climb. Some argue, as I write this, that farmland has remained an economic bubble. I disagree. I believe that these values reflect the surging demand for food around the globe. Population growth has serious ramifications on the price of all commodities, particularly agricultural commodities, which in turn impacts the state of nations. Just as the French Revolution of 1789 began with a grain shortage and the subsequent rise in the price of bread, the Arab Spring in 2011 also began as a response to higher bread prices. Governments around the world are aware of the link between the rising price of food staples, social unrest, and, ultimately, their own time in power.

Agricultural commodity prices are rising, driven by unstoppable, global demographic forces. However, it is the unknown that causes the price volatility, the massive spreads between the highs and lows. This is where weather, crop deterioration, and substitution become key factors for investors in the sector. Drought, excessive moisture, hurricanes, tornados, monsoons, fungus, mold, plant disease, and frost all wreak havoc on crops and, consequently, on crop prices. In a market where supply and demand is so fragile, weather can cause extraordinary nosedives and spikes in prices in very short periods of time.

Crop substitution is another factor in agricultural price volatility. We have already seen how U.S. farmers in 2008 made the economic decision to plant corn in lieu of cotton. However, while corn prices made them more money that year, global demand for cotton was left dissatisfied, and in 2011, cotton prices skyrocketed by more than 500 percent. These types of substitutions and price reactions have occurred many times over the course of history.

EASY TIP

When the price of one commodity moves dramatically, think about the impact on related commodities, both in terms of production and consumption. Often, your initial intuitive conclusion based on common sense will yield a profitable opportunity that others will not see until it is too late.

Likewise, in 2012, farmers decided to plant more corn than soybeans, and, as I write this, soybean prices are climbing. Thanks to crop substitution, the market fears that more corn in 2012 could potentially cause a soybean deficit. Intercommodity spreads tell an important story and pave a path to future prices and opportunities.

Spoilage and crop deterioration also affect the supply-and-demand picture for grains, meats, and soft commodities. (Luxury commodities such as coffee, sugar, and cotton are often referred to as soft commodities.) A fungus or rust in the coffee crop in Brazil or Colombia will cause the price of Arabica coffee to soar. If Hans Kilian, the cocoa-pod counter, saw mold spores on the Ivorian cocoa crop, his report would cause an immediate price spike, which in turn would likely cause problems for companies like Hershey and Nestlé, which rely on cocoa beans to produce their chocolate goods.

Conversely, oversupply in an agricultural market can have a devastating impact on prices. In the mid-1980s, the sugar price, which in mid-2012 traded at more than 20 cents a pound, dropped to less than 2.3 cents a pound because of oversupply. My friend, Charlie Nedoss, a commodity broker in Chicago, tells the story about how a bumper potato crop sent the price of potatoes to zero on the futures exchange. Traders on the exchange who bought at zero took physical delivery of the potatoes in burlap bags. In the end, the traders dumped the potatoes in the river and sold the burlap bags for a profit.

The supply-and-demand equation for agricultural commodities is highly fragile. Therefore, time spreads, location spreads, quality spreads, and intercommodity spreads are also volatile. Monitoring news events and an understanding of this sector's market structure will save and make an investor a lot of money. Take a minute to consider the many types of companies with exposure to the agricultural sector—food processors, biofuel producers, fast food chains, an energy refiner consuming ethanol made from corn, a manufacturer of farming tools and machinery, and a fertilizer producer, to name just a few.

Each month the U.S. Department of Agriculture issues crop forecasts, information on crop stockpiles, and crop progress on all major grains, meats, and perishable commodities grown in the United States and abroad. These reports are available free, and the prudent investor will study them carefully. They not only provide clues to future trends, but their publication often has an immediate effect on cash and futures prices of agricultural commodities.

However, it is important to remember that commodities are a highly integrated and interconnected sector. For example, the cost of manufacturing a box of Wheaties does not simply depend on the price of wheat. Other costs include the energy required to bring the wheat to the factory, processing, and transportation to market. Also to be considered is cost of the metals to construct the machinery that makes the cereal. Inter-commodity spreads are at play all over the place. And everything moves around, often dramatically—including production and consumption factors, as well as import and export variables. Bad harvests are just as likely as bumper harvests when looking into the future. Forecasting crop production in the long term is nothing more than a coin toss. In the end, agricultural production is only as certain as the weather and the ability to get crops to market before they perish. The most important *known* factor when it comes to the long-term prospects for agricultural commodities is rising global food demand.

THE GRAINS

Types of grain markets include corn, wheat, soybeans, rice, and assorted others.

Corn

Corn is endemic to the Americas. Native Americans grew corn thousands of years before Christopher Columbus set sail for the New World from Spain. Petrified cobs in ancient villages in North and South America date back more than 5,000 years. When Columbus landed in what is now the West Indies, he traded with the Native Americans and returned home with corn. Some early settlers in North America in the 1700s used corncobs for personal hygiene before the advent of toilet paper.

Corn futures and options trade on the Chicago Board of Trade (CBOT). There is also a corn contract offered on the London International Financial Futures and Options Exchange (LIFFE). The corn futures and options market is highly liquid. The United States is the world's largest producer of corn. In 2009 and 2010 it produced 39 percent of the global supply. Other significant corn-producing nations are China, the European Union, Brazil, Argentina, Mexico, India, and Ukraine. The top five importers are Japan, South Korea, Mexico, Egypt, and Taiwan.

Corn is a basic staple, a cereal crop, and a member of the grass family. Varieties of corn are required to produce numerous food products and animal feed. High-fructose corn syrup, corn starch, corn oil, and lysine are direct corn products. Ethanol, a biofuel, is also a corn product. All gasoline sold in the United States contains ethanol. The demand for ethanol-based fuels is just one more reason for rising corn prices.

The process of separating corn into its component parts to create the high number of related products has been going on for centuries. Dry milling produces corn flour, meal, grits, and other products. Wet milling is the process by which corn is separated into starch (syrup, ethanol, corn starch), germ (oil), and gluten (animal feed).

Corn is deliverable in various grades on CBOT against futures contract positions. Each grade commands a premium or discount, depending on the quality. The exchange has a number of approved and registered warehouses for delivery of all traded grains, including corn. These warehouses are sometimes called elevators, silos, terminals, or grains bins.

Corn does not trade every month. Corn's future contracts reflect the harvest seasons, so contracts exist only for March, May, July, September, and December on the U.S. exchange.

As with other grains, corn trades in old crop and new crop months. The *old crop* already exists; the *new crop* has not yet been grown (or has been planted but has not yet been harvested). Traders also pay close attention to the *carrying charge*, which is the price differential between months. Like all other agricultural commodities, corn can swing back and forth between contango and backwardation, depending on supplies and success of harvest. *Carryover stocks*, or stored grains, are also a key indicator. There may be carryover stocks after a bumper crop, and these impact the price of the commodity. *Stock-to-use ratio* is the amount of carryover relative to the total demand for a crop. The formula for the stock-to-use ratio is:

(Carryover/Total Use) $\times$ 100 = Stock-to-Use Ratio

The *basis* is the relationship between the physical cash market and the futures price. And just as successful management of basis risk can add to a producer's bottom line, it can also help investors and traders understand and exploit agricultural trends that can impact any number of holdings in a portfolio. A strengthening basis means that supplies are low and cash prices are high, relative to futures prices. A weakening basis means that supplies are ample, as they may be during a bumper harvest.

Backwardation reflects a supply shortage and is a condition of strong basis. Contango reflects a weak basis. At the farm level, the basis is generally weak. Farmers must make many decisions during the crop year—which crop they should plant or hedge, to whom they should sell, and for how much. Market conditions often guide these decisions.

Like most agricultural commodities, corn prices can be extremely volatile. There are instances in which they move in unexpected ways for unexpected reasons. In March 2011, Japan suffered a devastating earthquake and tsunami. The knee-jerk reaction of markets was eliminate risk and sell everything. Corn prices plunged in the days that followed the earthquake—until the market remembered an important fact: Japan is the world's largest importer of corn. The earthquake and subsequent tsunami destroyed some of the country's stockpiles. Once the market realized this, the price of corn soared. Any investor with an understanding of corn-market fundamentals would have seen that Japan would need to import more corn to feed its people. The initial market reaction was based on emotion, not reality.

Seasonality, weather conditions, perishability, crop substitution, innovation, and the fickle nature of demand can all result in tremendous volatility. As Figure 7.3 illustrates, historical volatility for corn was low for many years as prices languished between $2 and $4 per bushel. But in 2007, the commodity's price surged as oil prices moved higher.

Corn is a biofuel, and ethanol demand has created new demand for this agricultural commodity. Ethanol futures contracts are traded on NYMEX. While they are fairly illiquid, investors can use the daily prices as a guide to help them understand the importance of corn in ethanol production. And ethanol's price relationship with both corn and oil can provide interesting clues for future movements of either commodity. Viewing corn in relation to ethanol is a processing spread, because in the United States the biofuel is a product of corn production. Additionally for those investors who hold stocks in companies that produce ethanol, such as Archer Daniels Midland (ADM), the

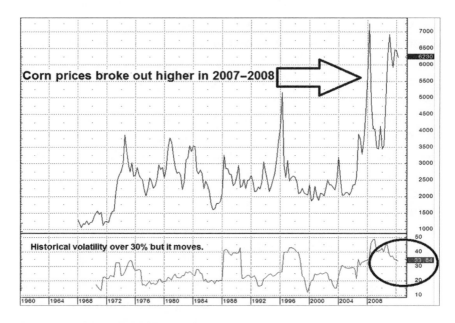

Figure 7.3 Quarterly CBOT corn chart
Source: CQG, Inc. © 2012. All rights reserved worldwide.

price relationships can tell you a tremendous amount about future profitability and earnings of companies in the processing business.

Indeed, the price of corn directly impacts your portfolio, no matter which assets you hold. Energy companies, food companies, and even fixed-income vehicles all have a relationship to the price of corn. Food prices are also a direct barometer of inflation. Watching the price of corn (and other grains) can amount to a real-time update on important economic data such as the consumer price index (CPI) and producer price index (PPI).

Wheat

Wheat was one of the first cereals to be domesticated. Archaeological records suggest that the cultivation of wheat began some 11,000 years ago in what is now southeastern Turkey. Wheat is a more volatile commodity than corn. The properties of wheat make it both foodstuff and a commodity with a multitude of industrial uses. Wheat is both gluten (protein) and a starch. Flour is required for the production of many foods, including cereals, bread, pasta, cakes, and cookies, just to name a few. At the same time, straw particle board, paper wheat starch, adhesives, and many other household products require wheat for their production.

In 2010, there were approximately 682 million tons of wheat produced in the world. The top global producers are the European Union, China, India, Russia, the United States, Canada, Pakistan, Australia, Ukraine, and Kazakhstan. The top ten consumers of wheat are China, India, Russia, the United States, Pakistan, Turkey, Iran, Egypt, Brazil, and Ukraine. The United States is the largest exporter of the staple. The top importers of wheat are Egypt, Iran, Brazil, Algeria, Japan, Indonesia, Morocco, Iraq, Nigeria, and Turkey.

Three different exchanges in the United States trade wheat futures and options. Wheat grown in different parts of the United States has different properties and uses. The largest futures exchange for wheat is CBOT, where contracts call for soft red winter wheat. This type of wheat is grown in central Texas, the northeastern Great Lakes area, and east to the Atlantic, and is suitable for cakes, cookies, snack foods, crackers, and pastries. However, most of the wheat grown in the United States is hard red winter wheat, which trades on the Kansas City Board of Trade (KBOT). Hard red winter wheat, which grows mainly in Kansas, Nebraska, Oklahoma, and the Texas panhandle, is primarily used for bread production. The third variety is hard red spring wheat, which grows on the northern plains states of Montana, Wyoming, North and South Dakota, and Idaho, and trades on the Minneapolis Board of Trade (MBOT), the least active of the three U.S. exchanges. Suitable for milling, this high-grade wheat is ideal for bread production. The United States also grows other forms of wheat. Durum has the hardest wheat kernels and contains the highest levels of protein. It is primarily used for the production of pasta.

Each futures exchange specifies a type and grade of wheat for delivery against its futures contract. Most of the exchanges allow for substitutions at variable premiums or discounts.

Wheat grown in other countries has different characteristics and differs in quality. The commodity also trades on futures exchanges in Canada, Europe, Asia, and Australia. Investors should be aware that when there is a weather issue or problem with a wheat crop anywhere in the world, there are ramifications on the price of wheat everywhere.

The price of wheat is volatile. Between July 2007 and January 2008, CBOT wheat moved from $5.63 to $13.35 per bushel, a move of more than 135 percent in six months. This was a result of poor harvests in Russia, Australia, and Ukraine.

The price spread between the various wheat contracts can also be very volatile. In 2011, the premium for KBOT over CBOT wheat reached as high as $1.40 a bushel. By the middle of 2012 that spread dropped to almost par. Intercommodity spreads between wheat contracts promise to be volatile in the future, and these spreads will have important ramifications for the price that food companies will pay for their raw materials. This price risk will directly impact the bottom line earnings for those companies and their stock prices. Those equities may be sitting in your portfolio or mutual funds. Time spreads or calendar spreads are also volatile in the wheat market. Seasonality, weather, perishability, and the effects of a good or bad harvest or an increase in demand will move agriculture markets back and forth between periods of backwardation and contango.

When it comes to the political nature of commodities, wheat is probably as important as oil. The price of bread is a direct reflection of wheat prices and is another political barometer for your portfolio. You may not notice when the price of a loaf rises by 100 percent because of a poor harvest, increased demand, or a general rise in the price of wheat because your expenditure on that loaf of bread is most likely only a small part of your total consumer spending, but your nest egg will certainly feel the impact. That is because other people around the world from less developed nations will notice a rise in the price of bread immediately—at higher prices they may no longer be able to afford to feed their families. We saw concrete evidence of this in 2011 as the Arab Spring uprisings started as a demonstration resulting from the rising bread prices in Tunisia. Certainly all our portfolios were affected by the upheaval in the Middle East in 2011. That upheaval began because the price of wheat (and bread) was on the rise. Wheat production is not concentrated in the United States; therefore, the price of wheat is subject to weather conditions and other factors around the globe. As the supply-and-demand equation for all foods and grains becomes more strained, wheat prices will continue to be more volatile as the production and export levels of even minor producing countries affect our ability to feed the world.

Soybeans

The soybean futures market is perhaps the most speculative of all the grain markets. Chinese farmers first grew soybeans around 1100 BC. Japanese farmers were growing the crop in the first century AD. In North America, soybean seeds were first planted in Georgia in 1765. The plains states of the United States began growing soybeans in 1851.

Among the many other innovations to his credit, U.S. inventor George Washington Carver discovered that soybeans were an excellent source of protein and oil in 1904. Henry Ford made plastic out of soybeans, and in 1935 he used one bag of soybeans for every car that he produced. Many of China's soybean fields were destroyed during World War Two. At that point, the United States began producing the crop on a large scale and has not looked back. In the 1950s, animal-protein producers began using soybean meal to feed hogs, cattle, chickens, and turkeys. Soybeans are now produced in 31 states in the United States, which together account for almost one-third of the world's annual soybean crop.

Soybeans are a multipurpose crop. Soybean-processing companies, such as Archer Daniels Midland, Cargill, Bunge, and others, crush the commodity to produce soybean oil and soybean meal, a high-protein fiber and major animal-feed product. Soybean oil has uses in cooking and the production of margarine, salad dressings, and mayonnaises, to name but a few. Soybeans also produce a clean-burning, nontoxic biodiesel fuel.

The United States is the world's number one producer of soybeans, followed by Brazil, Argentina, China, India, Paraguay, Canada, Indonesia, Bolivia, and Italy. The United States is also the world's largest consumer of soybeans, followed by Brazil, China, Argentina, India, and Japan, which is the number one importer of the commodity. The United States and China usually have the largest amount of carryover stocks of soybeans each year.

Soybeans trade on CBOT, which also offers a contract on South American soybeans as well as soybean oil and meal contracts. Other exchanges around the world, including those in Brazil and Australia, also offer futures contracts on soybeans.

Soybean crops are planted at different times of the year around the world, depending upon seasons. The commodity's futures fluctuate the most during growing season, because expectations of crop size and yield changes with the weather. Time spreads in soybeans can also be as volatile as the underlying commodity price because of the potential for oversupply or deficits.

Soybean crush spreads operate exactly like oil refinery spreads and reflect the value of processed soybean products versus the underlying commodity. When crushed, soybeans yield meal and oil, and the spreads can be volatile—but they are important indicators of profitability for the companies involved in the processing of soybeans. Like refining spreads, the wider the crush spread, the more profitable it is to process soybeans.

Crush-spread futures and options trade on the Chicago Mercantile Exchange (CME). A long crush contract reflects a short position in soybeans and a simultaneous long position in soybean meal and oil. A short crush spread reflects a long position in soybeans and a simultaneous short position in soybean meal and oil. CBOT also trades futures and options in soybean meal and soybean oil. Meanwhile, the underlying soybean market price often will determine the earnings of companies that use the commodity. A plethora of information is available on the CME website.

Soybeans are volatile, and the market attracts large speculative interest, particularly during growing season, when volatility tends to peak. As with many other commodities, spreads can be more volatile than the nominal price of the commodity. However, volatility often signals an opportunity for profit.

Crop substitution creates some interesting trading opportunities and even more interesting data. Crop substitution is often a function of intercommodity spreads. As we have seen, farmers will plant the crop that is the most profitable for them. Often, farmers have a choice between planting corn or soybeans, because both crops grow in similar soil. The corn versus soybean spread, while highly volatile, is one on which farmers base trading and planting decisions. Because of its volatility, this intercommodity spread attracts significant speculative interest. In 2012, farmers chose to plant a record corn crop in the United States, the biggest planting since 1944 when a bumper crop was planted to help feed war-torn Europe. This decision by farmers had an immediate effect on the corn-soybean intercommodity spread, as did the final results of the harvest of both corn and soybeans.

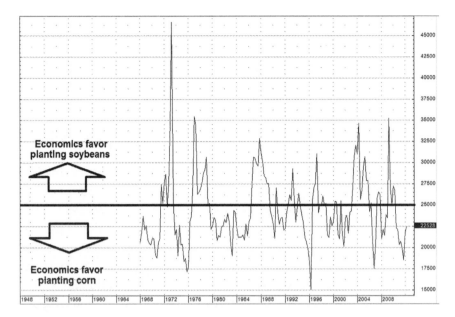

Figure 7.4 **Quarterly corn-soybean ratio chart. The historical average ratio has been 2.5 bushels of corn for 1 bushel of soybeans.**

Source: CQG, Inc. © 2012. All rights reserved worldwide.

As I write this in mid-2012, soybean prices have rallied on the back of farmers' decisions to plant more corn, and the corn-soybean ratio has corrected back to more than 2:1 from 1.8:1. Historically, this ratio has averaged 2.5 bushels of corn for each bushel of soybeans. A ratio of less than 2.5:1 can be interpreted as a market in which corn is expensive relative to soybeans. (See Figure 7.4.) This information is very valuable to investors. More corn and less soybeans may well throw off the international balance of supply and demand and create a shortage in the soybean market, thanks to the giant 2012 corn plantings.

The potential for higher soybean prices creates investment opportunities in companies that rely on soybean production, processing, and equipment.

Following current events is of paramount importance. In 2011, an international development caused soybean prices to rise. (This information was available to anyone watching grain prices, reading the business section of a newspaper, or keeping up with television business news.) China, fearing food-price inflation, sold soybeans to local edible-oil processors from the country's strategic stockpile at below-market prices. This action kept 2011 food-price inflation under control in China. However, it also caused China to have to replace strategic stockpiles with imports from the international market at a time when soybean prices were rising. Understanding the actions of the world's largest consumer of commodities and the world's third largest and most influential importer of soybeans provided an opportunity for profits to anyone who followed this story and grasped its ramifications. As an example, an investor could have bought shares in a company like Bunge Limited (BG) when it became clear that China would need to buy soybeans. An agribusiness giant such as Bunge would surely see an increase in business flows and profits from increased Chinese participation and buying in the global soybean market. For those investors more willing to trade commodities directly, falling Chinese stockpiles of soybeans was a clear signal of future Chinese demand and higher soybean prices. A purchase of soybean futures or call options in 2011 would have yielded an investor some spectacular profits!

Back in the 1980s when I was a precious-metal options trader, I noticed that the price of silver had developed an interesting correlation with the price of soybeans. You might wonder what a precious metal has in common with the price of a grain. The answer, while not readily apparent, is simple. Silver and soybeans are both active and liquid futures markets, and they are both commodities that attract speculative interest. As speculators took long and short positions in the markets, they would often go to silver and soybeans to trade perceived inflationary or deflationary pressures. For a time, the price of silver and soybeans moved in tandem. Moreover, in the mid–1980s, a silver futures contract traded in Chicago. The silver and soybean open outcry trading pits were close to one another. When one would start to rally or dip, traders and market makers who could not cover their risks hedged with the other commodity. The price relationship developed into a self-fulfilling prophecy.

I used to hear that the traders who were bullish on soybeans would say they were looking for "beans in the teens." This meant that they believed the price of the commodity would rally to $13 or higher. It was a pretty bold call in the 1980s and 1990s when soybeans traded between $6 and $8. Today, beans are in the teens. Given the global trend, I wonder whether one day "beans in the teens" will actually be a bearish market projection when soybean prices exceed $20 a bushel.

Rice

Dennis Gartman, the respected commodity trader and analyst, once said rice "only trades by appointment on the futures exchange." Rice futures are not liquid trading instruments. Nonetheless, it is an important commodity and staple around the world—even though rice futures have never gained critical mass. Rice is a physical commodity market. Rough rice futures trade on CBOT, but open interest is low and volumes are anemic.

Rice has been a food source as far back as 2500 BC. Production began in China and spread to India and Sri Lanka. Alexander the Great's armies introduced rice to Western Asia and Greece in 300 BC. America's first shipment of 200 tons of rice to England took place in 1700.

Rice is a staple consumed by 60 percent of the world's population. While the average American eats around 25 pounds of rice each year, the average Asian consumes between 200 and 400 pounds a year. Rice is probably the most important crop in the world. Some 3.3 billion people get up to 80 percent of their total caloric intake from the commodity. Rice starch produces ice cream, custard powder, puddings, gelatin, and distilled potable alcohol. Rice bran is contained in breads, cereals, snacks, cookies, and cakes. Rice bran is also found in cattle feed and organic fertilizer, and it even has some medicinal applications.

Global rice production stands at around 700 million tons a year. The largest producer is China, followed by India, Indonesia, Bangladesh, Vietnam, Thailand, Myanmar, the Philippines, Brazil, and Japan. The largest producers of rice are also its largest consumers. In 2010, Thailand was the world's leading exporter of rice followed by Vietnam, Pakistan, India, Cambodia, Uruguay, China, Egypt, Argentina, and Brazil. The leading importer was the Philippines followed by Nigeria, Iran, Saudi Arabia, and Iraq.

Local markets in China, Thailand, and Japan trade rice futures. Singapore has been contemplating an international rice futures trading platform. The size of the rice market in Asia is $160 billion per annum. A liquid market in its futures could attract both the hedging and speculative activity necessary to create a successful trading platform for this worldwide food source. While Asian diets are changing with the consumption of more complex grains and animal proteins, it will remain a dominant rice producer and consumer for many years to come. The price of rice has appreciated along with many other food staples in recent years. As price volatility for all foods increases, the need for a liquid and effective futures trading platform for rice is imperative.

Other Grains

In addition to the liquid markets in Chicago that trade futures and options on corn, wheat, and soybeans, other grains trade on exchanges around the world. The CME offers an oats and a crude palm oil contract. The Intercontinental Exchange (ICE), an electronic trading platform, offers futures contracts in western barley and Canadian canola. At the same time, the Winnipeg Commodity Exchange (WCE) trades futures on commodities including flaxseed and feed wheat.

Meanwhile, the London International Financial Futures Exchange (LIFFE) offers futures contracts in corn, malting barley, rapeseed, feed wheat, and mill wheat. The Dalian Commodity Exchange (DCE) in China trades soybeans, soybean meal and corn. The Zhengzhou Commodity Exchange (ZCE) in China trades futures on wheat (hard white and strong gluten), rapeseed oil, and early long-grain nongluten-ous rice. The Tokyo Grain Exchange (TGE) offers futures contracts in corn, soybeans, nongenetically modified (non-GMO) soybeans, and red azuki beans. And, finally, the Australian Securities Exchange (AXE) offers futures contracts in western Australian wheat, milling wheat, feed barley, sorghum, and canola. All these exchanges offer information and data on the commodities they trade. Futures exchanges are excellent sources of data for investigating current or potential investments.

Grain demand is ubiquitous around the world. Many alcoholic beverages such as whiskey and beer require grains for production. The global demand for grains has a perfect correlation with the growth in global population. Grains (and all food stuffs for that matter) are a commodity sector that will become more and more important and volatile in the years ahead.

ANIMAL PROTEIN

As carnivores or omnivores, many human beings rely on the meat of animals in their daily diets. Two of the most popular sources of meat; cattle and hogs, trade on futures exchanges.

Cattle

Cattle were first domesticated more than 10,000 years ago in Mesopotamia. By 2500 BC, several different breeds of cattle were established. Modern-day domesticated cattle fall into two groups—*Bos Taurus*, or European cattle, and *Bos Indicus*, cattle that originated on the Indian subcontinent. Both types are decedents from now-extinct *aurochs*. Breeding cattle raised for their meat began in the middle of the eighteenth century.

Futures and options on feeder cattle (steers) trade on the CME. Feeder cattle futures are cash settled contracts. There is no physical delivery mechanism for this contract. Meat and meat products come from slaughtered feeder cattle, ranging in age from 18 to 24 months.

Meanwhile, futures and options on live cattle, which are raised from calf to weights of between 600 and 800 pounds, trade on the CME. Live cattle futures contracts have a physical delivery mechanism. Live cattle become feeder cattle when they mature.

India, where cows are sacred, has the world's largest cattle population, followed by Brazil, China, the United States, the European Union, Argentina, Australia, Russia, and Mexico. When it comes to meat production, the United States is the largest producer followed by Brazil. The United States also leads the world in per capita meat consumption and is by far the world's largest importer of cattle. Meat consumption in Asia has been rising steadily.

Many different grades of beef trade at discounts and premiums in the physical market. While beef is the meal of choice for many, it is also an inefficient food source. Cattle must eat a lot of grain before they are slaughtered. It takes a great deal of grain to produce that juicy steak or chop.

Prices for live and feeder cattle can be very volatile. The outbreak of mad cow disease in 1986 and 1987 caused cattle prices to disintegrate rapidly. Recently, the growth of wealth in the emerging markets has resulted in an ever-increasing demand for beef and other meats. Figure 7.5 shows that, although feeder and live cattle prices have risen over time, there have been some wild moves, in spite of historical low volatility. This means that the commodity tends to trend slowly up and slowly down. A commodity that trends for long periods of time will give investors plenty of chances to hop onboard.

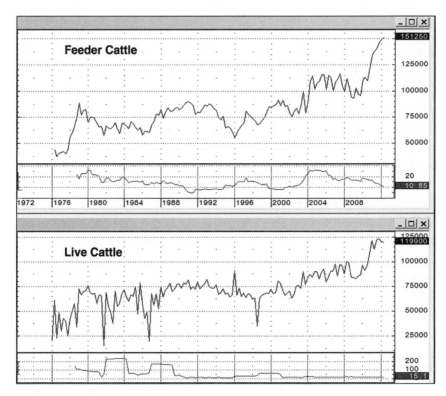

Figure 7.5 **Quarterly charts for (above) feeder cattle and (below) live cattle**
Source: CQG, Inc. © 2012. All rights reserved worldwide.

The rally in live and feeder cattle since 1998 has been steady. The global demand for beef is greater than ever before. Although there has been the occasional correction, cattle prices have moved slowly higher for a decade and a half. The same is not true when it comes to time spreads in cattle, where the moves can be vicious in both directions. (See Figure 7.6.)

The daily chart of live cattle prices shows historical volatility of future prices at 11.08 percent. The lower chart in Figure 7.6 represents a time spread in live cattle, which shows the relationship between the active month contract and the following deferred contract. The daily historical volatility of the live cattle futures spread is a whopping 189 percent. As usual, futures market spreads are more volatile than the underlying price. Notice how the live cattle market spread moves back and forth between contango and backwardation.

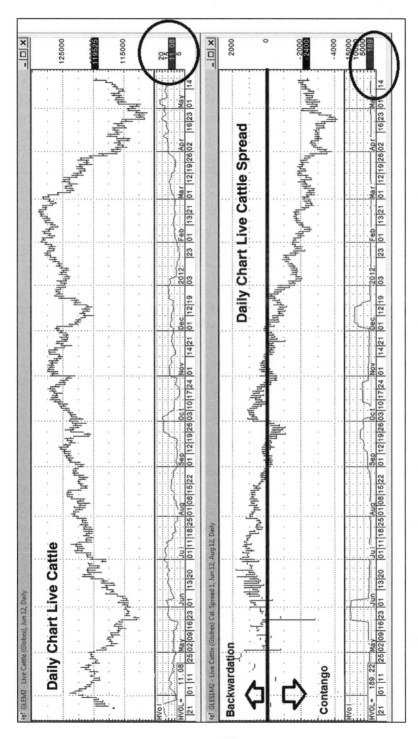

Figure 7.6 Daily chart for (above) live cattle (daily historical volatility = 11.08 percent) and (below) live cattle spread (daily historical volatility = 189 percent).

In the case of cattle, spreads between different futures months is where the action lies.

Importantly, the cattle market can uncover clues to other investments. Sharp moves in cattle spreads indicate periods of oversupply or deficit. A sudden upward price spike often indicates a shortage of beef supplies which affects price and availability. A sudden and sharp downward move in price will highlight that there is more beef available than is demanded at a specific time or that there a problem in the beef market as we witnessed during the era of mad cow disease. Food processing companies and food servicing companies are all sensitive to cattle prices. Imagine if McDonald's could not source beef patties because of a deficit in the cattle market. That would most certainly impact earnings, sales, and ultimately its share price.

The price of beef is also directly impacted by the price of grains, particularly corn and soybean meal. If grain prices rise, it costs more to produce animal protein. Higher production costs lead to higher prices or substitution. In 2012, cattle were slaughtered earlier and at lighter weights because of skyrocketing feed costs. While this is a depressing factor in terms of the price of cattle (more short-term supplies), it may increase cattle prices in the future because there will be less cattle available for future slaughter. Also, if the number of heads of cattle decreases, the demand for grains for feed will decrease.

Hogs

Pigs are descended from wild boars and were first domesticated around 5000 BC in either the Near East or China. They were a food source, and their hides produced shoes and shields. Their bones were made into tools and weapons, and their bristles were turned into brushes. Pigs also had other roles. They churned the ground as they fed, making it easier to plow. The Chinese invented bacon in 1500 BC by salting pork bellies.

Pork is one of the most widely eaten meats around the world, accounting for 38 percent of total meat consumption. However, pork is shunned by certain religious groups, such as Muslims, Jews, Seventh Day Adventists, Rastafarians, and members of the Ethiopian Orthodox Church. Many Muslim countries have banned imports of pork. Other pig products include medicines, heart valves for transplantation into humans, insulin, chalk, weed killers, fertilizer, cosmetics, floor wax, crayons, antifreeze, glass, china, adhesives, plastics, shoes, paint, and chewing gum.

China is the world's top hog producer, followed by the United States, the European Union, Brazil, Canada, Russia, and Poland. The largest consumers are China, the United States, Germany, and Spain. Worldwide pork consumption exceeds 100 million tons each year. Significant hog exporting countries include Denmark, Canada, and the United States

For many years, the CME traded futures in pork bellies, a boneless cut of fatty meat cut from the belly of a hog. Bacon is a product of a pork belly. Pork-belly futures trading began in 1961. However, the CME delisted pork-belly contracts in 2011 because of illiquidity and replaced them with lean-hog futures contracts, which are cash-settled. The CME also offers options on lean hog futures contracts. As in cattle futures, most of the action in the lean hog futures contract is in the time spreads.

Monthly historical volatility is close to 25 percent, and lean hog prices have gone higher in recent years as worldwide demand for pork has increased. As usual, lean hog time spreads are more volatile than hog prices themselves. The commodity has also swung back and forth between contango and backwardation as supply-and-demand factors compete with one another.

A friend, who trades futures on the CME, told me a story in 2011 about one of his customers, who visited China and spent some time in the regions away from the major cities. On his trip, he discovered a major shortage of pork. Even hog bones, used to make soup, were selling for huge premiums. I read about this phenomenon in U.S. newspapers and knew it would soon affect prices. Indeed, the price for lean hog futures rallied from 80 cents a pound to more than $1.07 in just seven months, a 33 percent rise. Events in the pork market offer interesting opportunities for all investors. Moves in lean hog futures prices and long-term price trends directly impact the food processing sector. Every savvy investor, like my friend on the CME, should have made a killing by buying at 80 cents as soon as the news story became public. The hog bone information from China was a call to action for those in the know. Sudden moves in prices and spreads can indicate problems in the hog market, which some companies depend on for their earnings—companies like Smithfield Foods (SFD), for example, is in the business of packaging meats for consumers as well as raising hogs.

EASY TIP

When analyzing a company for potential investment, look beyond the financial numbers everyone else is looking at. Study the core business and see where commodity-price risks lie. How will a move in the related commodity impact the cost of goods sold? The answer to this question will provide a map of future earnings and where the price of the stock in question is going.

Meat can be incredibly volatile in terms of its market structure. As perishable commodities, meat is susceptible to disease, the risks of wide-ranging feed prices, and rising global demand. However, it is precisely this kind of volatility that presents investors with opportunity. Remember to pay attention to intracommodity spreads as well as intercommodity spreads in relation to the feed that sustains the animals.

CHAPTER 8

Soft Commodities

AGRICULTURAL LUXURY

Coffee makes it possible to get out of bed. Chocolate makes it worthwhile.

—AUTHOR UNKNOWN

Soft commodities are the luxury area of the agricultural sector. That satisfying cup of coffee after a good meal, a piece of delicious chocolate, the sugar in a sweet treat, the glass of morning orange juice, and the cotton in the soft, comfortable garments you wear—all trade as soft commodities and have a major role in futures markets.

They are *feel-good* commodities. In prosperous regions of the world, people often take these goods for granted. In poverty-stricken parts of the world, where pleasures are few, these same commodities can bring joy and a sense that life is worth living. Like other agricultural products, soft commodities are perishable.

For the investor, knowledge of soft-commodity markets provides important information for analyzing a food company like Hershey (HSY) or a beverage company like Starbucks (SBUX). The production of soft commodities is restricted to certain areas of the world, and weather plays a key role during planting and harvesting. Political issues within producing countries also have a direct impact on the prices of these goods. Thus, historically, soft commodities can be heavily volatile.

COFFEE

Legend has it that a goat herder in Ethiopia named Kaldi discovered coffee during the ninth century. According to the myth, Kaldi noticed that when his goats ate the bright red berries from one of the bushes in his field, they became highly energetic. The goat herder decided to try the berries for himself, and, as he chewed, he became full of vigor. Kaldi then brought the berries to his local monastery, where the imam threw them into a fire, disapproving of the goat herder's obvious exhilaration. However, as the berries burned, they emitted a fragrant aroma. Kaldi raked the roasted beans from the embers, ground them up, dissolved them in hot water, and thus created the world's first cup of coffee.

The use of coffee soon spread from Ethiopia to Egypt and Yemen. The earliest documented account of coffee consumption comes from the Sulfi monasteries in Yemen in the fifteenth century. From there, coffee spread to the rest of the Middle East, Persia, Turkey, and North Africa. The custom of drinking coffee then spread to Italy and the rest of Europe, Indonesia, and the Americas during the sixteenth century. By the late seventeenth century, coffee drinking had spread throughout Europe and was sometimes associated with rebellious political activities. At the same time, the beverage was banned in Ottoman Turkey for political reasons.

Coffee farmers or producers pack coffee beans in 69 kilo (152 pound) bags. Total global coffee production in 2011 was approximately 131 million bags. Brazil is by far the largest coffee producer in the world and supplies around 33 percent of the annual global crop. The other major producers, in order of production, are Vietnam, Colombia, Ethiopia, Indonesia, and India. The top coffee consumer in the world by far is the European Union, which imported 70 million bags in 2011. The United States was the second largest consumer that year, importing around 24 million bags, followed by Japan (7.5 million bags) and Switzerland (2.4 million bags).

Arabica coffee, which accounts for 75 to 80 percent of all coffee beans produced, comes from an evergreen bush or tree (*Coffea arabica*), which is indigenous to the mountains of Yemen. Robusta coffee, which contains more caffeine than arabica, is indigenous to West Africa and is also grown in Java, in Indonesia. Robusta has a high resistance to coffee rust, a devastating disease that can ruin crops. Starbucks and Dunkin' Donuts use 100 percent arabica beans. Robusta beans generally produce Italian-style espresso coffees.

The process of harvesting coffee involves picking coffee berries either by hand or with machines and then exposing the seed, or the bean. Coffee producers then ship the beans to processors or roasters. Roastmasters are in charge of roasting. Different styles of roasting will produce coffees with different flavors. Coffee beans are ground in the final step of preparation.

Coffee buying is a specialized skill. Buyers from around the world often travel to producing countries to smell and taste different coffee beans from a variety of producers. If you are as old as I am, you may recall the choosy coffee buyer in the Savarin ad from the 1960s and 1970s. Juan Valdez or El Exijente was called "the demanding one." He would taste the coffee and, upon his approval, the locals would cheer.

A key distinction for coffee futures traders is the two different types of coffee that are traded on the world's exchanges. Arabica coffee futures and options are traded in New York on the Intercontinental Exchange (ICE). These were traded on the New York Board of Trade prior to the exchange's merger with ICE in 2007. The contract on ICE is a liquid futures market that producers and consumers use to hedge and that speculators use to trade. Countries exporting superior coffee command premiums, while those exporting inferior coffees trade at discounts to futures prices. ICE also determines approved delivery points at licensed warehouses in the United States and Europe. The size of the coffee futures contract on ICE is 37,500 pounds.

Meanwhile, robusta futures are traded in London on the Euronext LIFFE exchange. The size of a LIFFE coffee futures contract is 10 metric tons. Some traders exploit the price difference (or arbitrage) between ICE and LIFFE, both of which are traded electronically.

The robusta contract is located in Europe, because Europeans tend to prefer robusta, while U.S. consumers tend to prefer arabica blends. A number of other international exchanges that trade coffee futures and options are the Tokyo Grain Exchange (TGE), which trades both arabica and robusta, the Singapore Commodity Exchange, which trades robusta, and the BM&F in Brazil, which trades arabica.

A number of factors can affect the price of this commodity. Besides coffee rust, the annual crop is susceptible to loss from frosts, droughts, and other weather disruptions. Coffee is also a perishable commodity over long periods of time. Seasonality also influences the price of coffee. As with many agricultural commodities, the futures market is most active during the growing seasons. The way in which coffee is produced, the delicate nature of the crop, and the ubiquitous demand all contribute to make this an extremely volatile commodity, in terms of nominal price and calendar spreads.

Over the past 40 years coffee prices have traded as low as 41.5 cents a pound and as high as $3.375 a pound. Figure 8.1 shows quarterly historical volatility of more than 33 percent.

When I worked for Philipp Brothers in the 1980s, the coffee traders worked down the hall from me. They all spoke Spanish and Portuguese, and they travelled regularly to Colombia and Brazil to source coffee beans. They also built a tasting room near the trading

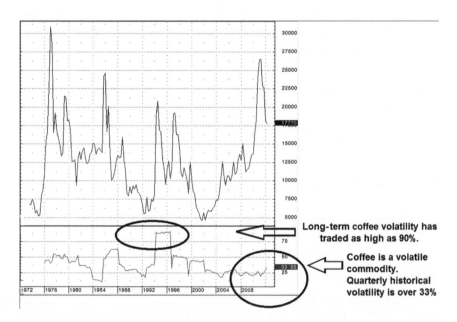

Figure 8.1 **Quarterly chart of coffee futures**

Source: CQG, Inc. © 2012. All rights reserved worldwide.

floor so they could sample potential cargos—the aromas that emanated from that room were delicious. On occasion, the coffee traders invited me to offer my opinion on taste. Some of the coffee varieties they let me sample were extraordinary, but others were awful. One of the biggest problems that coffee traders encountered in the 1980s was the relationship between coffee and drug smugglers, whose vessels often carried huge coffee shipments to mask the aroma of the drugs. I recall one occasion when a dead body arrived with a massive coffee shipment, along with a large cache of marijuana and cocaine.

Many companies in food-servicing businesses use coffee beans in the manufacturing of their products. When the price of coffee rises or falls it affects both the cost of goods sold and ultimate bottom line profits of these companies. Long-term price movements are absorbed by the coffee consumer, while short-term spikes caused by weather problems, crop deterioration, coffee rust, fungus, and other coffee growing issues can cause price volatility that can't be passed along to consumers. As an example, sudden moves in the price of coffee can directly impact companies like Starbucks (SBUX) and Green Mountain Coffee Roasters (GMRC). A sudden rally or dip in coffee price will impact company earnings and consequently share prices.

SUGAR

Some time around 8000 BC, the people of the large Pacific island of New Guinea first domesticated sugarcane. The first documented historical evidence of the commodity as a solid substance was recorded in India in 500 AD. Cultivation of sugar spread quickly to southern China. By the seventh century, sugar cultivation had reached Persia. From Persia it spread to the Arab world and the Mediterranean. While sugar has been a luxury, providing happiness to human beings, the Greek and Roman civilizations used sugar for medicinal purposes, not as a food.

In ancient times, it was time consuming and difficult to produce sugar from sugarcane. Growing the plant was a labor-intensive process. Moreover, the cane was bulky and costly to transport. Primitive refineries were set up in areas where the cane grew. Crushing the cane and boiling the liquid created raw crystallized sugar.

European explorers spread sugar production to the New World as they colonized and discovered ideal weather conditions for growing sugarcane. Sugar became extremely popular in the 1700s, and prices fluctuated widely with availability. Sugar also became expensive as demand outstripped supply. By 1750, sugar surpassed grains as the most valuable commodity. As Europeans established sugar production in the 1800s in areas like the Caribbean, the supplies of the commodity rose and prices fell. Nonetheless, some of the greatest architecture of the eighteenth century British industrial revolution was built as a result the fortunes accumulated from the trade in sugar and the ships that transported it.

In 1747, German chemist Andreas Marggraf identified sucrose in the sugar beet root, which established a new source for the commodity. While sugarcane requires hot tropical climates, sugar beets grow in temperate conditions. Sugarcane grows best in countries like Brazil, India, China, and Thailand where strong sun and hot temperatures make for ideal growing conditions. Sugar beets, on the other hand, grow best in countries like France, Germany and Russia, where, during the growing season, there are long days of temperate sunshine.

While sugar has traditionally been used as an ingredient to produce sweets, cakes, and jellies, technology has developed the ability to create fuel from sugar. Sugar-based ethanol has become a popular fuel in places like Brazil.

Sugarcane production in 2009 was around 1.7 billion tons. The largest producers of cane sugar in the world are Brazil, India, China, Thailand, Pakistan, Mexico, and Colombia. Brazil is by far the largest raw sugar producer in the world. Sugar beet sugar production in 2009 was around 230 million tons. The ratio of cane sugar to beet sugar varies year to year. The largest producer of beet sugar in the world is France followed by the United States, Germany, Russia, Turkey, Poland, Ukraine, and the United Kingdom.

Many sugar-producing nations consume the bulk of their own production. More than 70 percent of global sugar production is consumed domestically. The world's top exporters of sugar are Brazil, the European Union, Australia, and Thailand. Some sugar-producing regions, like the United States and Europe, employ a system of subsidies, tariffs, and quotas to aid domestic sugar producers. These result in higher prices for local consumers.

The European Union and the United States are the world's largest sugar importers. Other major importers include Canada, Sweden, Hong Kong, and Japan. In recent years, because of high oil prices, Brazil has used a greater proportion of its domestic sugar crop to produce sugar-based ethanol, and it has thus decreased its dependence on foreign sources of energy. However, this has resulted in less Brazilian sugar being exported and has driven up the price of international sugar.

Sugar futures and options trade on U.S., European, and Asian markets. NYMEX offers financially settled sugar futures. Financially settled futures do not have a mechanism for delivery rather they are ultimately settled against the final price on an expiration date established for the contract. The most active market for futures and options trading in the world is the ICE #11 sugar contract, which reflects the worldwide price of raw cane sugar. The #16 sugar contract reflects the U.S. domestic price of sugar which is influenced by subsidies. Like coffee, sugar also trades on the LIFFE exchange in London, as well as on exchanges in Tokyo and China.

Sugar is the most volatile agricultural commodity that trades. The crop is highly susceptible to weather conditions. Bad weather can wipe out a sugar crop, and the commodity is also perishable. Over time, sugar prices can be a wild ride. During the course of my career, I have seen sugar prices trade as low as 2.29 cents a pound in 1985, compared with a historic high of more than 66 cents in the 1970s. The price in the fall of 2012 was around 22 cents a pound. When I was a junior commodity options trader back in 1985, I asked my boss if we should take a long position in sugar, and he said, "Why would you ever want to buy something restaurants give away free?"

Nonetheless, quarterly historic volatility in sugar is 44 percent, which is high, and there have been numerous instances of sugar volatility exceeding 100 percent. Time spreads in sugar are even more volatile than the price of the commodity, because sugarcane grows in tropical regions that are susceptible to hurricanes, monsoons, and other bad weather events. It is not unusual for a sugar crop to get wiped out. At the same time, global sugar demand is ubiquitous, and a dramatic decline in supply will cause the price to spike.

Always keep an eye on this sweet commodity. The price of sugar can affect your nest egg, as well as how much you pay for related goods at the supermarket. Many foods contain sugar, and the companies that produce those foods present investment opportunities.

COCOA

The Olmec, the first major civilization in Mexico (1500–400 BC) ate cocoa beans. They crushed the beans, mixed them with water, and added spices. The Olmec are believed to have been the first people in the world to consume chocolate. A ritual beverage called *chocolatl*, containing cocoa beans, was prepared and shared during Mayan marriage ceremonies a few hundred years later on the Yucatan Peninsula, now in southern Mexico. This is the first known link between romance and chocolate. Christopher Columbus is said to have brought the first cocoa beans back to Europe from his fourth visit to the New World between 1502 and 1504. However, it was Spanish conquistador Hernán Cortés, who first realized their commercial value and brought cocoa beans back to Spain in 1528. By the eighteenth century confections containing cocoa had become popular in Europe, particularly as a drink. In South America cocoa beans were also used as currency. While visiting Central America, Cortés found that four cocoa beans could buy a pumpkin and that ten could buy a rabbit.

The cocoa bean is the original source of all chocolate—from chocolate liqueurs and candy bars to cocoa butter and cocoa powder for hot chocolate. Raw cocoa beans contain flavonoids, which are thought to improve cardiovascular health. Pharmaceuticals, makeup, soap, and scar removal products also contain cocoa beans.

The ideal climate for growing cocoa beans is found in countries within 10 degrees, north or south, of the equator. Between 5 and 6 million cocoa farmers in the world produce an annual crop of around 3 million tons. Some 50 million people around the world depend on cocoa for their livelihood. The world's largest producers of cocoa beans are the Ivory Coast, Ghana, Indonesia, Nigeria, Brazil, and Cameroon. Around 70 percent of global cocoa supplies come from West Africa. The largest importers are the European Union and the United States. Annual cocoa demand has been growing at 3 percent each year since the 1990s, with the largest increases coming from Asia.

The price of this commodity changes every year, depending on the size of the global cocoa crop. This is why, as I outlined in Chapter 1, cocoa pod counter Hans Kilian was such an important player in the cocoa market. A direct examination of the cocoa fields revealed enough supply information to affect the price.

However, cocoa is not just a food commodity. It is also political. It was a political event, rather than Kilian's numbers, that caused cocoa prices to soar in 2011. A hotly contested election in the Ivory Coast, the largest cocoa producer in the world, resulted in a great deal of civil unrest. Even though 2011 was a bumper crop year, the election issues caused cocoa prices to jump. Localized violence prevented the majority of the cocoa beans from traveling from the farms to the ports for export. Consequently, cocoa prices surged from $2,600 per ton to $3,800 in six months. Once the violence had subsided and the new leader took power, cocoa prices returned to earth because the commodity once again flowed from the country before it perished. In this sense, the Ivory Coast was lucky, because it depends on its cocoa crop for economic survival, and cocoa rots quickly beneath the equatorial sun.

Cocoa futures and options trade on the ICE. NYMEX offers financially settled futures on the commodity. Cocoa beans from some areas of the world trade at a premium for physical delivery. The exchange determines premiums based on industry input. The spot month (or cash price) for cocoa beans is used for calculating the physical delivery price. The delivery mechanism (as with many other commodities) allows for a smooth convergence of futures and physical prices over time. Cocoa futures also trade on the LIFFE. Professional cocoa traders often trade arbitrage between the ICE and LIFFE cocoa futures. The arbitrage is essentially an intracommodity and location spread; the trader buys cocoa on one exchange and sells it on the other. Because cocoa is an agricultural commodity produced in lesser-developed countries, prices can move around quite a bit.

Cocoa prices move much like the prices of many of the other soft commodities. Long-term historical volatility in cocoa is just under 20 percent, but there have also been periods when volatility exploded. As an investor, think about the origin of that piece of chocolate cake on your fork or that candy bar in your hand. Also think about the companies like Nestlé, Hershey, and M&M Mars, which all have their earnings tied to the price they pay for cocoa beans, the primary input in their production process.

FROZEN CONCENTRATED ORANGE JUICE

Oranges have been eaten by people for least 4,000 years. By the 1800s, the orange-growing business took off in the state of Florida. However, it was not until 1945 that frozen concentrated orange juice (FCOJ) was developed. Almost immediately, the United States became the main producer of FCOJ. Squeezed fresh orange juice is filtered and pasteurized, and then vacuumed and evaporated. Finally, the liquid is frozen and packaged in cans.

Total production of FCOJ is just over 51 million metric tons each year. Brazil is the largest producer of oranges, accounting for some 34 percent of world production. The United States (and Florida in particular) produces around 15.5 percent of the world's annual supply. Mexico is also a significant producer, contributing some 8 percent. Demand for orange juice exists all over the world; it's increasing at the fastest rate in Asia.

Orange growing comes with certain risks. Orange crops are especially susceptible to frost and fungus. A frost in Florida can destroy an entire orange crop in just a few days. Orange juice futures prices tend to spike during the hurricane season and winter in the Sunshine State. The perishability and fragility of the orange crop coupled with the uncertainty of weather results in FCOJ being a very volatile commodity. The USDA reports monthly on the status of orange production.

FCOJ trading was the subject of a popular movie back in the early 1980s. *Trading Places* was the story of several characters at a fictitious commodities brokerage firm, Duke and Duke. The Dukes arranged to steal a USDA crop report and use the information to control the market in FCOJ. The report revealed that the orange crop would be lower than expected, and the Dukes proceeded to buy up all of the FCOJ contracts on the futures market. However, it turned out they got the wrong report. The Dukes owned a lot of futures contracts and the price plummeted. When trading stopped on the exchange, they needed to come up with all of the money they had lost:

President of exchange: Margin call, gentlemen. You know the rules, all accounts must be settled at the end of the day, without exception.

Randolph Duke: You know perfectly well we do not have $394 million in cash!

President of exchange: Oh, I am sorry. (*To his assistants*) Put the Dukes' seats on the exchange up for sale and seize all holdings and property of Mortimer and Randolph Duke.

I have included these few lines from the movie because they exemplify beautifully how the futures markets work. The Dukes bought many contracts of FCOJ, and then the price went lower. At the end of trading, they had to pay the clearinghouse the difference between the prices at which they bought the FCOJ and the current, lower market price. The Dukes went bankrupt as a result of their FCOJ trade.

The ICE futures exchange offers futures and options contracts on FCOJ. The futures contract is the worldwide benchmark for FCOJ prices. The contract allows for physical delivery of FCOJ from the United States, Brazil, Mexico, and Costa Rica.

As I said, weather, perishability, and seasonality contribute to the volatility of FCOJ. Long-term volatility is above 25 percent, but that is only one part of the story. This commodity tends to really move during the growing season, and any whiff of a frost or a hurricane will cause prices to soar. Calendar spreads in the FCOJ market can also be very volatile.

PepsiCo-owned Tropicana is the leading supplier of orange juice in the United States. Tropicana also exports orange juice to Latin America, Central Asia, and Europe. Minute-Maid, the other dominant orange juice supplier, is owned by the Coca-Cola Company. Any investor involved in these companies should keep an eye on this market.

COTTON

The earliest cotton threads date back 7,000 years to western Pakistan. Other old traces of cotton are seeds and rope found in Peru dating back to 4500 BC. The use of cotton to produce garments played an important role in the growth and economic influence of the British Empire, India, and the United States.

The British Empire imported cotton to make garments in the 1600s. By1664, the East India Company was importing a quarter of a million pieces of cotton into Britain each year. The country's cotton imports grew by leaps and bounds during the following decades as the country became a large producer of clothing.

In India, Gandhi used cotton for political purposes. In 1920, Gandhi launched a boycott of British cotton goods and urged Indians to wear only homespun clothing. Cotton became an important symbol of Indian independence from colonial Britain.

Cotton played a key role during the American Civil War. "King Cotton" was a phrase used by Southern politicians to explain economic independence after secession from the Union. The cotton-growing industry was the epicenter of the Civil War, as the North sought to free slaves on Southern plantations.

The commodity continues to be an important crop today. Many textiles contain cotton. Yarns, threads, fishing nets, filters, tents, explosives, paper, and bookbinding use this commodity, as well as a number of medicinal and cosmetic products.

Total worldwide cotton production in 2011 was about 120 million bales, each weighing around 500 pounds. China was the leading cotton producer in the world in 2011, producing 33 million bales, followed by India, the United States, Pakistan, Brazil, Uzbekistan, and Australia. These seven countries produce almost 90 percent of the world's cotton. The top consumers are China, India, and Pakistan.

The United States is by far the world's largest exporter of cotton. Typically the United States exports more than seven times more cotton than the second largest exporter, Australia. Thus, the U.S. cotton crop can have a massive impact on global prices. Thanks to crop substitution among U.S. farmers, the reduced number of cotton exports in 2008 caused a deficit in the market. Global demand for the commodity simply outstripped supply and moved prices from less than 40 cents a pound in October 2008 to $2.27 a pound in March 2011, an increase of more than 515 percent. The price climbed so rapidly that Chinese garment manufacturers substituted synthetic fibers for the commodity rather than pay the prohibitive prices. The commodity has since come back to earth after U.S. farmers began planting cotton again. As I write this, cotton trades at around 70 cents a pound.

The U.S. government subsidizes its cotton farmers, which affects global planting behavior. Without subsidies, free market prices dictate planting behavior. The subsidies lower world market prices, making cotton production uneconomical for Chinese farmers, as well as others around the world. Subsidies and tariffs can also result in artificially high prices for consumers of some commodities. European Union sugar subsidies, which serve to keep prices higher than the global free market would otherwise allow, in many cases cut out unsubsidized competitors. As we have seen, commodity prices are efficient. If they rise too high, consumers find substitutes; if they fall too low, producers cut back on output. Subsidies and tariffs are political tools and run contrary to the efficiency of free markets.

Cotton futures and options trade on the ICE. The Zhengzhou Commodities Exchange in China also offers cotton futures contracts, and NYMEX in New York offers financially settled futures on cotton. As with all agricultural commodities, calendar spreads in cotton can be more volatile than the underlying price of the commodity. Cotton swings back and forth between backwardation and contango. The cotton futures and options market attracts a reasonable level of volume, but liquidity suffers when the market becomes highly volatile.

Cotton prices have ranged from between just under 30 cents to just over $1.15 for the past 40 years. The move to $2.27 in 2011 was an anomaly. Watch out for changes in U.S. or other government subsidies to farmers which could impact the price of the commodity if it were ever allowed to trade in a free market. Such actions change the fundamental supply and demand equation, and hence the price.

OTHER SOFT COMMODITIES

A number of other soft commodities such as milk, butter, eggs, and cheese trade on exchanges in the United States and around the world. These commodities are less liquid. However, knowledge of their existence can prove useful to investment analysis and may help illuminate some of the key variables in your investment calculus.

LIFFE trades futures on skimmed milk powder futures. The CME offers futures and options on milk, skimmed milk powder, nonfat dry milk, dry whey, as well as cash-settled butter and cheese.

CHAPTER 9

Other Commodities

You can observe a lot by just watching.

—YOGI BERRA

The price of essential goods has an impact on the economics and fortunes of each company we invest in, sometimes directly and sometimes indirectly. Often these essential commodities provide clues to the future viability and profitability of investments. A few more globally traded commodities that investors should keep their eyes on are essentials such as steel, rare earth metals, lumber and pulp, and fertilizers as well as some lesser-known commodities.

STEEL

Steel contains iron, which defines it as a ferrous metal. Steel ironware dating back 4,000 years turned up at an archaeological dig in Turkey. Sickle-shaped weapons from the fourth century BC have been found on the Iberian Peninsula. Nordic steel was used by the Roman military. Today, many different steel products are used by industry. Steel is one of the key building materials of modern infrastructure. Steel is an essential in the manufacture of cars, ships, pipelines, and many kinds of machinery, tools, and appliances.

Steel production begins with iron, which is found in the crust of the earth. Naturally occurring iron ore contains iron, carbon, and other elements. To produce steel, iron ore first goes into a blast furnace, which produces pig iron with a carbon content of between 2 and 4 percent. The pig iron can then be further refined to produce various grades of steel. Ferrous scrap metal can also be refined into steel. The biggest cost associated with the production of steel is energy. When energy costs rise, so does the cost of producing steel.

Total global steel production in 2011 was around 1.5 billion tons. China is by far the world's largest producer of steel—almost 700 million tons in 2011, exceeding the world's second-largest producer, the European Union, by more than 500 million tons. China is also the world's biggest steel consumer. Other big steel-producing countries include Japan, the United States, India, Russia, South Korea, and Germany.

Emerging-market countries use the commodity to build infrastructure as they grow. On the back of this greater demand, the steel price increases. However, steel prices, which are sensitive to global economic expansion and contraction, can be as volatile as other metals traded on futures exchanges.

A number of different steel contracts are traded on markets around the world. NYMEX offers a financially settled contract on so-called U.S. Midwest Domestic Hot-Rolled Coil Steel Index futures. The LME offers a contract on steel billets, ICE offers a futures contract on iron ore, and the Shanghai Futures Exchange (SHFE) offers futures contracts in steel rebar (reinforcing bar) and steel wire rod.

Steel futures and options contracts are rarely liquid. However, they are useful for keeping track of steel prices around the world. Watching intercommodity spreads (steel versus forms of energy, such as natural gas, oil, coal, and electricity) gives an investor a feel for the production costs, which can be a key factor in deciding whether or not to invest in a particular company.

MOLYBDENUM

Alloys that need to withstand extreme heat, such as aircraft parts and industrial motors, require the metal molybdenum. This commodity is also used in radioisotopes and biological staining. About 220,000 tons of molybdenum are produced each year. The world's leading producer is China, followed by the United States, Chile, and Peru. Molybdenum is mined as a principal ore, and it is recovered as a by-product of copper and tungsten mining. Thus, a price relationship exists between copper and molybdenum.

COBALT

Cobalt is a by-product of nickel production. Some alloys that require cobalt are found in blades for gas turbines and jet engines. Cobalt is also required in the production of lithium ion battery cathodes, as oxidation catalysts, as radioisotopes, for electroplating, and as ground coats for porcelain enamels. In 2010 there was approximately 88,000 tons of cobalt produced in the world. The world's leading producer of cobalt in 2010 was the Democratic Republic of Congo, formerly known as Zaire. High-tech demand has caused the United States to become the largest consumer of cobalt in the world.

Both molybdenum and cobalt are thinly traded commodities on the LME. However, companies that use these metals, and companies that produce them, such as the U.S. mining firm Molycorp, trade on exchanges around the world. Investing in this sector has become popular over the past few years as the prices for minor metals and rare earth metals have rallied along with the rest of the commodity sector.

Many investors have been attracted to companies involved in these commodities without understanding the underlying commodities themselves. Understanding the basic supply-and-demand equation for these commodities is key to understanding and profiting from investment opportunities. Because they are so thinly traded, they are subject to a high degree of volatility.

EASY TIP

Familiarize yourself with and watch the prices of lesser-known commodities because very few investors do. Pay particular attention when prices of minor metals and rare earth metals trade lower and present cheap opportunities around the price of production. When prices turn and begin to move, it's time to jump in before the pack. Trading ranges in these commodities are wide, and market action is cyclical. Once they are in the news, it's time to take profits. Smart money gets in before the pack and gets out when most investors are getting in.

RARE EARTH METALS

Rare earth metals are a collection of 17 elements. Technology has dramatically increased demand for these metals over the past few years, and in many ways they are the metals of the future. Many of these metals are toxic and environmentally hazardous to mine. The vast amount of mining activity for rare earth metals today takes place in China. There are ETFs available to invest in this sector, but the metals themselves are highly illiquid.

Here is a list of rare earth metals and their major uses:

- **Scandium:** Used in fuel cells, added to mercury-vapor lamps to give a natural sunlight appearance. Used as an alloy with aluminum for aerospace components and some sporting goods, such as baseball bats and racquets.
- **Yttrium:** Produces color in many TV picture tubes. Used to conduct microwaves and acoustic energy, simulates diamond gemstones, and strengthens ceramics, glass, and some alloys.
- **Lanthanum:** Used in carbon arc lamps for the film and TV industries, in batteries, cigarette-lighter flints, and specialized types of glass; in hydrogen storage; and as a fluid cracking catalyst for oil refineries.
- **Cerium:** The most common of all rare earth metals. Used in catalytic converters and diesel fuels to reduce carbon monoxide emissions. Used in carbon arc lights, flints for lighters, glass polishers, and self-cleaning ovens.
- **Praseodymium:** Used to make rare earth magnets. An alloying agent (with magnesium) to produce high-strength metals for aircraft engines. Used as a signal amplifier in fiber-optic cables and to make glass for welding goggles.
- **Neodymium:** Used in rare earth magnets—powerful magnets for computer hard disks, wind turbines, hybrid cars, ear bud headphones, and microphones. Used to produce colored glass, lighter flints, and welding goggles.
- **Promethium:** Artificially produced via uranium fission. Used in luminous paint and nuclear batteries. Potential uses in portable X-rays.
- **Samarium:** Together with cobalt creates a permanent magnet with the highest demagnetization resistance of any known material. Used for "smart" missile production, lasers, neutron capture, and masers for amplifying microwaves.
- **Europium:** The most reactive rare earth metal. Employed as a red phosphor in TV sets, computer monitors, mercury vapor lamps, and some types of lasers.

- **Gadolinium:** Has a medical application in magnetic resonance imaging (MRI). Used in control rods at nuclear power plants; improves workability of iron, chromium, and various other metals. Also used in high-refractive index glass, lasers, X-ray tubes, computer memories, and neutron capture.
- **Terbium:** Used in solid-state technology, advanced sonar systems, small electronic sensors, and fuel cells designed to operate at high temperatures. Produces laser light and green phosphors in television tubes.
- **Dysprosium:** Used for control rods at nuclear power plants and lasers, high-intensity lighting, and high-powered permanent magnets, such as those in hybrid vehicles.
- **Holmium:** Highest magnetic strength of any known element—useful for industrial magnets and some nuclear control rods. Used in solid-state lasers and to help color cubic zirconia and certain types of glass.
- **Erbium:** Used as a photographic filter and as a signal amplifier in fiber-optic cable.
- **Thulium:** Rarest of all naturally present rare earth metals. Used in some surgical lasers. Used in portable X-ray technology.
- **Ytterbium:** Used in portable X-ray devices. Used in certain types of lasers, stress gauges for earthquakes, and as a chemical reducing agent.
- **Lutetium:** Used in the calculation of the age of meteorites, used to perform positron emission tomography (PET) scans. Has also been used as a catalyst for the process of "cracking" petroleum products at oil refineries and for high-refractive index glass.

China has only 30 percent of the world's rare earth metal reserves, but it controls 97 percent of the world's production through investments and joint ventures. However, these metals are so important for future technological advances that China has put itself in the driver's seat. Have no doubt that technological advances over the coming years will find more uses for these rare earth metals. They are the commodities for tomorrow, so keep your eye on this important emerging commodity sector for profitable investment opportunities in the future.

LUMBER AND PULP

Just as copper diagnoses the state of the global economy's health, lumber is a commodity that diagnoses the state of the housing industry. The U.S. government issues a report on the number of newly built homes each month, and this tends to move markets. But the lumber market is aware of these numbers before the government report is released. The lumber market has long been a crucible for trends in home-building and the general economic condition.

The United States is the world's top producer of timber, followed by India, China, Brazil, Canada, Russia, and Indonesia. China is the largest importer of soft wood lumber in the world. Building infrastructure in China requires more lumber each year.

There are futures and options contracts on lumber that trade on the CME. The CME also offers futures and options contracts on northern bleached softwood kraft pulp. Paper made from kraft pulp is a strong paper used principally for wrapping or packaging. The lumber market is not terribly liquid, but price data provide excellent information on trends and the economy as a whole. Keeping track of lumber prices will open your eyes to price changes that may portend developments in the economy and the future value of your home.

FERTILIZERS

Fertilizers are a key component and a complementary commodity in the production of agricultural commodities. Fertilizers can be organic or inorganic substances. They supply one or more nutrients essential to the growth of plants when they are added to soil. The three major types of fertilizer used are nitrogen, phosphorus, and potassium (potash).

As the demand for food increases around the world, so does the need for fertilizers. The largest consumers of fertilizers in the world are the countries with the biggest populations and most arable land for growing crops, such as China, India, the United States, and Brazil.

While there are no futures contracts on fertilizers offered as I write this book, the CME does offer swaps in fertilizer products; granular urea, urea ammonium nitrate (UAN), and diammonium phosphate (DAP). In commodity swaps, parties exchange a fixed price for a floating price over a specific period of time (see Chapter 2). While no futures data are available, there is information on swaps published on the CME website as well as via fertilizer trade association websites and the USDA.

OTHER COMMODITIES WORTH KEEPING AN EYE ON

In order to round out your knowledge base, it is worth taking a look at a few other staples, commodities, and derivatives that trade.

Swaps in *uranium*, which is used mainly for nuclear power or weaponry, trade on NYMEX. It is also a target for X-rays and it is used in gyroscope compasses. Global production of uranium in 2010 was approximately 53,000 tons. The largest producer in the world is Kazakhstan. Other significant producers include Canada, Australia, Namibia, Niger, Russia, Uzbekistan, and the United States. Countries maintain strategic stockpiles of uranium for obvious defensive and offensive reasons. Surprisingly, the country with the largest stated stockpile in the world as of 2009 was Australia, which holds 31 percent of the world's known stocks.

As the demand for nuclear fuel has increased around the world, so has the price of uranium. Uranium prices are very volatile. In July 2007, the price of the commodity was $131.50 per pound, while in April 2012 the price had dropped to $51.30 per pound. New supplies have depressed the price over the past few years, but uranium prices are sure to move around over the coming years as demand increases for the production of nuclear energy.

Unlike uranium, there is an active trading market in *emission allowances*. Cap and Trade, as this market is known, emerged from the need to address pollution by providing market-based incentives for reductions. A central authority (a government or a supranational institution) sets a limit on the gross amount of a pollutant allowed. Companies that emit pollutants, particularly those that burn coal, receive a number of permits that is a portion of the overall cap. Companies are allowed to sell their unused permits if they emit less pollution then they are allocated. If a company emits more than its allocation, it must buy additional permits as a penalty. Carbon dioxide, sulfur dioxide, and nitrogen oxide are the three types of pollutants covered by emission allowances.

The over-the-counter market for the trading of these allowances is highly active. In 1997 and 1998, I ran the commodities brokerage business for Cantor Fitzgerald, at the time, home to traders Carlton Bartels and Jude Moussa, both of whom were in part responsible for the birth of the emissions trading markets. Both Carlton and Jude perished on September 11, 2001, on the 105th floor of the World Trade Center, along with many others. I sat next to both of these gentlemen for more than a year and travelled with them on several occasions. They taught me a great deal about the emissions allowance markets.

Futures and options contracts on emission allowances can be traded on the GreenX (a division of the CME), the Chicago Climate Exchange (a division of ICE), the European Climate Exchange, and the European Energy Exchange. A number of exchanges in Asia also offer these products. All these exchanges offer valuable information on the price of emission allowances. When an economy is growing and expanding, more pollution credits are necessary for industry. During these times prices of allowances should go higher. Conversely, during times of economic contraction, allowance prices should fall.

There is an active and growing futures market in *weather derivatives*. The CME offers a wide range of futures and options products based on temperatures in various locations around the world. Weather derivatives provide market participants with the opportunity to hedge heating days, cooling days, rainfall, snowfall, and even hurricanes. These are financially settled insurancelike contracts used by industry to protect against the financial ramifications of temperature and weather events. Products like these can be very useful to farmers and others involved in the agricultural sector. The energy industry and operators of seasonal businesses, such as ski resorts and beach resorts, can also make use of these products.

The Australian Securities Exchange offers contracts in *wool*. There are a lot of sheep in Australia and New Zealand, and wool is a big business there. Futures and options trading is available on the exchange.

The Tokyo Commodity Exchange and the Shanghai Futures Exchange offer futures and options contracts on *rubber*. The largest producers of rubber in the world are in Asia. The three largest producing countries are Thailand, Indonesia, and Malaysia. Think about them the next time you buy tires for your car or invest in an automobile manufacturing company.

Finally, the LME offered *plastics* (polypropylene and polyethylene) futures and options in 2005, but the contracts were delisted in 2010 because of a general lack of open interest. Only one market in Dalian, China, offers a market in plastics.

CHAPTER 10

The Future of Commodity Markets

Study the past, if you would divine the future.

—CONFUCIUS

The dynamics of government regulation in the commodities markets are changing, as are the roles of speculators and traders in commodities markets. In addition, how these regulations tie in with the emergence of China as an economic superpower is key to the future. The question now becomes this: What is the future relationship between commodity essentials and your portfolio?

REGULATION

The formation of capital, a hedging mechanism, and the opportunity to invest are the reasons why financial markets exist. The efficient operation of financial markets depends on the identification and removal of unscrupulous and criminal elements. A free market is one in which there are transparency and a level playing field.

Regulation is administrative legislation that constitutes or constrains rights and allocates responsibilities. Various governments around the world regulate the financial markets that trade on their soil. Certainly there is a need for some degree of regulation because a small investor needs protection from the controllers of huge pools of capital that have the ability to manipulate and influence markets by virtue of their size.

In the United States, regulation is a maze of bureaucracy. The Securities and Exchange Commission (SEC) regulates the stock market, Treasury securities, and the municipal bond markets. The Commodity Futures Trading Commission (CFTC) regulates commodity and financial futures and options. We have seen how interrelated these markets are. The U.S. regulatory agencies operate under the auspices of the federal government. The president appoints the commissioners and chairs of both the SEC and CFTC, although the charters of both agencies call for an apolitical mix of commissioners.

The mission of each agency is logical. The SEC, according to its website, must "protect investors, maintain fair, orderly, and efficient markets, and facilitate capital formation."

The CFTC, according to its website, should "protect market users and the public from fraud, manipulation, abusive practices, and systemic risk related to derivatives that are subject to the Commodity Exchange Act, and to foster open, competitive markets."

The SEC has been around since 1934, and the CFTC since 1974. Contrary to popular belief, regulation is an art, not a science. Depending on the political climate, regulators at the CFTC and SEC have had different powers under different presidential administrations. As a rule, Republican administrations tend to favor a more lax regulatory environment, while Democratic administrations favor more regulation.

Other governmental bodies have been involved in regulation from time to time. The Senate Banking Committee and the House Committee on Financial Services are the watchdogs of the Senate and House of Representatives, respectively. Allegations of abuse in the financial markets generally lead to an investigation. At the inception of an investigation, the FBI usually also becomes involved. If criminal activity is uncovered, the U.S. Justice Department gets in on the act to prosecute an alleged crime. As you can see, the government is all over the financial market. Its aim is to protect you, the investor.

There has been much financial legislation written and rewritten—voted into law and repealed—since the Great Depression. The Security Exchange Act of 1934 created the SEC, and the Commodity Futures Trading Act of 1974 created the CFTC. The Glass-Steagall Act of 1933 separated commercial and investment banking after the Great Depression. However, Treasury Secretary Robert Rubin and the Clinton administration orchestrated its repeal in 1999.

Meanwhile, the Foreign Corrupt Business Practices Act (FCBPA) became law in the United States in 1977. The two defining provisions of the FCBPA relate to accounting transparency and the banning of U.S. citizens from bribing foreign officials. FCBPA is a well-intentioned piece of legislation, but it places U.S. companies at a distinct disadvantage in relation to companies elsewhere. The agent in Taiwan who wanted me to give him $1 million in cash in exchange for an order to buy gold for the Central Bank of Taiwan did not care about the FCBPA. The oil producer in Nigeria does not care about the FCBPA. The cocoa producer in Ghana and the uranium producer in Kazakhstan do not care either. The FCBPA has inadvertently put U.S. companies out of the running when it comes to securing commodity staples in many parts of the world. The big question posed by the FCBPA is this: Can the United States impose its morality on other countries through legislation? The Sarbanes-Oxley Act, passed in 2002, sets new standards, rules, and regulations for publicly traded companies.

Many people have claimed that the repeal of the Glass-Steagall Act was at least partly to blame for the financial crisis that began in the summer of 2007, giving members of the banking community license to increase their risk-taking activities. The response to the financial crisis was the adoption of the Dodd-Frank Wall Street Reform and Consumer Protection Act of 2010. While the name may be long, it is not as long as the legislation itself—at 2,300 pages, this set of rules and regulations has effectively changed the free market status of trading and banking in the United States. In the wake of Dodd-Frank, the only area for employment growth in the U.S. banking and financial industry has been the compliance departments of the institutions themselves. Wall Street, banks, and other financial service providers continue their attempts to decipher Dodd-Frank and what the requirements are for compliance. While there is a tremendous amount of confusion about

Dodd-Frank, the act has expanded the power and reach of both the SEC and the CFTC.

Historically, increases in regulations are a direct result of increasing numbers of financial scandals. The SEC and the Glass-Steagall Act were a direct result of the Great Depression and abuses in the stock market that caused the 1929 crash. The creation of the CFTC was a reaction to the development of financial engineering and the use of new market products such as options and futures. The 2002 Sarbanes-Oxley Act was a result of the increasing number of corporate fraud scandals, such as the Enron, Tyco and WorldCom debacles.

The point here is that all these legislative developments have been reactive. There has yet to be a proactive piece of financial legislation. The U.S. government and its elected leaders, as a matter of course, have always rushed to make new rules after the fact. This is at the heart of the problem. Regulators have become firefighters. Proactive regulation prevents fires or market abuses by looking for smoke before a fire is blazing, while reactive regulation seeks to locate a fire that has already caused destruction. The problem is that it is usually too late "to protect" when the fires are found. Much of the legislation is long-winded and complicated, often the result of the political wrangling that gave birth to the regulations in the first place. Simple, easy-to-follow, commonsense rules and regulations will allow business to prosper and regulators to regulate. The biggest problem with the current state of U.S. regulation is that it has become difficult to really understand what the rules are and how to comply with them.

The majority of the world's liquid commodity futures markets are located in the United States and denominated in the greenback. The question becomes, but for how long? Regulators are present in other countries, such as the United Kingdom's Financial Services Author-ity and the European Parliament's 2003 Market Abuse Directive, which are in the process of being strengthened to include the com-modity markets. The trend of increasing market regulation continues in the United States and Europe. However, the financial might has been shifting steadily from the United States and Europe to Asia, and countries like China are not likely to subject themselves to the rules of the West. Philipp Brothers, the now defunct once largest commodity trading house in the world, which I worked for, could not compete in today's markets. New regulation has created an environment in which

U.S. companies must report all activities in detail in the various commodity markets. Historically commodity markets have been highly secretive—producers, consumers, and governments are particularly sensitive when it comes to reporting or publicity surrounding their activities. Many of these market participants do not believe that the laws of the United States or Europe should apply as they are doing business in parts of the world where the basis and foundations for these rules and regulations are not contained in the political and economic systems. If Philipp Brothers had been forced to disclose all activities across the globe that came across the desks of its offices in the United States and Europe, it would have been impossible for them to compete with foreign trading houses. These days, some of the most influential groups that specialize in physical commodity trading are based offshore— Glencore is based in Switzerland, and Nobel, another large commodity trading company, is based in Hong Kong.

Even with the increased regulation in the United States, scandal and market manipulation continue. A case in point is MF Global, a 200-year-old commodities brokerage firm that suffered scandal and bankruptcy in October 2011. The CFTC regulated MF Global directly and, in spite of Dodd-Frank directives, the regulator became aware of MF Global's indiscretions only after it was too late. Its demise was brought about by losses on speculative bets in European debt. The damage was already done by the time the CFTC arrived. This is but one example; there are many more.

As long as the majority of commodity futures exchanges remain in the United States, regulatory bodies will increase rules and regulations. More exchanges are opening all over the world each year. It is possible these exchanges will pull business and liquidity away from the heavily regulated U.S. (and European) exchanges in the future.

THE ROLE OF SPECULATORS AND TRADERS IN COMMODITIES

A lot of stones have been thrown at speculators and traders, particularly in recent years as commodity prices have risen. In fact, the Dodd-Frank legislation seeks specifically to limit the amount of speculation in commodity markets.

Joseph P. Kennedy II, the former congressman from Massachusetts, was quoted in the *New York Times* (April 11, 2012) as saying: "There are factors contributing to the high price of oil that we can do something about. Chief among them is the effect of 'pure' speculators—investors who buy and sell oil futures, but never take physical possession of actual barrels of oil. These middlemen add little value and lots of cost as they bid up the price of oil in pursuit of financial gain. They should be banned from the world's commodity exchanges, which could drive down the price of oil by as much as 40 percent and the price of gasoline by as much as $1 a gallon."

What Congressman Kennedy failed to understand is that speculators go short as often as they go long. As often as speculative activity in the commodity markets results in higher prices for consumers, the activity results in lower prices for consumers. Over time speculation is a zero sum game, so the congressman's comment indicates a naïveté in that he is highlighting only one side of a speculator's effect on the price of essential goods, in this case crude oil.

President Barack Obama remarked on April 17, 2012, during a speech from the Rose Garden of the White House that: "Rising gas prices means a rough ride for a lot of families. We can't afford a situation where speculators artificially manipulate markets by buying up oil, creating the perception of a shortage and driving prices higher, only to flip the oil for a quick profit."

Vermont Senator Bernie Sanders wrote on April 3, 2012, "Our bill requires the CFTC to invoke its emergency powers within 14 days to: (1) curb immediately the role of excessive speculation in any contract market ... on or through which energy futures are traded; and (2) eliminate excessive speculation, price distortion, sudden or unreasonable fluctuations or unwarranted changes in prices, or other unlawful activity that is causing major market disturbances that prevent the market from accurately reflecting the forces of supply and demand for energy commodities."

Senator Sanders takes the issue one step further. The senator's bill is in direct contrast to the free market system that results in fair market equilibrium prices over time. Think of the other ways that government influences prices of commodities; through farming subsidies, tariffs, tax breaks, and incentives. All these policies influence the price of many commodities. Senator Sanders's bill is not a free market solution but rather a system in which government agencies will manipulate prices that should ultimately be determined by buyers and sellers in a free, open, and transparent exchange of essential goods.

What all these well-meaning public officials fail to understand is that demographics, low interest rates, and increasing standards of living across the globe are causing commodity prices to rise. It is easy to blame the speculators, and it is a populist theme that resonates with voters. However their arguments and legislative proposals are fatally flawed in that the price of any commodity will ultimately be determined by supply-and-demand fundamentals. The "evil" speculators are short-term players in the larger context of the market, and their activities in buying and selling have little effect over time.

As you can see, there are many critics of speculation. However, the speculator's corner is defended by commodity trader, hedge fund manager, and best-selling author Victor Niederhoffer. He wrote in an article titled "The Speculator As Hero" published in February 1993, "Let's consider some of the principles that explain the causes of shortages and surpluses, and the role of speculators. When a harvest is too small to satisfy consumption at its normal rate, speculators come in, hoping to profit from the scarcity by buying. Their purchases raise the price, thereby checking consumption so that the smaller supply will last longer. Producers encouraged by the high price further lessen the shortage by growing or importing to reduce the shortage. On the other side, when the price is higher than the speculators think the facts warrant, they sell. This reduces prices, encouraging consumption and exports and helping reduce the surplus." (See http://www.fff.org/freedom/0293c.asp.)

Victor Niederhoffer has been trading commodities for many decades, and his comments represent a level-headed understanding of the role of speculators in the commodity markets.

In my opinion, commodity speculation is a zero-sum game and a short-term influence on markets, at best. I believe that speculators provide a market with liquidity when producers want to sell and consumers do not want to buy, and also when consumers want to buy but producers do not want to sell. This makes it possible for hedgers (producers and consumers), as well as arbitrageurs to transact. It is also worth noting that speculators risk their own capital. Sometimes they make money, and sometimes they lose.

The critics of speculation point only to markets that go up in price, such as crude oil and oil products in 2008 and 2011 to 2012 or grains in 2008. They have no interest in markets that fall on speculative activity, such as natural gas in 2011 and 2012. Think back to the comments of Guy Adami in the foreword to this book, "Commodity speculators today are often ridiculed and lambasted in the press for driving the prices of goods higher . . . These critics, however, often forget that speculators speculate on prices going higher *and* lower. During the spring and early summer of 2012, for example, there was a 30-percent–plus drop in the price of crude oil. Not surprisingly, there was no public outcry that accompanied such a dramatic move."

They also forget that commodity producers, like miners who invest huge sums of money in holes in the ground to mine metal, oil drillers who invest fortunes to drill, or farmers who plant seeds and pray for good growing conditions, are also big speculators.

Speculation will continue to be a hot-button topic with arguments on both sides. New products, such as ETFs and ETNs, have increased trading, individual investment, and liquidity for certain commodity futures. New trading techniques, such as high-frequency trading (HFT), have added volume, liquidity and action to the commodity markets. Both ETF/ETN investing and HFT are certainly forms of speculation.

Drawing a line between speculative and investment-related trading is not an easy task for a regulator. Nonetheless, I believe that the most efficient and effective markets are those that are free from all but simple and proactive regulation. There is a role for all types of market participants because the market price at any time is the right price. I believe that the role of the speculator is an important one that needs to be protected.

CHINA AND THE EMERGING MARKETS

China is a commodity powerhouse in terms of both production and consumption, and that gives it tremendous power in the markets. China also exploits its powerful position in the futures and physical commodity markets as a master manipulator of price. When China shows up in the grain or base metals markets, for example, its traders often play both sides of the market. Sometimes they are sellers, and sometimes they are buyers. When China is a buyer of a commodity, as it was with soybeans during 2012, after selling its strategic stockpiles the year before, it often stands aside when prices begin to drop. To make matters worse, China will sometimes sell into a weak market in which it eventually needs to buy, thus flushing out weak holders of a commodity through its selling. The Chinese method of trading is particularly dangerous to technical traders who rely solely on price patterns to take market positions. This allows China to buy at rock-bottom prices, as frustrated traders get stopped out of risk positions. Fear and greed are what drive most traders, and China is a master at recognizing and capitalizing on both. China's power in the commodity markets comes by virtue of the fact that it is the largest consumer in the world.

Moreover, China's massive consumption of commodities has resulted in another method of sourcing the commodities it needs. This rising economic powerhouse has made strategic investments all over the world to secure future supplies. For example, China has 30 percent of annual global production of rare earth metals within its borders and controls 97 percent of production in Africa, where many of these metals are found. China is also active in financing and investing in burgeoning commodity mining operations in regions in the Middle East and South America where natural resources abound, but capital for mining and developing industry is scarce. China knows that its vast and growing population will require these essential commodities for many years to come, and it is doing its best to lock in flows of staples and natural resources, rather than be dependent on the rest of the world. Indeed, given the current level of activity, the rest of the world will become dependent on China for commodity supplies in the future.

However, China is not the only powerhouse in the commodities game today. Emerging countries with huge populations like India, Indonesia, Brazil, Pakistan, and Nigeria will all require more essential goods in the coming years. With populations growing, commodity production costs rising, and wealth spreading to emerging markets, competition for commodities is sure to intensify and become fierce.

THE FUTURE OF COMMODITIES TRADING IN THE UNITED STATES

To be sure, the value of the U.S. dollar has plunged dramatically over the past three decades, causing the price of dollar-based commodities to rise. Government deficits in the United States and Europe have caused monetary authorities to keep interest rates low. Commodity prices feed on low interest-rate environments. However, it is hard to imagine that a rising $16 trillion U.S. deficit and sovereign debt issues in Europe, coupled with weakening paper currencies, will end well. Europe and the United States can ill afford entitlement programs and the loose fiscal management of yesteryear. Nonetheless, the road ahead appears to lead to inflation. Commodity prices, across the board, are showing signs of inflationary pressures.

At the same time, population growth and emerging wealth will create fierce competition for commodities in the years ahead. It is also quite possible that regulation, if too onerous, will backfire and cause commodity markets to move away from U.S. shores. Moreover, the U.S. dollar may not be the future currency of choice for pricing commodities, and that would only hasten the decline of the greenback as the reserve currency of the world. It may be just a matter of time.

The world is changing rapidly. Only a few years ago, the emerging markets were China, India, and Brazil. Now they include African countries, the Middle East, and nations like Burma, Cambodia, and Sri Lanka.

Commodity prices will continue to be volatile, as demand and populations grow and wealthier nations emerge. The fundamental supply-and-demand equation for most commodities is today more fragile than ever before, and that trend will continue tomorrow. The fragility of finite supplies and growing demands will have a profound impact on your investment portfolio in the years to come.

CHAPTER 11

How to Trade Commodities

Take calculated risks. That is quite different from being rash.
GENERAL GEORGE S. PATTON

This book is intended as a road map to help you improve your investment results and, consequently, your portfolio's yield. There is only one way to profit directly from a move in a commodity market, and that is to invest directly in commodity-related instruments, such as physical commodities, futures contracts, and options on futures contracts. This chapter offers advice on how to set up a trading account for commodity futures and options or derivatives. Also, please see the appendix, "Commodity Contracts and Exchanges," which provides you with contract information for many of the major liquid commodity futures and options markets covered in this book, as well as a list of commodity exchanges and the products they trade.

TRADING COMMODITIES DIRECTLY

You can trade commodity futures and options with or without a full-service broker. A number of electronic trading platforms offer commodities trading, and there are many full-service brokers who will execute, advise, and even trade for you. Some brokers offer managed accounts, in which professional traders or certified commodities trading advisors (CTAs) either pool or separately manage customer investment funds.

Commodity brokers and CTAs must pass a competency exam and register with the National Futures Association (NFA) to execute customer transactions. The exam ensures that a broker understands the market risks and the regulations surrounding futures trading, clearing, and brokerage. Brokers and CTAs are regulated by the CFTC. When selecting brokers, make sure they are licensed and that they clear futures and options transactions through a solid regulated clearing firm. The steps involved in setting up a trading account are as follows:

- **Selecting a broker:** Brokers advertise all over the Internet. It is a good idea to call the broker and speak to him or her directly. Ask for references. When setting up an electronic trading account in which commissions are much cheaper, you should always speak with a customer service representative as you go through the steps. Also, always check the NFA website (www.nfa.futures.org) to make sure that the broker is registered and has a clean record.
- **Paperwork:** A broker will require that you fill out account-opening forms, disclosure statements, and other documentation required by regulation. They are likely to ask for identity verification and proof of income.
- **Approval process:** You will generally have to wait a few days for approval. The broker will forward your paperwork to a compliance officer to make sure the paperwork is in order. If you are rejected, make sure to ask why. Some brokerage companies cater only to high-net-worth individuals. If this is the case, try another broker.
- **Funding your account:** Do not fund your account until you are approved. Check the funding instructions with your broker or a customer account representative in the case of electronic brokerage companies. Checks and wire transfers are generally accepted.

After your account is open and funded, you are ready to trade. But remember that markets move quickly and they are not for the faint of heart. It may be a good idea to start with buying options and then work up to buying and selling futures. When you buy an option, losses are minimal—all you can lose is the premium. Although options and futures markets move quickly and often violently, risk and opportunity always coexist.

TRADING AND INVESTMENT TIPS

Following is a list of some of the investment tips provided in this book. You may find that these tips are nothing more than common sense. These tips apply to many investment activities. I list them here because as a professional trader for many years I have always needed to remind myself of these concepts. During the heat of market action, it is human nature to get caught up in the moment and forget the important guiding principles that will enhance profits and limit losses:

- **Most people are lazy investors:** Do your homework before trading.
- **Practice discipline:** Before you enter a trade, decide exactly how much you want to risk and how much profit you desire. As a rule, make sure that the risk, at the very minimum, equals the reward (only risk a dollar to make a dollar or more; never risk a dollar to make 50 cents). Use stop orders and profit targets at the time of the trade. Enter orders to take profits and losses as soon as you enter a trade. Use GTC (good until cancelled orders) so that if you get distracted, you will not miss your levels.
- **Volatility analysis:** If you are buying options, check the historical versus implied volatility for the life of the option. As an example, if the option is a one-month option, check one-month historical volatility. If the implied volatility is equal to or lower than historical volatility, the option is fairly priced or cheap. If the implied volatility of the option is much greater than historical volatility, it is expensive. This is particularly true when it comes to at-the-money options.

- **Open interest and volume:** Check the open interest and volume figures for the future or option that you are contemplating. Refer to Chapter 1, "Technical Analysis," for a review of these concepts. Make sure that there is liquidity in the option or future that you select.
- **Supply-demand:** Make sure that you have an understanding of supply-and-demand fundamentals. The more information you have, the better your odds of making money.
- **Technical analysis:** Always keep an eye on price charts. Charts are a road map of whether other traders are buying or selling. Technical analysis will help you avoid getting run over by a herd.
- **Markets move for one reason:** Markets rise when there are more buyers than sellers, and markets move down when there are more sellers than buyers. Never forget this rule!
- **Options versus futures:** There are times when options are better investment vehicles than futures, and there are times when the opposite is true. Usually this depends on the relationship of historic versus implied volatility. Futures markets provide immediate pain or pleasure, while long options require patience and an extended move in order to realize profits. Only advanced investors and traders should consider selling options on commodity futures contracts.
- **Liquidity:** When trading futures and options, only trade in liquid markets. A liquid market will have a fair amount of volume and open interest. Try to avoid trading around the release of economic or commodity specific data. Markets tend to move violently in both directions upon the release of data.
- **Execute electronically or pick an excellent broker:** If you are comfortable with trading on an electronic platform, it is the cheaper method of execution. However, if you are new to this game or if you are more comfortable dealing with a person who will make your trades, make sure that you develop chemistry and a trusting relationship with your broker. If your broker makes you uncomfortable in any way or pressures you, find a different broker.

- **Always expect the unexpected:** The unexpected in futures and options trading is the norm. Markets move quickly, and there are many opportunities for profits. Wherever there is the opportunity for profit, there is also a risk of loss.
- **No one is smarter than the market:** Remember the market price is always the right price. If you are in a losing position and you feel uncomfortable, get out and take a fresh look later.
- **Discipline:** The most important characteristic of a successful commodity trader and investor is discipline. All traders get the market wrong, and they do so often. Good traders realize they are in the wrong position quickly and have the discipline to get out. The mistake that many traders and investors make is that they become like deer in the headlights and do not take their lumps early enough.
- **Information is power:** Read everything you can get your hands on. Make sure that you receive research reports from your broker. Become an information sponge.
- **Investment pace:** Always remember that investing is a long-term proposition. Slow and steady profits and small losses will win the race every time.

CHAPTER 12

Final Thoughts

The only true wisdom is in knowing you know nothing.
—SOCRATES

History tends to repeat itself, and markets are cyclical. Therefore, many of the concepts contained in this book are evergreen. This book is meant to serve as a ready reference and resource guide that you can apply to your investment knowledge base, while also providing you with the knowledge of how commodities can affect your investments overall. No matter what investments you contemplate to strengthen your portfolio, remember to always look at the commodity risk.

Analyze the commodity components of every company in your portfolio as well as every investment you add in the future. Watch the effect of commodity prices on your everyday life. You cannot imagine how useful your daily actions and observations as a commodity consumer will be once you sensitize yourself. It will add a new dimension to your investing, present new investment ideas and opportunities, and produce results. Your new knowledge is an investment calculus that, if used wisely, will allow you to navigate the markets with ease and confidence, and—best of all—profit handsomely.

Glossary

active month: The term for the nearby futures contract.

arbitrage: The process in which professional traders simultaneously buy and sell the same or equivalent commodities or securities for a riskless or limited risk profit. A technique employed to take advantage of differences in price. Arbitrage involves the simultaneous purchase of one futures, forward, or options contract and the sale of another, to profit from disparity in price relationships. Variations include simultaneous purchases and sales of futures contracts in the same asset with different delivery months or different exchanges (intracommodity spreads).

ask: The price at which a person is ready to sell. The ask price normally quoted is the lowest price at which anyone is willing to sell a commodity future, forward, or option.

assignment: The receipt of an exercise notice by an option writer (seller) that obligates him or her to sell (in the case of a call) or purchase (in the case of a put) the underlying commodity or security or to effect cash settlement at the specified strike price.

at-the-money option: The strike price of the option is equal to the market price of the underlying security or commodity.

backwardation: A market condition in which prices are lower in the future than they are in more immediate months.

basis: The price differential between the physical and futures markets.

bear market: A market in which prices are moving lower or the perception that prices will move lower.

bid: Often referred to as a quotation or quote, a bid is an offer to buy at a specific price. The bid is the highest price anyone has declared that he or she will pay for a commodity.

Black-Scholes option pricing formula: Described in F. Black, and M. Scholes, *Options Pricing Formula* (University of Chicago, 1973). This option pricing formula assumes that the underlying stock price follows a geometric Brownian motion with constant volatility. In the original option pricing formula published by Black and Scholes, values are established for a call price *c* and put price *p*. Log denotes the natural logarithm, and:

s = the price of the underlying stock

x = the strike price

r = the continuously compounded risk-free interest rate

t = the time in years until the expiration of the option

σ = the implied volatility for the underlying stock

Φ = the standard normal cumulative distribution function

breakout: A breakout occurs when a market moves outside of the trading range; below support or above resistance.

bull market: A market in which prices are moving higher or the perception that prices will move higher.

buy on close: To buy at the end of the trading session within a closing range of prices.

buy on opening: To buy at the beginning of the trading session at a price within the opening range of prices.

calendar spread: Simultaneous purchase and sale of futures contracts in the same asset with different delivery months (intracommodity spreads).

call option: An options contract that gives the holder the right, but not the obligation, to buy a specified amount of a commodity or security at a specified price for a specific period of time in the future.

cash market: The current cash price for the underlying market.

cash settlement: The process by which the terms of an option or futures contract are fulfilled through the payment or receipt of the amount by which the option or future is in the money and has intrinsic value.

cash settlement future: A future settled on a cash basis against a predetermined benchmark price or index.

clearing: The process by which the clearinghouse becomes the buyer to each seller and the seller to each buyer of a futures or options contract. The clearinghouse assumes responsibility for the performance of each contract and protects the buyer and seller from contractual default.

clearinghouse: The part of a futures exchange that acts as a buyer for all sellers and a seller for all buyers.

closing order: The buying back or selling of a position that closes out all or part of an existing position.

contango: A market condition in which prices are higher in the future than they are nearby.

contract month: The month in which delivery or settlement will occur in accordance with the terms of a futures or options contract.

contract trading volume: The number of contracts traded in a commodity or commodity delivery month during a specific period of time.

contract unit: The standardized amount for a commodity futures contract.

convergence: The term used to describe the price of a commodity gravitating to the underlying price of that commodity as delivery approaches.

crack spreads: Reflect the cost of processing or refining a barrel of crude oil into oil products.

crush spreads: Reflect the cost of processing soybeans into soybean meal and soybean oil.

day order: An order that will expire automatically at the end of each trading day or session.

deficit: A market condition in which demand exceeds supply.

delta: A value for the amount by which an option's price will change for a one-point change in price by the underlying entity. Call options have positive deltas, while put options have negative deltas.

electronic market: A computerized platform or medium that matches bids to buy and offers to sell.

equity: The total cash value of an account including the amount of unrealized profits and/or losses on existing positions.

equity market: A market in which equity securities trade, such as stocks.

exchange traded: Futures and options traded on a regulated exchange.

exercise: The act of taking advantage of the right to buy or sell the underlying futures contract at the agreed-upon strike price of an option.

expense ratios: Fees charged for exchange-traded fund (ETF) products.

expiration date: The day or time on which an option contract becomes void. Holders of options should indicate their desire to exercise, if they wish to do so, by this date.

exponential moving average: A method for calculating the moving average for a large distribution or a large number of periods.

fill or kill order: An order to execute a transaction immediately or to cancel the order.

forward market: A market for the trading of cash forward contracts, that is non-exchange contracts, for any amount of a commodity or security, for any quality, delivered or cash settled at a time and place mutually agreed upon by the buyer and seller.

forward transaction (forward contract): A principal-to-principal contract between a buyer and seller in which all terms are negotiated and mutually agreed upon between the two parties.

forward value: The price agreed upon by a buyer and a seller in a forward contract.

front to back spread: Simultaneous purchase and sale of futures contracts in the same asset with different delivery months (intracommodity spreads).

fundamental analysis: The examination of underlying factors of supply and demand in an attempt to determine market behavior and, therefore, allows one to profit from anticipating price trends.

futures price: The price of a commodity or a security determined by public auction on a futures exchange or an electronic medium.

futures transaction (futures contract): A contract traded on a futures exchange for delivery of a specified amount of a commodity or security, or for settlement on a cash basis at a future date.

gamma: A value for how fast or how much the delta of an option changes as the underlying futures change.

good until cancelled order (GTC): A buy or sell order that remains active until executed or cancelled.

hedge: A conservative strategy used to limit loss by effecting a transaction that offsets an existing position.

hedging: The use of a futures, forward, or options position to reduce price risk. It involves the purchase or sale of a forward contract, a futures contract, or an options contract as a temporary substitute for a cash market transaction that will occur later.

high-frequency trading (algorithmic trading): The use of quantitative models to trade large volumes at a high frequency; often used in a futures market.

historical volatility: The measure of volatility or variance that a market has exhibited through historical behavior.

implied volatility: A measure of the volatility of the underlying stock or commodity determined by using option prices currently existing in the market at the time rather than using historical data on the price changes of the underlying stock or commodity; the option market's perception of future volatility.

index: A compilation of the prices of several common entities into a single number.

index option: An option whose underlying entity is an index.

intercommodity spread: The purchase of one commodity futures contract for a particular month and the simultaneous sale of another related commodity futures contract for exactly the same time period.

in-the-money option: Any option that has intrinsic value. A call option is in the money if the underlying security or commodity is higher than the strike price of the call, and a put option is in the money if the security or commodity is below the strike price of the put.

intracommodity spread: The purchase of a futures contract and the simultaneous sale of another futures contract for a different month in the same commodity on the same exchange.

intrinsic value: The value of an option if it were to expire immediately with the underlying stock or commodity at its current price. For call options, this is the difference between the stock or commodity forward or futures price and the strike price, if that difference is a positive number, and zero otherwise. For put options, this is the difference between the strike price and the stock or commodity forward or futures price, if that difference is positive, and zero otherwise.

leverage: The control of a large amount of an asset with a small amount of capital.

limit order: An order to buy or sell at a specified price or better. Also called a *resting order.*

liquid market: An actively traded market; a market that has a large number of buyers and sellers.

liquidation: The offsetting of a futures or options position.

location spread: The simultaneous purchase and sale of a commodity of the same or similar quality in two different locations.

long position: A position in which an investor's interest in a particular series of forwards, futures, and/or options is as a net holder (i.e., the number of contracts bought exceeds the number of contracts sold).

margin: A good-faith deposit or performance bond that acts as collateral against futures or options positions.

mark to market: An accounting process in which the prices of securities or commodities held in an account are valued each day to reflect the last sale price or market quote if the last sale is outside the market quote.

market if touched (MIT) order: An order that becomes a market order when the commodity or security touches a specified price or better. An MIT order to sell becomes a market order when the commodity or security trades or is bid at or above the MIT price. An MIT order to buy becomes a market order when the commodity or security trades or is offered at or below the MIT price. Also called a *board order.*

market maker: Provides a two-way price (bid and offer) to other market participants.

market on close order: An order to buy or sell during the close.

market on opening order: An order to buy or sell during the opening.

market order: A buy or sell order executed at the best available prevailing market price.

model: A mathematical formula designed to price an option as a function of certain variables—generally stock or commodity price, strike price, volatility, time to expiration, dividends (if any) to be paid, and the current risk-free interest rate. A mathematical algorithm used in high-frequency trading or algorithmic trading.

moving average: A series of calculations used to spot trends that develop over time. This technique offsets the effect of a widely varying range by identifying the typical past experience and likely future experience.

nearby months: Months with the shortest maturity in terms of futures contracts.

offer: A proposal to sell at a given price (versus bid).

offset: The liquidation of a long or short futures or options position.

on close: An order instructing the broker to buy or sell during the close of the trading session.

on opening: An order instructing the broker to buy or sell during the opening of the trading session.

open interest: The total number of long and short positions.

open outcry: Brokers calling out in a loud, clear voice for any other broker to hear their bids and offers in the trading pits or rings of commodity exchanges.

opening: That specific period of time designated by an exchange at the start of the trading session during which all transactions are considered made "at the opening."

opening order: An order to buy or sell at a price that is within the opening range.

option: The right, but not the obligation, to purchase or sell a specified amount of a commodity or security at a specified price within a specified period of time.

option premium: The price the buyer pays and the seller gets for transacting the option.

original margin (or **initial margin**): The amount of money that is required to be deposited in an account when a futures or options position is established.

out-of-the-money option: Any option that has no intrinsic value. For example, a call option is out of the money if the strike price is greater than the market price of the underlying security or commodity, and a put option is out of the money if the strike price is less than the market price of the underlying security or commodity.

over the counter (OTC): An option or future traded off-exchange, as opposed to a listed stock or commodity option or future. The OTC future or option has a direct link between buyer and seller, has no secondary market, and has no standardization of strike prices and expiration dates or quantity.

pin risk: The risk associated with being long or short on an at-the-money option on expiration day. The long or short does not know whether or not the option will be exercised until the final market price is known.

position: An interest in the market demonstrated by buying or selling futures, forwards, or option contracts. One with a long position has bought the futures, forwards, or options. One with a short position has sold the futures, forwards, or options.

position limit: The maximum number of contracts a speculator may control in a particular futures contract at any time.

processing spread: The difference between two related commodities where one traded commodity is the product of another. Crack spreads between oil and oil products, crush spreads between soybeans and soybean products, and ethanol versus corn spreads are examples of processing spreads.

put option: An options contract that gives the holder the right, but not the obligation, to sell a specified amount of a commodity or security at a specified price for a specific period of time in the future.

quality spread: The exchange of one grade of a commodity for another.

resistance: A level that is above the current price. Resistance means that at a certain price technical analysts believe that sellers will outnumber buyers.

rho: A value of the option's sensitivity to changes in interest rates.

roll: The transfer of one futures contract to another futures contract in the same commodity on the same exchange.

scalper: A member of the exchange who day trades for his or her personal account many times in a single trading session in hopes of making a small profit on each day trade.

settlement price: The price a clearinghouse employs to determine the unrealized profit or loss on all open contracts on a daily basis. Also called the *clearing price*.

short position: A position in which a person's interest in a particular series of forwards, futures, and/or options is as a net writer or seller (i.e., the number of contracts sold exceeds the number of contracts bought). It refers to one who sells and does not own the underlying commodity or security.

speculation: The process of buying and selling forwards, futures, and options for the purpose of making a profit. A speculator will buy forwards, futures, and/or options if he or she expects that the price will rise and will sell forwards, futures, and/or options if he or she expects that the price will fall.

spot transaction: This occurs when the seller transfers title to the buyer for cash.

spread: (1) The simultaneous purchase of one commodity forward or futures contract against the sale of the same or a related commodity forward or future. (2) The purchase or sale of puts and calls on the same forward or futures contract with different expiration dates and/or strike prices.

stop-limit order: An order to buy or sell at a specified price or better if the contract trades at or through a specified price. A sell stop-limit order becomes a limit order once the commodity trades at or below the specified price. A buy stop-limit order becomes a buy limit order if the contract trades at or above the specified price.

stop order: An order to buy or sell at the market if the contract trades at or through a specified price (the stop price).

strike price (exercise price): The stated price per share or unit for which the underlying security or commodity may be purchased (in the case of a call option) or sold (in the case of a put option) by the option holder upon exercise of the options contract, as defined in the terms of the options contract.

strike price gravitation: The tendency of futures prices to gravitate to the put and call strike prices with the largest total open interest on the day of expiration of the options.

substitution: The process of using another related commodity for economic reasons. Substitution can be supply- or demand-driven.

support: A level below the current price. Support means that at a certain price technical analysts believe that buyers will outnumber sellers.

surplus: A market condition in which supply exceeds demand.

swap transaction: The exchange of a fixed price for a floating price.

technical analysis: The study of past price movements.

theoretical value: The price of an option, or a combination of options, as computed by a mathematical model.

theta: A value for the rate at which an option loses its value as time passes; that is, a measure of the rate of change in an option's theoretical value for a one-unit change in time to the option's expiration date. Also known as *time decay* of an option.

tick value: The minimum price fluctuation per futures contract.

time spreads: Simultaneous purchases and sales of futures contracts in the same asset with different delivery months (intracommodity spreads). Also called a *calendar spread*.

time value: The amount of option premium that exceeds its intrinsic value.

trend: Occurs when a market moves and continues to follow in the same direction.

valuation: The attribution of worth to a commodity or security.

variation margin: A deposit in a futures account that restores the equity in the account back to the original margin requirement.

vega: A value for how much an option will increase in value as the volatility rises.

volatility (variance): The degree of deviation in a distribution of values, in this case, a measure of how spread out a distribution of prices is from a mean price.

volume: The total number of purchases and sales (trades) made during a trading session.

Commodity Contracts
and Exchanges

Market specifications for *selected* commodity contracts are found in Table A.1. Any commodity not listed can be found on its exchange website. A selected list of commodity exchanges around the world can be found in Table A.2.

Table A.1 **Selected Market Specs for Future Reference**

Commodity	Exchange	Symbol	Pit Hours *	Electronic Hours *, †
Gold	COMEX on GLOBEX	GC	8:20 AM - 1:30 PM	6:00 PM - 5:15 PM
Mini Gold	GLOBEX	MQO	Electronic Only	6:00 PM - 5:15 PM
Micro Gold	COMEX on GLOBEX	MGC	Electronic Only	6:00 PM - 5:15 PM
Silver	COMEX on GLOBEX	SI	8:25 AM - 1:25 PM	6:00 PM - 5:15 PM
Mini Silver	COMEX on GLOBEX	MQI	Electronic Only	6:00 PM - 5:15 PM
Platinum	NYMEX on GLOBEX	PL	8:20 AM - 1:05 PM	6:00 PM - 5:15 PM
Palladium	NYMEX on GLOBEX	PA	8:30 AM - 1:00 PM	6:00 PM - 5:15 PM
Copper	COMEX on GLOBEX	CP	8:10 AM - 1:00 PM	6:00 PM - 5:15 PM
Copper	E-Mini COMEX	MQC	8:10 AM - 1:00 PM	6:00 PM - 5:15 PM
Copper	LME	LDKZ	10:00 PM - 2:00 PM	10:00 PM - 2:00 PM
Copper	LME Mini	MCD	10:00 PM - 2:00 PM	10:00 PM - 2:00 PM
Aluminum	LME	LALZ	10:00 PM - 2:00 PM	10:00 PM - 2:00 PM
Aluminum	LME Mini	MAD	10:00 PM - 2:00 PM	10:00 PM - 2:00 PM
Nickel	LME	LNIZ	10:00 PM - 2:00 PM	10:00 PM - 2:00 PM
Lead	LME	LEDZ	10:00 PM - 2:00 PM	10:00 PM - 2:00 PM
Zinc	LME	LZHZ	10:00 PM - 2:00 PM	10:00 PM - 2:00 PM
Zinc	LME MINI	MZD	10:00 PM - 2:00 PM	10:00 PM - 2:00 PM
Tin	LME	LTIZ	10:00 PM - 2:00 PM	10:00 PM - 2:00 PM
Steel	LME	FDMZ	10:00 PM - 2:00 PM	10:00 PM - 2:00 PM
Crude Oil (WTI)	NYMEX on GLOBEX	CL	9:00 AM - 2:30 PM	6:00 PM - 5:15 PM
Mini Crude	NYMEX on GLOBEX	NQM	9:00 AM - 2:30 PM	6:00 PM - 5:15 PM
Crude Oil (Brent)	ICE Futures	B	7:55 PM - 6:00 PM	7:55 PM - 6:00 PM
Heating Oil	NYMEX on GLOBEX	HO	9:00 AM - 2:30 PM	6:00 PM - 5:15 PM
RBOB Gasoline	NYMEX on GLOBEX	RB	9:00 AM - 2:30 PM	6:00 PM - 5:15 PM
Natural Gas	NYMEX on GLOBEX	NG	9:00 AM - 2:30 PM	6:00 PM - 5:15 PM
Wheat	CBOT on GLOBEX	ZWA	10:30 AM - 2:15 PM	7:00 PM - 8:15 AM
Mini Wheat	CBOT on GLOBEX	XW	10:30 AM - 2:45 PM	7:00 PM - 8:15 AM
Kansas City Wheat	KC Board of Trade-GLOBEX	KW	10:30 AM - 2:15 PM	7:00 PM - 8:15 AM
Minneapolis Spring Wheat	Minn Grain Exch-GLOBEX	MW	10:30 AM - 2:30 PM	7:00 PM - 8:15 AM
Corn	CBOT on GLOBEX	ZC	10:30 AM - 2:15 PM	7:00 PM - 8:15 AM

Contract Size	Active Months	Quoted In	Tick Value	Options
100 ounces	GJMQVZ	$ per ounce	10 cents = $10	YES
50 ounces	GJMQVZ	$ per ounce	25 cents = $12.50	NO
10 ounces	GJMQVZ	$ per ounce	10 cents = $1	NO
5,000 ounces	HKNUZ	cents per ounce	0.5 cents = $25	YES
2,500 ounces	HKNUZ	cents per ounce	1.25 cents = $31.25	NO
50 ounces	HKNUZ	$ per ounce	10 cents = $5	YES
100 ounces	HMUZ	$ per ounce	5 cents = $5	NO
25,000 pounds	All	cents per pound	0.05 cents = $12.50	YES
12,500 pounds	All	cents per pound	0.02 cents = $5.00	NO
25 tons	90-day forward	$ per ton	25 cents = $6.25	YES
5 tons	All	$ per ton	25 cents = $1.25	NO
25 tons	90-day forward	$ per ton	25 cents = $6.25	YES
5 tons	All	$ per ton	25 cents = $1.25	NO
6 tons	90-day forward	$ per ton	$1 = $5.00	YES
25 tons	90-day forward	$ per ton	$1 = $6.00	YES
25 tons	90-day forward	$ per ton	25 cents = $6.25	YES
5 tons	All	$ per ton	25 cents = $1.25	NO
5 tons	90-day forward	$ per ton	$1 = $5.00	YES
65 tons	90-day forward	$ per ton	10 cents = $6.50	NO
1,000 barrels	All	$ per barrel	1 cent = $10	YES
500 barrels	All	$ per barrel	2.5 cents = $12.50	NO
1,000 barrels	All	$ per barrel	1 cent = $10	YES
42,000 gallons	All	cents per gallon	.01 cent = $4.20	YES
42,000 gallons	All	cents per gallon	.01 cent = $4.20	YES
10,000 mmbtu	All	cents per mmbtu	.1 cent = $10	YES
5,000 bushels	HKNUZ	cents per bushel	.25 cent = $12.50	YES
500 bushels	HKNUZ	cents per bushel	.25 cent = $1.25	NO
5,000 bushels	HKNUZ	cents per bushel	.25 cent = $12.50	YES
5,000 bushels	HKNUZ	cents per bushel	.25 cent = $12.50	YES
5,000 bushels	HKNUZ	cents per bushel	.25 cent = $12.50	YES

Table A.1 **Selected Market Specs for Future Reference (Continued)**

Commodity	Exchange	Symbol	Pit Hours *	Electronic Hours *, †
Mini Corn	CBOT on GLOBEX	XC	10:30 AM - 2:45 PM	7:00 PM - 8:15 AM
Soybeans	CBOT on GLOBEX	ZS	10:30 AM - 2:15 PM	7:00 PM - 8:15 AM
Mini Soybeans	CBOT on GLOBEX	YK	10:30 AM - 2:45 PM	NA
Soybean Oil	CBOT on GLOBEX	ZL	10:30 AM - 2:15 PM	7:00 PM - 8:15 AM
Soybean Meal	CBOT on GLOBEX	ZM	10:30 AM - 2:15 PM	7:00 PM - 8:15 AM
Rice	CBOT on GLOBEX	ZR	10:30 AM - 2:15 PM	7:00 PM - 8:15 AM
Oats	CBOT on GLOBEX	ZO	10:30 AM - 2:15 PM	7:00 PM - 8:15 AM
Sugar	ICE Futures	SB	8:10 AM - 1:30 PM	3:30 AM - 2:00 PM
Coffee	ICE Futures	KC	8:00 AM - 1:30 PM	3:30 AM - 2:00 PM
Cocos	ICE Futures	CC	8:00 AM - 11:50 AM	4:00 AM - 2:00 PM
Orange Juice	ICE Futures	OJ	10:00 AM - 2:00 PM	8:00 AM - 2:00 PM
Cotton	ICE Futures	CT	8:15 AM - 2:15 PM	9:00 PM - 2:30 PM
Lumber	CME on GLOBEX	LBS	10:00 AM - 2:55 PM	6:00 PM - 5:00 PM
Live Cattle	CME on GLOBEX	GL	10:05 AM - 2:00 PM	6:00 PM - 5:00 PM
Feeder Cattle	CME on GLOBEX	GF	10:05 AM - 2:00 PM	6:00 PM - 5:00 PM
Lean Hogs	CME on GLOBEX	HE	10:05 AM - 2:00 PM	6:00 PM - 5:00 PM

* All market hours are Eastern Standard Time and are subject to change. Monday–Thursday maintenance shutdown from 5:30 PM to 6:00 PM.
  Sunday trading begins at 6 PM.

*, † Multiple closes and reopenings during electronic session. Electronic grains also trade during day session alongside open outcry pit trading.

Contract Size	Active Months	Quoted In	Tick Value	Options
500 bushels	HKNUZ	cents per bushel	.25 cent = $1.25	NO
5,000 bushels	FHKNQUX	cents per bushel	.25 cent = $12.50	YES
500 bushels	FHKNQUX	cents per bushel	.25 cent = $1.25	NO
60,000 pounds	FHKNQUVZ	cents per pound	.01 cent = $6.00	YES
100 tons	FHKNQUVZ	cents per ton	10 cents = $10	YES
2,000 CWT	FHKNUX	cents per CWT	.5 cents = $10	YES
5,000 bushels	HKNUZ	cents per bushel	.25 cent = $12.50	YES
112,000 pounds	HKNV	cents per pound	.01 cent = $11.20	YES
37,500 pounds	HKNUZ	cents per pound	.05 cents = $18.75	YES
10 tons	HKNUZ	$ per ton	$1 = $10	YES
15,000 pounds	FHKNUX	cents per pound	.05 cents= $7.50	YES
50,000 pounds	HKNVZ	cents per pound	.01 cents = $5	YES
110,000 board feet	FHKNUX	cents per BF	.01 cents = $11	YES
40,000 pounds	GJMQVZ	cents per pound	.025 cents = $10	YES
50,000 pounds	FHUKQUVX	cents per pound	.025 cents = $12.5	YES
40,000 pounds	GJKMNQVZ	cents per pound	.025 cents = $10	YES

Table A.2   **Global Commodity Exchanges**

Continent	Exchange	Location
Africa	Africa Mercantile Exchange	Nairobi, Kenya
Africa	Ethiopia Commodity Exchange	Addis Ababa, Ethiopia
Africa	Agricultural Commodity Exchange for Africa	Lilongwe, Malawi
Africa	Mercantile Exchange of Madagascar	Antananarivo, Madagascar
Americas	Brazilian Mercantile and Futures Exchange	São Paulo, Brazil
Americas	Chicago Board of Trade (CME Group)	Chicago, United States
Americas	Chicago Mercantile Exchange (CME Group)	Chicago, United States
Americas	Chicago Climate Exchange	Chicago, United States
Americas	Houston Street Exchange	New Hampshire, United States
Americas	Intercontinental Exchange	Atlanta, Georgia, United States
Americas	Kansas City Board of Trade	Kansas City, United States
Americas	Memphis Cotton Exchange	Memphis, United States
Americas	Mercado a Termino de Buenos Aires	Buenos Aires, Argentina
Americas	Mercado a Termino de Rosario Financial	Rosario, Argentina
Americas	Minneapolis Grain Exchange	Minneapolis, United States
Americas	North American Derivatives Exchange	Chicago, United States
Americas	New York Mercantile Exchange (CME Group)	New York, United States
Asia	International Commodity Exchange Kazakhstan	Almaty Kazakhstan
Asia	Agricultural Futures Exchange of Thailand	Bangkok, Thailand
Asia	Asian Derivative Exchange	Kathmandu, Nepal
Asia	Borsa Malaysia	Malaysia
Asia	Cambodian Mercantile Exchange	Phnom Penh, Cambodia
Asia	Central Japan Commodity Exchange	Nagoya, Japan
Asia	Dalian Commodity Exchange	Dalian, China
Asia	Derivatives and Commodity Exchange	Kathmandu, Nepal
Asia	Dubai Mercantile Exchange	Dubai, UAE
Asia	Dubai Gold & Commodities Exchange	Dubai, UAE
Asia	Hong Kong Mercantile Exchange	Hong Kong
Asia	Iran Mercantile Exchange	Tehran, Iran
Asia	Iranian Oil Bourse	Kish Island, Iran
Asia	Kansai Commodities Exchange	Osaka, Japan
Asia	Commodities & Metal Exchnage Nepal Ltd.	Nepal

Exchange Abbreviation	Commodities Offered
AfMX	Agricultural and energy products
ECX	Agricultural products
ACE	Agricultural products
MEX	Agricultural products
BMF	Agricultural products, Biofuels, Precious Metals
CBOT	Grains, Ethanol, Metals
CME	Animal Protein (Meats)
CCX	Emission Allowances
NA	Crude Oil, Distillates
ICE	Energy, Emission Allowances, Agricultural Products, Biofuels
KCBT	Agricultural products
NA	Agricultural products
MATba	Agricultural products
ROFEX	Agricultural products
MGEX	Agricultural products
NADEX	Metals, Energy, Agricultural products
NYMEX or COMEX	Energy, Precious Metals, Industrial Metals
NA	Spot Trading in a variety of commodities
AFET	Agricultural products
ADX	Energy, Industrial Metals, Precious Metals
MDEX	Biofuels
CMEX	Energy, Metals, Rubber, Precious Metals, Agricultural products
NA	Energy, Industrial Metals, Rubber
DCE	Agricultural products, Energy & Agricultural Commodities
DCX	Agricultural products, Energy & Agricultural Commodities
DME	Energy
DGCX	Precious Metals
HKMEx	Gold, Silver
IME	Minerals, Oil products, Petrochemicals, Agricultural products
IOB	Oil, Gas, Petrochemicals
KANEX	Agricultural products
COMEN	Gold and Silver

Table A.2 **Global Commodity Exchanges (Continued)**

Continent	Exchange	Location
Asia	National Spot Exchange Limited	Mumbai, India
Asia	Nepal Derivative Exchange Limited	Kathmandu, Nepal
Asia	Mercantile Exchange Nepal Limited	Kathmandu, Nepal
Asia	Nepal Spot Exchange Limited	Kathmandu, Nepal
Asia	Indian Commodity Exchange Limited	India
Asia	Multi-Commodity Exchange	India
Asia	National Multi-Commodity Exchange of India Ltd.	India
Asia	Pakistan Mercantile Exchange Limited	Pakistan
Asia	Bhatinda Om & Oil Exchange Ltd.	India
Asia	Pakistan Mercantile Exchange	Pakistan
Asia	Shanghai Futures Exchange	Shanghai, China
Asia	Shanghai Gold Exchange	Shanghai, China
Asia	Singapore Commodity Exchange	Singapore
Asia	Singapore Mercantile Exchange	Singapore
Asia	Tokyo Commodity Exchange	Tokyo, Japan
Asia	Tokyo Grain Exchange	Tokyo, Japan
Asia	Zhengzhou Commodity Exchange	Zhengzhou, China
Asia	Vietnam Commodity Exchange	Ho Chi Minh City, Vietnam
Asia	Buon Ma Thuot Coffee Exchange Center	Buon Ma Thuot, Vietnam
Europe	APX-ENDEX	Amsterdam, Netherlands
Europe	Commodity Exchange Bratislava, JSC	Bratislava, Slovakia
Europe	Climex	Amsterdam, Netherlands
Europe	NYSE LIFFE	Europe
Europe	European Climate Exchange	Europe
Europe	Energy Exchange Austria	Vienna, Austria
Europe	London Metal Exchange	London, UK
Europe	Risk Management Exchange	Hannover, Germany
Europe	European Energy Exchange	Leipzig, Germany
Oceania	Australian Securities Exchange	Sydney, Australia
Oceania	Australian Bullion Exchange	Brisbane, Australia

Exchange Abbreviation	Commodities Offered
NSEL	Spot Trading in commodites
NDEX	Agricultural products, Precious Metals, Base Metals, Energy
MEX	Agricultural products, Precious Metals, Base Metals, Energy
NSE	Agricultural products, Precious Metals
ICEK	Energy, Precious Metals, Base Metals, Agricultural products
MCX	Precious Metals, Metals, Energy, Agricultural products
NMCE	Precious Metals, Metals, Agricultural products
PMEX	Precious Metals, Agricultural products
BOOE	Agricultural products
PMEX	Metals, Agricultural products, other commodities
SHFE	Industrial metals, Gold, Fuel Oil, Rubber
SHFE	Gold, Silver, Platinum
SICOM	Agricultural products, Rubber
SMX	Precious Metals, Base Metals, Agricultural products, Energy
TOCOM	Energy, Precious Metals, Industrial Metals, Agricultural products
TGE	Agricultural products
CZCE	Agricultural products, Terephthalic acid
VNX	Coffee, Rubber, Steel
BCEC	Coffee
APX-ENDEX	Energy
CEB	Emission Allowances, Agricultural products, Diamonds
CLIMEX	Emission Allowances
LIFFE	Agricultural products
ECX	Emission Allowances
EXAA	Electricity, Emission Allowances
LME	Industrial Metals, Plastics
RMX	Agricultural products
EEX	Energy, Emission Allowances
ASX	Agricultural products, Electricity, Thermal Coal & Natural Gas
ABX	Precious Metals

The exchange symbols used on U.S. exchanges for each of the twelve months of the year are as follows:

Month	Symbol
January	F
February	G
March	H
April	J
May	K
June	M
July	N
August	Q
September	U
October	V
November	X
December	Z

Commodity exchanges and references around the world are listed here by commodity and sector:

Energy
ASX: http://www.asx.com.au/
ICE: https://www.theice.com/homepage.jhtml
NYMEX division of CME: http://www.cmegroup.com/trading/energy/
TOCOM: http://www.tocom.or.jp/

Industry/Government/Supranational Websites
API: http://www.api.org/
EIA: http://www.eia.gov/
OPEC: http://www.opec.org/opec_web/en/
Platts: http://www.platts.com/
World Coal: http://www.worldcoal.org/

Precious Metals Exchange Websites
BM&FBOVESPA: http://www.bmfbovespa.com.br/en-us/home
    .aspx?idioma=en-us
COMEX division of CME: http://www.cmegroup.com/trading/metals/
SMX: http://www.smx.com.sg/
TOCOM: http://www.tocom.or.jp/

Industry/Government/Supranational Websites
IMF: http://www.imf.org/external/index.htm
LBMA: http://www.lbma.org.uk/pages/index.cfm
LCH: http://www.lchclearnet.com/
LPPM: http://www.lppm.com/

The Silver Institute: http://www.silverinstitute.org/site/
World Gold Council: http://www.gold.org/

Base Metals
COMEX division of CME: http://www.cmegroup.com/trading/metals/
LME: http://www.lme.com

Industry/Government/Supranational Websites
LCH: http://www.lchclearnet.com/
The Aluminum Assoc.: http://aluminum.org/
American Tin Trade Assoc.: http://tintrade.org/
Copper Development Assoc.: http://www.copper.org/
The International Zinc Assoc.: http//www.zinc.org/
Lead Sheet Manufacturers: http://www.leadsheetassociation.org.uk/
    lsa-members
The Nickel Institute: http://www.nickelinstitute.org/

Grains/Meats/Soft Commodities Exchange Websites
ASX: http://www.asx.com.au/products/commodities.htm
BM & FBOVESPA: http://www.bmfbovespa.com.br/en- us/home
    .aspx?idioma=en-us
CBOT division of CME: http://www.cmegroup.com/trading/agricultural/
DCE: http://www.dce.com.cn/portal/cate?cid=1114494099100
ICE: https://www.theice.com/homepage.jhtml
KCBT: http://www.kcbt.com/
LIFFE: https://globalderivatives.nyx.com/
MGE: http://www.mgex.com/
TGE: http://www.tge.or.jp/english/index.shtml
ZCE: http://english.czce.com.cn/

Industry/Government/Supranational Websites
American Assoc. of Cereal Chemists: www.aaccnet.org
American Corn Growers Assoc.: www.acga.org
Cocoa Merchants Assoc. of America: http://www.cocoamerchants.com/
Corn Refiners Assoc.: www.corn.org
European Cocoa Association: http://www.eurococoa.com/
Florida Citrus Processors Assoc.: http://www.fcplanet.org/members.html
International Cocoa Association: http://www.icco.org/
International Coffee Organization: http://www.ico.org/
National Corn Growers Assoc.: www.ncga.com
National Livestock Assoc.: http://www.nlpa.org/
North American Millers Assoc.: www.nama.org
The Sugar Association: http://www.sugar.org/
USDA: http://www.usda.gov/wps/portal/usda/usdahome
U.S. Grains Council: www.grains.org

Other Commodities Exchange Websites
CBOT division of CME: http://www.cmegroup.com/trading/agricultural/
CME Fertilizer Swaps: http://www.cmegroup.com/trading/agricultural/
    fertilizer-swap-futures.html
CME Uranium: http://www.cmegroup.com/trading/metals/other/uranium.html
CME Weather: http://www.cmegroup.com/trading/weather/
COMEX division of CME: http://www.cmegroup.com/trading/metals/
EEX: http://www.eex.com/
GreenX: http://www.thegreenx.com/products/index.html
ICE: https://www.theice.com/homepage.jhtml
LME: http://www.lme.com/
LME Minor Metals: http://www.lme.com/minormetals/index.asp
SHFE: http://www.shfe.com.cn/Ehome/index.jsp

Industry/Government/Supranational Websites
ISSB: http://www.issb.co.uk/global.html
LCH: http://www.lchclearnet.com/
National Cotton Council of Am.: http://www.cotton.org/
World Steel Organization: http://www.worldsteel.org/

Commodities Regulatory Agencies
CFTC: http://www.cftc.gov/index.htm
FSA: http://www.fsa.gov.uk/
NFA: http://www.nfa.futures.org
SEC: http://www.sec.gov/

Resources and
Further Reading

The following URLs and bibliographical references indicate source material for content throughout the chapters, along with useful further reading and information.

Introduction
Jim Rogers, *JimRogers.com*, "Breakfast of Champions?" 2012, http://www.jimrogers
.com/content/stories/articles/Breakfast_Cereals.html
http://www.guardian.co.uk/business/2010/aug/16/chinese-economic-boom)
http://blogs.ft.com/the-world/2011/01/when-will-china-become-the-worlds-largest
-economy/#axzz1rwwhxyf9)
http://rationalview.homestead.com/files/us_mad_cow_scare.htm)
http://europeanhistory.about.com/od/thefrenchrevolution/a/hfr7.htm
http://thehistorybox.com/ny_city/riots/riots_article11a.htm

Chapter 1
http://www.futuresmag.com/2008/07/15/funnymentals
http://topics.nytimes.com/topics/reference/timestopics/subjects/s/strategic_
petroleum_reserve_us/index.html
http://www.ft.com/intl/cms/s/0/9fac1c44–7cb7–11e1–8a27–00144feab49a
.html#axzz1sLU
http://www.forextradingplus.com/chart-patterns.htm#Cup%20and%20Handle
http://candlestickforum.com/PPF/Parameters/16_20_/candlestick.asp
http://www.acrotec.com/ewt.htm

Chapter 2

http://www.globelawandbusiness.com/Interviews/Detail.aspx?g=14be1e71-4b20
-421b-bcc2-6f86f51f809d

http://legal-dictionary.thefreedictionary.com/bill+of+lading

http://www.efinancialnews.com/story/2011–11–16/otc-derivatives-top–700-trillion

http://www.optiontradingpedia.com/history_of_options_trading.htm

https://www.etrade.wallst.com/v1/stocks/snapshot/snapshot.asp?YYY220_/
UfRI8EalsDNDoN+yIV40qr5WVGEn8cQzW9xSdWWCGroVsRTAdKeD
-JzNAwM5xeMSVDlEGxLGfu9m8k0Lrka7VHSsGMEaof+30H7GgyWlEF
-szME8MeqWa5CrTRj7DtZMMKqIA40mGiDn4oLvQmvusmnkW5Yr/
M3xSux59nsnZVrJ4yI8Dh9OYBzI+VPQWyQohRyxcIUw/U7ROSb4JK
-j9A+jCiN4aSiwuSNpV5VCtRrmI=

https://www.etrade.wallst.com/v1/stocks/snapshot/snapshot.asp?YYY220_/
UfRI8EalsDAUXwwn7MPZWS+auOOgc4Bxe8NzgriuP+BM
-m1TBdd9RCHHpBDrqMKTPa9di0z2vJWVUrSxiSvknC9C0I03BxIH
-SJWT+C/moj+KOGhG7jPXlv6FSUVLYER3BVvSiHTnFsfGQ+mREG/
BEFuYakR8JUQ+Wh5b29AfrgSfc7E5wyqD6pXJcMIwHX2PHTkJpMzWOY
-h7WiVBa1X50eo7Sr1NVnM1

http://www.mnprogressiveproject.com/diary/2682/warren-buffett-derivatives-are
-financial-weapons-of-mass-destruction

http://www.cbsnews.com/8301–503983_162–20003377–503983.html

http://www.moneynews.com/Companies/berkshire-hathaway-buffett-railroad/
2011/02/26/id/387546

Chapter 3

Andrew Hecht, "Contango's Curse and the Beauty of Backwardation," *Barron's*,
1997, http://mwelsh.com/hhmcommodities/press_news.htm

Chapter 4

http://www.bloomberg.com/news/2012–06–17/jindal-power-to-invest–7–7-billion
-in-hydro-corporate-india.html

http://www.opec.org/opec_web/en/about_us/24.htm

http://www.indexmundi.com/energy.aspx

http://americanhistory.si.edu/powering/generate/gnmain.htm

https://www.cia.gov/library/publications/the-world-factbook/rankorder/2179rank
.html

http://www.ogj.com/articles/print/volume–108/issue–46/special-report/total
-reserves-production-climb-on-mixed.html

http://petroleuminsights.blogspot.com/2012/01/worlds-top–15-natural-gas-proven
.html

http://www.nationmaster.com/graph/ene_nat_gas_con-energy-natural-gas
-consumption

http://www.energyfromshale.org/what-is-fracking

http://www.nationmaster.com/graph/ene_nat_gas_con-energy-natural-gas
-consumption
https://www.cia.gov/library/publications/the-world-factbook/fields/2181.html
http://www.china.org.cn/business/2012–02/26/content_24733674.htm
http://www.thestreet.com/story/11253879/1/japan-china-igniting-natural-gas
-prices.html
http://205.254.135.7/coal/news_markets/
http://www.worldcoal.org/resources/coal-statistics/

Chapter 5

http://whiskeyandgunpowder.com/why-gold-really-is-money/
http://www.onlygold.com/tutorialpages/historyfs.htm
http://www.goldsheetlinks.com/production.htm
http://www.china.org.cn/top10/2012–02/13/content_24585877.htm
http://www.gold.org/media/press_releases/archive/2012/02/gold_demand_trends_
q4_2011_pr/
http://www.lbma.org.uk/pages/index.cfm?page_id=55&title=gold_
forwards&show=1992
http://247wallst.com/2011/06/22/rising-gold-production-cost-very-uneven-from
-miner-to-miner-abx-nem-au-gfi-hmy-gdx-gdxj-gld/
http://www.kitco.com/pop_windows/stocks/xau.html
http://www.onlygold.com/tutorialpages/historyfs.htm
The Ascent of Money, Ferguson, pp. 20–27.
http://www.silverinstitute.org/site/supply-demand/silver-demand/
http://books.google.com/books?id=uHjijRpTUSYC&pg=PA30&lpg=PA30&dq=
what+are+the+total+government+holdings+of+silver?&source=bl&ots=
HDd1wckvC6&sig=c9Xbo1gIvgfb3xEUpLa8zIc1FEA&hl=en&sa=X&ei=q4
-pT4iNO8rC2QXLuv2TBw&ved=0CFsQ6AEwCQ#v=onepage&q=what%20
are%20the%20total%20government%20holdings%20of%20silver%3F&f=false
http://www.lbma.org.uk/pages/index.cfm?page_id=17&title=market_basics
http://www.gotgoldreport.com/2010/06/endeavours-report-on-silver.html
http://www.platinummetalsreview.com/resources/view-questions-answers/when
-were-the-six-platinum-group-metals-discovered/
http://large.stanford.edu/courses/2010/ph240/usui1/
http://www.mineweb.com/mineweb/view/mineweb/en/
page35?oid=130361&sn=Detail
http://heraeus-trading.com/en/bankenundanleger/edelmetalleheute/platin_1/Edel
-metalle_heute_Platin.aspx
http://commentaries.argmaur.com/platinum2012.html
http://www.lppm.com/statistics.aspx
http://www.lppm.com/
http://seekingalpha.com/article/277249-investors-flocking-to-palladium
-platinum-etfs

http://www.marketwatch.com/story/platinum-demand-up-in–2011-but-surplus
    -still-seen–2011–11–15
http://articles.marketwatch.com/2011–05–16/markets/30698117_1_platinum
    -prices-palladium-demand
http://www.kitco.com/scripts/hist_charts/yearly_graphs.cgi
http://heraeus-trading.com/en/bankenundanleger/edelmetalleheute/palladium_1/
    Edelmetalle_heute_Palladium.aspx
http://www.tocom.or.jp/

Chapter 6
http://www.lme.com
http://www.lme.com/who_ourhistory.asp
WSY Blog–5/29/12. "The Source: LME Warehousing Looks East."
http://www.lme.com/
http://www.rameria.com/inglese/history.html
http://www.copper.org/education/production.html
http://www.life123.com/career-money/commodities–2/copper/what-is-copper-used
    -for.shtml
http://www.bloomberg.com/apps/news?pid=newsarchive&sid=aERBG3FANNMw
http://www.historyofaluminum.com/
http://curiosity.discovery.com/question/what-is-aluminum-used-for
http://www.businesswire.com/news/home/20110705006032/en/Research-Markets
    -Aluminum-Industry (2011 report)
http://www.rocksandminerals.com/aluminum/process.htm
http://www.webelements.com/nickel/history.html
http://www.bloomberg.com/news/2011–06–07/world-s–10-biggest-nickel
    -producing-countries-in–2010-table-.html
www.investorideas.com/Research/PDFs/Nickel_Feb_2009.pdf
http://corrosion-doctors.org/Elements-Toxic/Lead-history.htm
http://www.infoplease.com/ce6/sci/A0859212.html
http://www.indexmundi.com/en/commodities/minerals/lead/lead_table14.html
http://www.madehow.com/Volume–2/Lead.html
http://www.lme.com/lead_industryusage.asp
http://www.zinc.org/basics/history_of_zinc
http://www.zinc.org/basics/zinc_uses
http://www.scribd.com/doc/903664/ZINC-REPORT-ORIGINAL
http://www.carondelet.pvt.k12.ca.us/Family/Science/GroupIVA/tin.htm
www.consolidatedtinmines.com.au/ . . . /Tin%20News/ . . . / . . .
http://books.google.com/books?id=NNlT5of3YikC&pg=PA22&lpg=PA22&dq=a
    nnual+tin+consumption+by+country&source=bl&ots=c2isPUMBVr&sig=cY
    cPkIf3zfUtRgLGKGYfGtriXzU&hl=en&sa=X&ei=As2zT5
    -dDoua8gTU3ZySCQ&ved=0CE8Q6AEwAw#v=onepage&q=annual%20
    tin%20consumption%20by%20country&f=false
http://www.indexmundi.com/minerals/?product=tin&graph=production

http://hecht.sovereignsociety.com/2011/03/09/more-bullish-news-for-metals/
http://newsfeed.time.com/2011/03/09/the-end-of-the-dollar-bill-high-cotton
   -prices-could-force–1-coin/#more–54764

Chapter 7
http://www.news.cornell.edu/releases/aug97/livestock.hrs.html
topsoil.nserl.purdue.edu/nserlweb-old/isco99/ . . . /P233-Beinroth.pdf
http://soils.usda.gov/use/worldsoils/papers/pop-support-paper.html
http://www.scientificamerican.com/article.cfm?id=organic-farming-yields-and
   -feeding-the-world-under-climate-change
http://www.dailymail.co.uk/sciencetech/article–1272838/Organic-farms-produce
   -HALF-food-conventional-ones.html
http://www.thegrainsfoundation.org/corn
http://www.soyatech.com/corn_facts.htm
http://www.nationmaster.com/graph/agr_gra_cor_exp-agriculture-grains-corn-exports
http://www.cmegroup.com/trading/agricultural/grain-and-oilseed/corn_contract_
   specifications.html
http://www.ag.ndsu.edu/pubs/agecon/market/ncr21718.htm
http://futures.tradingcharts.com/learning/stocks_to_use.html
American Association of Cereal Chemists: www.aaccnet.org
American Corn Growers Association: www.acga.org
Corn Refiners Association: www.corn.org
National Corn Growers Association: www.ncga.com
North American Millers Association: www.nama.org
U.S. Grains Council: www.grains.org
http://www.agricorner.com/world-top-ten-wheat-producers–2010/
http://www.kswheat.com/consumerspageid261_UsesofWheat.shtml
http://www.agricorner.com/world-top-ten-wheat-producers–2010/
http://www.nationmaster.com/graph/agr_gra_whe_con-agriculture-grains-wheat
   -consumption
http://in.reuters.com/article/2009/07/13/wheat-trade-idINSP49082020090713
http://www.commodityseasonals.com/types_of_wheat.htm
http://www.cmegroup.com/trading/agricultural/grain-and-oilseed/soybean-crush_
   contract_specifications.html
http://www.spectrumcommodities.com/education/commodity/statistics/
   soybeantable.html
http://www.ncsoy.org/ABOUT-SOYBEANS/History-of-Soybeans.aspx
http://www.ncsoy.org/ABOUT-SOYBEANS/Uses-of-Soybeans.aspx
http://top5ofanything.com/index.php?h=69ee35b6
http://www.soystats.com/2011/page_30.htm
http://www.cmegroup.com/trading/agricultural/grain-and-oilseed/soybean_
   contract_specifications.html
http://www.cmegroup.com/trading/agricultural/grain-and-oilseed/soybean_
   contract_specifications.html

http://www.tradertech.com/information/soybeanstrading.asp
http://www.duke.edu/web/soc142/team3/Group%20Rice/History.htm
http://www.shilpaagro.com/rice_uses.php
http://daniel-workman.suite101.com/top-rice-producing-countries-a50588
http://uk.reuters.com/article/2011/01/28/uk-rice-exporters-idUK
    -TRE70R1LY20110128
http://oryza.com/Rice-News/14700.html
http://www.cmegroup.com/company/cbot.html
http://www.indexmundi.com/commodities/glossary/commodities-exchanges
    -around-the-world
http://www.financialadvisory.com/dictionary/term/live-cattle/
http://www.mapsofworld.com/world-top-ten/world-top-ten-meat-consumer
    -countries.html
http://www.spectrumcommodities.com/education/commodity/statistics/cattletable
    .html
http://chartsbin.com/view/bhy
http://www.spectrumcommodities.com/education/commodity/statistics/hogtable.html
http://www.nationmaster.com/graph/agr_hog_pro-agriculture-hog-production
http://www.murphybrownllc.com/ABOUT/HOG-PRODUCTION/index.html
http://oklahoma4h.okstate.edu/aitc/lessons/extras/facts/swine.html

Chapter 8

http://shine.yahoo.com/green/20-unusual-uses-coffee–183200501.html
http://www.ico.org/prices/po.htm
http://www.ico.org/prices/m4.htm
http://www.merriam-webster.com/dictionary/arabica
http://www.coffeeresearch.org/agriculture/coffeeplant.htm
http://www.risk.net/energy-risk/news/1512153/ice-nybot-merger-complete
https://www.theice.com/productguide/ProductSpec.shtml;jsessionid=C1A16F14256
    6696F1221B56ECEEB9EC0?specId=15
http://www.euronext.com/trader/contractspecifications/derivative/wide/contract
    -specifications–2864-EN.html?euronextCode=RC-LON-FUT
http://www.boyds.com/news/coffee-buying-the-importance-of-differentials/
http://www.thecoffeeguide.org/88-Futures-markets-Singapore-Exchange-Ltd
    -the-SGX-Robusta-Coffee-Contract/
http://www.wisegeek.com/what-is-raw-sugar.htm
http://www.sugarinds.com/2011/06/world-top–10-sugar-producing-countries.html
http://daniel-workman.suite101.com/top-ten-sugar-exporters-a24351
http://www.nationmaster.com/graph/eco_wor_tra_imp_sug_con-world-trade
    -imports-sugar-confectionery
http://www.worldcocoafoundation.org/learn-about-cocoa/history-of-cocoa.html
http://worldagroforestry.org/treesandmarkets/inaforesta/history.htm
http://www.ehow.com/list_6037610_uses-cocoa-beans.html
http://www.zchocolat.com/chocolate/chocolate/cocoa-production.asp

https://www.theice.com/productguide/ProductSpec.shtml?specId=7

http://www.euronext.com/trader/contractspecifications/derivative/wide/contract
-specifications–2864-EN.html?euronextCode=C-LON-FUT

http://www.orangesfacts.com/2009/09/06/the-history-of-orange-juice-and
-its-varieties/

http://www.spectrumcommodities.com/education/commodity/oj.html

http://www.top5ofanything.com/index.php?h=886acb20

https://www.theice.com/productguide/ProductSpec.shtml?specId=30

http://www.indexmundi.com/commodities/glossary/commodities-exchanges
-around-the-world

http://www.worldsteel.org/media-centre/press-releases/2012/2011-world
-crude-steel-production.html

http://articles.economictimes.indiatimes.com/2010–05–28/news/27580521_1_
steel-consumption-value-added-steel-global-steel

http://www.issb.co.uk/global.html

http://www.indexmundi.com/commodities/?commodity=cold-rolled
-steel&months=360

http://www.lme.com/minormetals/cobalt.asp

http://www.mapsofworld.com/minerals/world-cobalt-producers.html

http://www.mapsofworld.com/minerals/world-cobalt-producers.html

http://www.somika.com/cobalt-properties-ores-minerals-lubumbashi.php

http://www.lme.com/minormetals/6782.asp

http://www.mnn.com/earth-matters/translating-uncle-sam/stories/what-are
-rare-earth-metals

http://www.dailytech.com/China+Cuts+Off+Worlds+Rare+Earth+Metal+
Supply/article23069.htm

http://www.cottoninc.com/corporate/Market-Data/MonthlyEconomicLetter/

http://daniel-workman.suite101.com/top-ten-cotton-countries-a30604

http://www.nationmaster.com/graph/agr_cot_exp-agriculture-

http://www.cottoninc.com/corporate/Market-Data/MonthlyEconomicLetter/

https://www.theice.com/productguide/ProductSpec.shtml?specId=254

http://www.cmegroup.com/trading/agricultural/lumber-and-pulp/wood-pulp_
contract_specifications.html

http://www.cmegroup.com/trading/agricultural/lumber-and-pulp/random-length
-lumber_contract_specifications.html

http://www.paperage.com/pulp_paper_terms.html

http://www.mapsofworld.com/world-top-ten/countries-with-most-timber
-producing-countries.html

http://www.cisionwire.com/wood-resources-international-llc-company/r/china-is
-now-the-world-s-largest-importer-of-softwood-lumber-and-logs-despite-a
-slowdown-in-imports-,c9213679

http://greenmarkets.pf.com.

http://cruonline.crugroup.com/FertilizersChemicals/FertilizerWeek/tabid/177/
Default.aspx.

United States Department of Agriculture
http://www.tfi.org/statistics/statistics-faqs
http://www.cmegroup.com/trading/agricultural/fertilizer/dap-fob-nola-swaps_
    contract_specifications.html
http://www.cmegroup.com/trading/metals/other/uranium_contract_specifications.
    html
http://uranium21.tripod.com/id5.html
http://www.uxc.com/review/uxc_Prices.aspx
http://www.indexmundi.com/commodities/?commodity=uranium&months=60
http://www.traditionenergy.com/green-energy/
http://www.thegreenx.com/products/index.html
https://www.theice.com/ccx.jhtml
http://www.eex.com/en/Download/Market%20Data/EU%20Emission%20Allowances
    %20-%20EEX
http://www.cmegroup.com/trading/weather/
http://www.lme.com/media_resources/10945.asp

Chapter 10
http://www.cftc.gov/About/MissionResponsibilities/index.htm
http://www.sec.gov/about/whatwedo.shtml
http://www.fsa.gov.uk/about/who
http://www.natlawreview.com/article/european-market-abuse-regulation-extended
    -to-commodities-sector
http://www.hellenicshippingnews.com/News.aspx?ElementId=ed6ae704-442e
    -4dfd-853e-a90a00c1a8c9
http://www.focac.org/eng/zxxx/t832788.htm
http://www.farmdocdaily.illinois.edu/2012/04/speculation_and_gasoline_price.html
http://www.opednews.com/articles/Statement-By-Senator-Berna-by-Bernie
    -Sanders-120403-490.html
http://money.cnn.com/2008/06/27/news/economy/The_onion_conundrum_Birger
    .fortune/?postversion=2008062713

INDEX

Note: Boldface numbers indicate illustrations or tables.